'Don't leave home without the 3rd edition! With new chapters and rigorous restructuring, this classic guide to critical tourism studies becomes even more useful to scholars and students across the social sciences and humanities. *The Tourist Gaze 3.0* takes us on a detailed tour of the major concepts and approaches to one of the world's largest culture industries. With fresh insights and new materials, this collaboratively written revision will immediately become required reading for those who pay attention to the world of travel, mobility, and visual culture.'
Caren Kaplan, Professor, Cultural Studies/Science and Technology Studies, UC Davis

'The original *Tourist Gaze* was a classic, marking out a new land to study and appreciate. This new edition extends into fresh areas with the same passion and insight of the object. Even more essential reading!'
Nigel Thrift, Vice-Chancellor, Warwick University

'The first edition of *The Tourist Gaze* was a landmark in the theoretical development of tourism studies, and it inspired waves of research and often fierce debates that have reverberated over the following two decades. This new edition of the book is not only thoroughly revised but has also been given renewed cutting edge, particularly by the addition of chapters on risk and on digital photography. At the same time, our understanding of the tourist gaze has been reframed and broadened by the infusion of ideas about mobility and embodiment, making this book an essential read for every tourism scholar.'
Allan Williams, Professor of Tourism Management, School of Management, University of Surrey

'A great classic remade to capture the lives of tourists in the 21st century. For two decades *The Tourist Gaze* has been one of the most influential books in tourist research. This new and thoroughly reworked version meets the challenges of a changing world of tourism and engages the lively contemporary debates in the field.'
Orvar Löfgren, Professor of European Ethnology at the University of Lund

D01162223

The Tourist Gaze 3.0

Theory, Culture & Society

Theory, Culture & Society caters for the resurgence of interest in culture within contemporary social science and the humanities. Building on the heritage of classical social theory, the book series examines ways in which this tradition has been reshaped by a new generation of theorists. It also publishes theoretically informed analyses of everyday life, popular culture and new intellectual movements.

EDITOR: Mike Featherstone, *Nottingham Trent University*

THE TCS CENTRE
The *Theory, Culture & Society* book series, the journals *Theory, Culture & Society* and *Body & Society*, and related conference, seminar and postgraduate programmes operate from the TCS Centre at NottinghamTrent University. For further details of the TCS Centre's activities please contact:

The TCS Centre
School of Arts and Humanities
Nottingham Trent University
Clifton Lane, Nottingham, NG11 8NS, UK
e-mail: tcs@ntu.ac.uk
web: http://sagepub.net/tcs/

Recent volumes include:

Education and Cultural Citizenship
Nick Stevenson

Inhuman Nature
Nigel Clark

Race, Sport and Politics
Ben Carrington

Intensive Culture
Scott Lash

The Media City
Scott McQuire

The Tourist Gaze 3.0

John Urry and Jonas Larsen

Los Angeles | London | New Delhi
Singapore | Washington DC

© John Urry and Jonas Larsen 2011

First edition first published 1990
Second edition first published 2002 (reprinted 2002, 2003, 2005 twice, 2006, 2008, 2009 twice, 2010)

This edition published 2011

SAGE Publications Ltd
1 Oliver's Yard
55 City Road
London EC1Y 1SP

SAGE Publications Inc.
2455 Teller Road
Thousand Oaks, California 91320

SAGE Publications India Pvt Ltd
B 1/I 1 Mohan Cooperative Industrial Area
Mathura Road, Post Bag 7
New Delhi 110 044

SAGE Publications Asia-Pacific Pte Ltd
33 Pekin Street #02-01
Far East Square
Singapore 048763

Library of Congress Control Number: 2010940108

British Library Cataloguing in Publication data

A catalogue record for this book is available from the British Library

ISBN 978-1-84920-376-0
ISBN 978-1-84920-377-7 (pbk)

Typeset by C&M Digitals (P) Ltd, Chennai, India
Printed in India by Replika Press, Pvt, Ltd.
Printed on paper from sustainable resource

Contents

List of Figures

About the Authors

John Urry graduated with a BA/MA in Economics and a PhD in Sociology from Cambridge. He has since worked at Lancaster University where he has been Head of Department, Founding Dean of the Social Sciences Faculty and University Dean of Research. He is a Fellow of the Royal Society of Arts, Founding Academician, UK Academy of Social Sciences, Member (1992) and Chair RAE Panels (1996, 2001). He has published 40 books and special issues his work is translated into 18 languages, and he has lectured in 30 countries. He is currently Director of the Centre for Mobilities Research at Lancaster. Recent books include: *Mobilities* (Polity, 2007); *After the Car* (Polity, 2009); *Mobile Lives* (Routledge, 2010); *Climate Change and Society* (Polity, 2011) as well as *The Tourist Gaze 3.0* (Sage, 2011).

Jonas Larsen is a senior lecturer in Geography at Roskilde University, Denmark. He is interested in mobility, tourism and media. He has published many articles in tourism, geography and mobility journals and co-authored *Performing Tourist Places* (Ashgate, 2004); *Mobilities, Networks, Geographies* (Ashgate, 2006) and *Tourism, Performance and the Everyday: Consuming the Orient* (Routledge, 2010).

Preface

I am very grateful for the advice, encouragement and assistance of the following, especially those who have provided me with tourist gems from around the world: Paul Bagguley, Nick Buck, Peter Dickens, Paul Heelas, Mark Hilton, Scott Lash, Michelle Lowe, Celia Lury, Jane Mark-Lawson, David Morgan, Ian Rickson, Chris Rojek, Mary Rose, Peter Saunders, Dan Shapiro, Rob Shields, Hermann Schwengel, John Towner, Sylvia Walby, John Walton and Alan Warde. I am also grateful to professionals working in the tourism and hospitality industry who responded to my queries with much information and advice. Some interviews reported here were conducted under the auspices of the ESRC Initiative on the Changing Urban and Regional System. I am grateful to that Initiative in first prompting me to take holiday-making 'seriously'.

John Urry
Lancaster, December 1989

Preface to the Second Edition

This new edition has maintained the structure of the first edition except for the addition of a new chapter (8) on 'Globalising the Gaze'. The other seven chapters have been updated in terms of data, the incorporation of relevant new studies and some better illustrations. I am very grateful for the extensive research assistance and informed expertise that has been provided by Viv Cuthill for this new edition. I am also grateful to Mike Featherstone for originally prompting a book on tourism, and Chris Rojek who suggested this second edition as well as for collaboration on our co-edited *Touring Cultures*.

Over the past decade I have supervised various PhDs at Lancaster on issues of tourism, travel and mobility. I have learnt much from these doctorates and especially from the conversations about the ongoing work. I would especially like to thank the following, some of whom commented very helpfully on Chapter 8: Alexandra Arellano, Javier Caletrio, Viv Cuthill, Saolo Cwerner, Monica Degen, Tim Edensor, Hernan Gutiérrez Sagastume, Juliet Jain, Jonas Larsen, Neil Lewis, Chia-ling Lai, Richard Sharpley, Jo Stanley and Joyce Yeh. I have also benefited from many discussions with the MA students who have taken my 'Tourist Gaze' module over the past decade.

Lancaster colleagues with whom I have discussed these topics (some also making very helpful comments on Chapter 8) include Sara Ahmed, Gordon Clark, Carol Crawshaw, Bülent Diken, Anne-Marie Fortier, Robin Grove-White, Kevin Hetherington, Vincent Kaufmann, Phil Macnaghten, Colin Pooley, Katrin Schneeberger and Mimi Sheller.

Working on graduate matters in the Sociology Department with Pennie Drinkall and Claire O'Donnell has been a pleasure over the past few years.

John Urry
Lancaster, April 2001

Preface to 3.0

The world of tourism is in constant flux and tourism theory needs to be on the move to capture such changes. This third edition of *The Tourist Gaze* radically restructures, reworks and expands the two first editions to make this book relevant for tourism researchers, students, planners and designers in the twenty-first century. There are many changes to the first two editions. Jonas Larsen, as co-author, has brought fresh eyes on the book. The original chapters have been thoroughly updated. Outdated data and studies have been deleted, new studies and theoretical concepts have been incorporated and the concept of the tourist gaze receives more theoretical consideration, including its 'darker' sides. Three *new* chapters examine the tourist gaze in relation to *photography* and *digitisation*, recent analyses of embodied *performances* within tourism theory and research, and the various *risks* of tourism, including global warming and peak oil, that problematise the desirability and future of the globalising tourist gaze.

We are very grateful for the inspiration, help and assistance in producing this new edition of *The Tourist Gaze*. We would particularly like to thank Jørgen Ole Bærenholdt, Monika Büscher, Javier Caletrio, Beckie Coleman, Anne Cronin, Viv Cuthill, Monica Degen, Kingsley Dennis, Pennie Drinkall, Tim Edensor, Michael Haldrup, Kevin Hannam, Allison Hui, Michael Hviid Jacobsen, Juliet Jain, Jennie Germann Molz, Mette Sandbye, Mimi Sheller, Rob Shields, David Tyfield, Amy Urry, Tom Urry, Sylvia Walby and Laura Watts. Photos were taken by Amy Urry and ourselves.

John Urry, Lancaster
Jonas Larsen, Roskilde

'To remain stationary in these times of change, when all the world is on the move, would be a crime. Hurrah for the Trip – the cheap, cheap Trip.' (Thomas Cook in 1854, quoted in Brendon, 1991: 65)

'A view? Oh a view! How delightful a view is!' (Miss Bartlett, in *A Room with a View*, Forster, 1955: 8, orig. 1908)

'[T]he camera and tourism are two of the uniquely modern ways of defining reality.' (Horne, 1984: 21)

'For the twentieth-century tourist, the world has become one large department store of countrysides and cities.' (Schivelbusch, 1986: 197)

'It's funny, isn't it, how every traveller is a tourist except one's self?' (an Edwardian skit, quoted in Brendon, 1991: 188)

'Since Thomas Cook's first excursion train it is as if a magician's wand had been passed over the face of the globe.' (*The Excursionist*, June 1897, quoted in Ring, 2000: 83)

'[The tourists] pay for their freedom; the right to disregard native concerns and feelings, the right to spin their own web of meanings. ... The world is the tourist's oyster ... to be lived pleasurably – and thus given meaning.' (Bauman, 1993: 241)

'Going by railroad, I do not consider travelling at all; it is merely being "sent" to a place, and no different from being a parcel.' (John Ruskin, quoted in Wang, 2000: 179)

'Wow, that's so postcard!' (Visitor seeing Victoria Falls, quoted in Osborne, 2000: 79)

1

Theories

The Importance of Tourism

> The clinic was probably the first attempt to order a science on the
> exercise and decisions of the gaze ... the medical gaze was also organ-
> ized in a new way. First, it was no longer the gaze of any observer, but
> that of a doctor supported and justified by an institution. ... Moreover,
> it was a gaze that was not bound by the narrow grid of structure ... but
> that could and should grasp colours, variations, tiny anomalies ...
> (Foucault, 1976: 89)

The subject of this book would appear to have nothing whatsoever
to do with the serious world of medicine and the medical gaze that
concerns Foucault. This is a book about pleasure, about holidays,
tourism and travel, about how and why for short periods people
leave their normal place of work and residence. It is about consuming goods and services which are in some sense unnecessary. They are
consumed because they supposedly generate pleasurable experiences which are different from those typically encountered in everyday life. And yet at least a part of that experience is to gaze upon or
view a set of different scenes, of landscapes or townscapes which are
out of the ordinary. When we 'go away' we look at the environment
with interest and curiosity. It speaks to us in ways we appreciate, or
at least we anticipate that it will do so. In other words, we gaze at
what we encounter. This gaze is as socially organised and systematised, as is the gaze of the medic. Of course it is of a different order
in that it is not a gaze confined to professionals 'supported and justified by an institution'. And yet even in the production of 'unnecessary' pleasure many professional experts help to construct and
develop one's gaze as a tourist.

The concept of the gaze highlights that looking is a learned ability
and that the pure and innocent eye is a myth. What the medic gaze
saw, and made visible, was not a simple pre-existing reality simply
waiting 'out there' according to Foucault. Instead it was an epistemic
field, constructed linguistically as much as visually. Seeing is what

the human eye does. Gazing refers to the 'discursive determinations', of socially constructed seeing or 'scopic regimes'. Foster refers to 'how we are able to see, allowed or made to see, and how we see this seeing or the unseen herein' (1988: ix). To depict vision as natural or the product of atomised individuals naturalises its social and historical nature, and the power relations of looking.

Just like language, one's eyes are socio-culturally framed and there are various 'ways of seeing'. 'We never look just at one thing; we are always looking at the relation between things and ourselves' (Berger, 1972: 9). People gaze upon the world through a particular filter of ideas, skills, desires and expectations, framed by social class, gender, nationality, age and education. Gazing is a performance that orders, shapes and classifies, rather than reflects the world. Jenks maintains:

> The world is not pre-formed, waiting to be 'seen' by the 'extro-spection' of the 'naked eye'. There is nothing 'out-there' intrinsically formed, interesting, good or beautiful, as our dominant cultural outlook would suggest. *Vision is skilled cultural practice.* (1995: 10, our italics)

Gazing at particular sights is conditioned by personal experiences and memories and framed by rules and styles, as well as by circulating images and texts of this and other places. Such 'frames' are critical resources, techniques, cultural lenses that potentially enable tourists to see the physical forms and material spaces before their eyes as 'interesting, good or beautiful'. They are not the property of mere sight. And without these lenses the beautiful order found in nature or the built world would be very different. These different ways of seeing have many consequences for physical and built worlds.

This book, then, is about how in different societies and especially within different social groups in diverse historical periods the tourist gaze changes and develops. We elaborate on processes by which the gaze is constructed and reinforced, and consider who or what authorises it, what its consequences are for the 'places' which are its object and how it interrelates with other social practices. The 'tourist gaze' is not a matter of individual psychology but of socially patterned and learnt 'ways of seeing' (Berger, 1972). It is a vision constructed through mobile images and representational technologies. Like the medical gaze, the power of the visual gaze within modern tourism is tied into, and enabled by, various technologies, including camcorders, film, TV, cameras and digital images.

There is no single tourist gaze as such. It varies by society, by social group and by historical period. Such gazes are constructed through difference. By this we mean not merely that there is no universal experience that is true for all tourists at all times. There are many ways of gazing within tourism, and tourists look at 'difference' differently. This is in part because tourist gazes are structured according to class, gender, ethnicity and age. Moreover, the gaze in any historical period is constructed in relationship to its opposite, to non-tourist forms of social experience and consciousness. What makes a particular tourist gaze depends upon what it is contrasted with; what the forms of non-tourist experience happen to be. The gaze therefore presupposes a system of social activities and signs which locate the particular tourist practices, not in terms of some intrinsic characteristics, but through the contrasts implied with non-tourist social practices, particularly those based within home and paid work.

Tourism, holidaymaking and travel are more significant social phenomena than most commentators have considered. On the face of it there could not be a more trivial subject for a book. And indeed since social scientists have had plenty of difficulty in explaining weightier topics, such as work or politics, it might be thought that they would have great difficulties in accounting for more trivial phenomena such as holiday-making. However, there are interesting parallels with the study of deviance. This involves the investigation of bizarre and idiosyncratic social practices which happen to be defined as deviant in some societies but not necessarily in others. The assumption is that the investigation of deviance can reveal interesting and significant aspects of 'normal' societies. Just why various activities are treated as deviant can illuminate how societies operate more generally.

This book is based on a similar analysis applying to tourism. Such practices involve the notion of 'departure', of a limited breaking with established routines and practices of everyday life and allowing one's senses to engage with a set of stimuli that contrast with the everyday and mundane. By considering the typical objects of the tourist gaze one can use these to make sense of elements of the wider society with which they are contrasted. In other words, to consider how social groups construct their tourist gaze is a good way of getting at just what is happening in the 'normal society'. We can use the fact of difference to interrogate the normal through investigating typical forms of tourism. Thus rather than being a trivial subject, tourism is significant in its ability to reveal aspects of normal practices which might otherwise remain opaque. Opening up the workings of the social world often requires the use of counter-intuitive and surprising methodologies; as in this case the investigation of the 'departures' involved in the tourist gaze.

Although we insist on the historical, geographical and sociological variations in the gaze, there are some minimal characteristics of the social practices which are conventionally described as 'tourism'. We set these out to provide a baseline for more historical, sociological, and global analyses developed later.

1   Tourism is a leisure activity which presupposes its opposite, namely regulated and organised work. It is one manifestation of how work and leisure are organised as separate and regulated spheres of social practice in 'modern' societies. Indeed, acting as a tourist is one of the defining characteristics of being 'modern' and is bound up with major transformations in paid work. This has come to be organised within particular places and to occur for regularised periods of time.

2   Tourist relationships arise from a movement of people to, and their stay in, various destinations. This necessarily involves some movement through space, that is, the journeys and periods of stay in a new place or places.

3   The journey and stay are to, and in, sites outside the normal places of residence and work. Periods of residence elsewhere are of a short-term and temporary nature. There is intention to return 'home' within a relatively short period of time.

4   The places gazed upon are for purposes not directly connected with paid work and they normally offer some distinctive contrasts with work (both paid and unpaid).

5   A substantial proportion of the population of modern societies engages in such tourist practices; new socialised forms of provision are developed in order to cope with the mass character of the gaze of tourists (as opposed to the individual character of 'travel').

6   Places are chosen to be gazed upon because there is anticipation, especially through daydreaming and fantasy, of intense pleasures, either on a different scale or involving different senses from those customarily encountered. Such anticipation is constructed and sustained through a variety of non-tourist technologies, such as film, TV, literature, magazines, CDs, DVDs and videos, constructing and reinforcing the gaze.

7   The tourist gaze is directed to features of landscape and townscape which separate them off from everyday experience. Such aspects are viewed because they are taken to be in some sense out of the ordinary. The viewing of such tourist sights often involves different forms of social patterning, with a much greater sensitivity to visual elements of landscape or townscape than normally found in everyday life. People linger over such a gaze, which is then often visually objectified or captured through photographs, postcards, films, models and so on. These enable the gaze to be reproduced, recaptured and redistributed over time and across space.

8   The gaze is constructed through signs, and tourism involves the collection of signs. When tourists see two people kissing in Paris what they

capture in the gaze is 'timeless romantic Paris'. When a small village in England is seen, what they gaze upon is the 'real olde England'. As Culler argues: 'the tourist is interested in everything as a sign of itself. ... All over the world the unsung armies of semioticians, the tourists, are fanning out in search of the signs of Frenchness, typical Italian behaviour, exemplary Oriental scenes, typical American thruways, traditional English pubs' (1981: 127).

9   An array of tourist professionals reproduce ever new objects of the tourist gaze. These objects are located in a complex and changing hierarchy. This depends upon the interplay between, on the one hand, competition between interests involved in providing such objects and, on the other hand, changing class, gender and generational distinctions of taste among potential visitors.

In this book we consider the development of, and historical transformations within, the tourist gaze. We mainly chart such changes in the past couple of centuries; that is, in the period in which mass tourism became widespread within much of Europe, North America and most other parts of the world. To be a tourist is one of the characteristics of the 'modern' experience. It has become a marker of status in modern societies and is also thought to be necessary for good health and a cosmopolitan outlook (see Feifer, 1985: 224; Urry, 2007).

There was organised travel in premodern societies, but it was very much the preserve of elites (see Towner, 1988). In Imperial Rome there was a fairly extensive pattern of elite travel for pleasure and culture. A travel infrastructure developed, partly permitted by two centuries of peace. It was possible to travel from Hadrian's Wall to the Euphrates without crossing a hostile border (Feifer, 1985: ch. l). Seneca maintained that this permitted city-dwellers to seek ever new sensations and pleasures. He said: 'men [sic] travel widely to different sorts of places seeking different distractions because they are fickle, tired of soft living, and always seek after something which eludes them' (quoted in Feifer, 1985: 9).

In the thirteenth and fourteenth centuries pilgrimages had become a widespread phenomenon 'practicable and systematized, served by a growing industry of networks of charitable hospices and mass-produced indulgence handbooks' (Feifer, 1985: 29; Eade and Sallnow, 1991). Pilgrimages often included a mixture of religious devotion and culture and pleasure. By the fifteenth century there were regular organised tours from Venice to the Holy Land.

The Grand Tour had become firmly established by the end of the seventeenth century for the sons of the aristocracy and the gentry, and by the late eighteenth century for the sons of the professional middle class. Over this period, between 1600 and 1800, treatises on travel shifted from a scholastic emphasis on touring as an opportunity for discourse, to travel as eyewitness observation. There was a visualisation of the travel experience, or the development of the 'gaze', aided and assisted by the growth of guidebooks which promoted new ways of seeing (see Adler, 1989). The character of the tour itself shifted, from the earlier 'classical Grand Tour' based on the emotionally neutral observation and recording of galleries, museums and high-cultural artefacts, to the nineteenth-century 'romantic Grand Tour' which saw the emergence of 'scenic tourism' and a much more private and passionate experience of beauty and the sublime (see Towner, 1985). Travel was expected to play a key role in the cognitive and perceptual education of the male English upper class (see Dent, 1975).

The eighteenth century had seen the development of a considerable tourist infrastructure in the form of spa towns throughout much of Europe (Thompson, 1981: 11–12; Blackbourn, 2002). Myerscough notes that the 'whole apparatus of spa life with its balls, its promenades, libraries, masters of ceremonies was designed to provide a concentrated urban experience of frenetic socialising for a dispersed rural elite' (1974: 5).

There have been periods in which much of the population engaged in play or recreation. In the countryside, work and play were particularly intertwined in the case of village or town fairs. Most towns and villages in England had at least one fair a year and many had more. People would often travel considerable distances and fairs involved a mixture of business and pleasure, normally especially centred around the tavern. By the eighteenth century the public house had become a major centre for public life in the community, providing light, heat, cooking facilities, furniture, news, banking and travel facilities, entertainment and sociability (Harrison, 1971; Clark, 1983).

But before the nineteenth century, few outside the upper classes travelled to see objects unconnected with work or business. And it is this which is the central characteristic of mass tourism in modern societies, namely that much of the population in most years travels somewhere else to gaze upon it and stay there for reasons basically unconnected with work. Travel is thought to occupy 40 per cent of available 'free time' in Britain (Williams and Shaw, 1988: 12). If people do not travel, they lose status: travel is the marker of status. It is a crucial element of modern life to feel that travel and holidays are necessary. 'I need a holiday' reflects a modern discourse based on the idea that people's physical and mental health will be restored if only they can 'get away' from time to time.

The importance of this can be seen in the scale of contemporary travel. There are around 880 million international passenger arrivals each year, compared with 25 million in 1950. It is predicted that this figure will rise to 1.6 billion by 2020, although it dipped by over 4 per cent in 2009 (www.unwto.org/index.php; accessed 31.03.10). At any one time there are 300,000 passengers in flight *above* the USA, equivalent to a substantial city (Gottdiener, 2001: 1). Half a million new hotel rooms are built annually, while there are 31 million refugees across the globe (Papastergiadis, 2000: ch. 2). 'Travel and tourism' is the largest industry in the world, accounting for 9.4 per cent of world GDP and 8.2 per cent of all employment (www.wttc. org/eng/Tourism_Research/Economic_Research/; accessed 31.03.10).

This travel occurs almost everywhere, with the World Tourism Organization publishing tourism/travel statistics for 204 countries with at least 70 countries receiving more than one million international tourist arrivals a year (www.unwto.org/index.php; accessed 31.03.10). There is more or less no country in the world that is not a significant receiver of visitors. However, the flows of such visitors originate very unequally, with the 45 countries with 'high' human development accounting for three-quarters of international tourism departures (UNDP, 1999: 53–5). Such mobilities are enormously costly for the environment (see many accounts in the journal *Tourism in Focus* and Chapter 9 below). There is an astonishing tripling of world car travel predicted between 1990 and 2050 (Hawken et al., 1999).

In the next section we consider some of the seminal theoretical contributions that have attempted to make sense of these extensive flows.

Theoretical Approaches

Making theoretical sense of 'fun, pleasure and entertainment' has proved a difficult task for social scientists. In this section we summarise some of the seminal contributions to the sociology of tourism. They are not uninteresting, but they leave much work still to be done. In the rest of the book we develop some of the notions relevant to theoretical understanding of tourist places and practices (see Jamal and Robinson, 2009, and Hannam and Knox, 2010, for state-of-the-art reviews).

One early formulation is Boorstin's analysis of the 'pseudo-event' (1964). He argues that contemporary Americans cannot experience 'reality' directly but thrive on 'pseudo-events', with tourism being the prime example (see Eco, 1986; Baudrillard, 1988). Isolated from the host environment and the local people, mass tourists travel in guided groups and find pleasure in inauthentic contrived attractions, gullibly enjoying 'pseudo-events' and disregarding the 'real' world outside. As a result tourist entrepreneurs and the indigenous populations are induced to produce ever more extravagant displays for gullible observers who are thereby further removed from local people. Over time, via advertising and the media, the images generated through different tourist gazes come to constitute a closed self-perpetuating system of illusions which provide tourists with the basis for selecting and evaluating potential places to visit. Such visits are made, says Boorstin, within the 'environmental bubble' of familiar American-style hotels that insulates them from the strangeness of the host environment.

A number of later writers develop and refine this relatively simple thesis of a historical shift from the 'individual traveller' to the 'mass society tourist'. Turner and Ash's *The Golden Hordes* (1975) fleshes out the thesis about how the tourist is placed at the centre of a strictly circumscribed world. Surrogate parents (travel agents, couriers, hotel managers) relieve the tourist of responsibility and protect him/her from harsh reality. Their solicitude restricts the tourist to the beach and certain approved objects of the tourist gaze (see Edensor 1998, on package-holidaymakers at the Taj Mahal). In a sense, Turner and Ash suggest, the tourists' sensuality and aesthetic sense are as restricted as they are in their home country. This is further heightened by the relatively superficial way in which indigenous cultures are presented to the tourist. They note about Bali: 'Many aspects of Balinese culture and art are so bewilderingly complex and alien to western modes that they do not lend themselves readily to the process of over-simplification and mass production that converts indigenous art forms into tourist kitsch' (Turner and Ash, 1975: 159; Bruner, 1995; and see Figure 1.1). The upshot is that in the search for ever-new places to visit, what is constructed is a set of hotels and tourist sights that are bland and lacking contradiction, 'a small monotonous world that everywhere shows us our own image … the pursuit of the exotic and diverse ends in uniformity' (Turner and Ash, 1975: 292).

Somewhat critical of this argument, Cohen maintains that there is no single tourist as such but various tourist types or modes of tourist experience (see 1972, 1979, 1988, mainly drawn from the sociology of religion). What he terms as the 'experiential', the 'experimental' and the 'existential' do not rely on the environmental bubble of conventional tourist services. To varying degrees such tourist experiences are based on rejecting such ways of organising tourist activity. Moreover,

Figure 1.1 *The tourist gaze in Bali, Indonesia*

one should also note that such bubbles permit many people to visit places which otherwise they would not, and to have at least some contact with the 'strange' places thereby encountered. Indeed, until such places have developed a fully-fledged tourist infrastructure much of the 'strangeness' of such destinations will be impossible to hide and package within a complete array of pseudo-events.

The most significant challenge to Boorstin is MacCannell, who is also concerned with the inauthenticity and superficiality of modern life (1999; orig. 1976). He quotes Simmel on the nature of the sensory impressions experienced in the 'metropolis': 'the rapid crowding of changing images, the sharp discontinuity in the grasp of a single glance, and the unexpectedness of onrushing impressions' (MacCannell, 1999: 49). He maintains these are symptomatic of the tourist experience but disagrees with Boorstin's account, which he regards as reflecting a characteristically upper-class view that 'other people are tourists, while I am a traveller' (MacCannell, 1999: 107; see Buzard 1993, on this distinction).

All tourists, for MacCannell, embody a quest for authenticity, and this quest is a modern version of the universal human concern with the sacred. The tourist is a kind of contemporary pilgrim, seeking authenticity in other 'times' and other 'places' away from that person's everyday life. Tourists show particular fascination in the 'real lives' of others that somehow possess a reality that is hard to discover in their own experiences. Modern society is therefore rapidly institutionalising the rights of outsiders to look into its workings. 'Institutions are fitted with arenas, platforms and chambers set aside for the exclusive use of tourists' (MacCannell, 1999: 49). Almost any sort of work, even the backbreaking toil of the Welsh miner or the unenviable work of those employed in the Parisian sewer, can be the object of the tourist gaze.

MacCannell particularly examines the character of the social relations which emerge from this fascination people have in the work lives of others. He notes that such 'real lives' can only be found backstage and are not immediately evident to us. Hence, the gaze of the tourist will involve an obvious intrusion into people's lives, which would be generally unacceptable. So the people being observed and local tourist entrepreneurs gradually come to construct backstages in a contrived and artificial manner. 'Tourist spaces' are thus organised around what MacCannell calls 'staged authenticity' (1973). The development of the constructed tourist attraction results from how those who are subject to the tourist gaze respond, both to protect themselves from intrusions into their lives backstage and to take advantage of the opportunities it presents for profitable investment. By contrast, then, with Boorstin,

MacCannell argues that 'psuedo-events' result from the social relations of tourism and not from an individualistic search for the inauthentic.

Pearce and Moscardo further elaborate the notion of authenticity (1986; Turner and Manning, 1988). They maintain it is necessary to distinguish between the authenticity of the setting and the authenticity of the persons gazed upon; and to distinguish between the diverse elements of the tourist experience of importance to the tourist in question. Crick, by contrast, points out that there is a sense in which all cultures are 'staged' and inauthentic. Cultures are invented, remade and the elements reorganised (Crick, 1988: 65–6). Hence, it is not clear why the apparently inauthentic staging for the tourist is so very different from the processes of cultural remaking that happens in all cultures anyway (Rojek and Urry, 1997).

Based on research at New Salem, where Abraham Lincoln spent some years in the 1830s, Bruner interestingly distinguishes conflicting senses of what is meant by 'authentic' (1994; Wang, 2000). First, there is the authentic in the sense of a small town that *looks* like it has appropriately aged over the previous 170 years, whether the buildings are actually that old or are newly, if sensitively, constructed. Second, there is the town that appears as it would have looked in the 1830s, that is, mostly comprising in fact *new* buildings. Third, there is authenticity in the sense of the buildings and artefacts that literally date from the 1830s and have been there ever since. And fourth, there are those buildings and artefacts that have been authorised as *authentic* by the Trust that oversees 'heritage' within the town. Holderness similarly describes the processes in Stratford-upon-Avon by which the Shakespeare Birthplace Trust has come to exert a hegemonic role in the town, determining which buildings, places and artefacts are authentically part of 'Shakespeare's heritage' and those which are not so 'authenticated' (1988). Bruner also notes that New Salem now is wholly different from the 1830s since in the previous period there would not have been camera-waving tourists wandering about in large numbers excitedly staring at actors dressed up as though they are residents of a previous and long-since disappeared epoch.

MacCannell also notes that, unlike the religious pilgrim who pays homage to a single sacred centre, the tourist pays homage to a large array of centres and attractions. These include sites of industry and work as work has become a mere attribute of society and not its central feature (MacCannell, 1999: 58). MacCannell characterises such an interest in work displays as 'alienated leisure'. It is a perversion of the aim of leisure since it involves a return to the workplace but now as leisure.

He also notes how each centre of attraction involves complex processes of production in order that regular, meaningful and profitable tourist gazes can be generated and sustained. Such gazes cannot be left to chance. People have to learn how, when and where to 'gaze'. Clear markers are provided and in some cases the object of the gaze is merely the marker that indicates some event or experience previously happened at that spot.

MacCannell maintains that there is normally a process of sacralisation that renders a particular natural or cultural artefact a sacred object of the tourist ritual (1999: 42–8). A number of stages are involved in this: naming the sight, framing and elevation, enshrinement, mechanical reproduction of the sacred object and social reproduction as new sights (or 'sites') name themselves after the famous. It is also important to note that not only are there many attractions to which to pay homage, but many attractions may only be gazed upon once. In other words, the gaze of the tourist can be amazingly fickle, searching out or anticipating something new or something different. MacCannell notes that 'anything is potentially an attraction. It simply awaits one person to take the trouble to point it out to another as something noteworthy, or worth seeing' (1999: 192).

The complex processes involved here are partly revealed in Turner's analysis of pilgrimage (1973, 1974). Important *rites de passage* are involved in the movement from one stage to another. There are three such stages: first, social and spatial separation from the normal place of residence and conventional social ties; second, liminality, where the individual finds him/herself in an 'anti-structure … out of time and place' – conventional social ties are suspended, an intensive bonding 'communitas' is experienced, and there is direct experience of the sacred or supernatural; and third, reintegration, where the individual is reintegrated with the previous social group, usually at a higher social status.

Although this analysis is applied to pilgrimages, other writers have drawn out its implications for tourism (see Cohen, 1988: 38–40; Shields, 1990; Eade and Sallnow 1991). Like the pilgrim, the tourist moves from a familiar place to a far place and then returns to the familiar place. At the far place both the pilgrim and the tourist 'worship' shrines which are sacred, albeit in different ways, and as a result gain some kind of uplifting experience. In the case of tourists, Turner and Turner talk of 'liminoid' situations where everyday obligations are suspended or inverted (1978). There is licence for permissive and playful 'non-serious' behaviour and the encouragement of a relatively unconstrained 'communitas' or social togetherness.

What is often involved is semi-routine action or a kind of routinised non-routine.

One analysis of such a pilgrimage is Shields' (1990) exploration of the 'honeymoon capital of the world', Niagara Falls. Going on honeymoon to Niagara did indeed involve a pilgrimage, stepping out into an experience of liminality in which the codes of normal social experience are reversed. In particular, honeymooners find themselves historically in a liminal zone where the strict social conventions of bourgeois families were relaxed under the exigencies of travel and of a relative anonymity and freedom from collective scrutiny. In a novel written in 1808, a character says of Niagara: 'Elsewhere there are cares of business and fashion, there are age, sorrow, and heartbreak; but here only youth, faith, rapture' (quoted in Shields, 1990). Shields also discusses how Niagara, like Gretna Green in Scotland, has become a signifier now more or less emptied of meaning, a commercialised cliché.

Some writers in this tradition argue that such playful or 'ludic' behaviour is restitutive or compensatory, revitalising the tourists for their return to familiar places of home and work (see Lett, 1983 on ludic charter-yacht tourism). Other writers argue that general notions of liminality and inversion have to be given a more precise content. It is necessary to investigate the nature of the social and cultural patterns within the tourist's day-to-day existence in order to see just what is inverted and how the liminal experience works out. Gottlieb argues, for example, that what is sought for in a vacation/holiday is inversion of the everyday. The middle-class tourist will seek to be a 'peasant for a day' while the lower middle-class tourist will be 'king/queen for a day' (1982). Although these are hardly profound examples, they do point to a crucial feature of tourism, namely the distinction between the familiar and the faraway and how such differences produce distinct kinds of liminal zones.

It therefore seems wrong to suggest that a search for authenticity is *the* basis for the organisation of tourism. Rather, one key feature would seem to be that there is a difference between one's normal place of residence/work and the object of the tourist gaze. Now it may be that a seeking for what we take to be authentic elements is an important component here, but that is only because there is in some sense a contrast with everyday experiences. Furthermore, it has been argued that some visitors – what Feifer (1985) terms 'post-tourists' – almost delight in the inauthenticity of the normal tourist experience. 'Post-tourists' find pleasure in the multiplicity of tourist games. They know that there is no authentic tourist experience, that there are merely a series of games or texts that can be played (see Chapter 5 later).

We argue in this book for the fundamentally visual nature of many tourism experiences. Gazes organise the encounters of visitors with the 'other', providing some sense of competence, pleasure and structure to those experiences. The gaze demarcates an array of pleasurable qualities to be generated within particular times and spaces. It is the gaze that orders and regulates the relationships between the various sensuous experiences while away, identifying what is visually out-of-ordinary, what are relevant differences and what is 'other'.

We can date the birth of the tourist gaze in the west to around 1840. This is the moment when the 'tourist gaze', that peculiar combining together of the means of collective travel, the desire for travel and the techniques of photographic reproduction, becomes a core component of western modernity. As we show in Chapter 7, photography is central within the modern tourist gaze. Tourism and photography commenced in the west in 1840, as Louis Daguerre and Fox Talbot announced their somewhat different 'inventions' of the camera (in 1839 and 1840 respectively). In 1841, Thomas Cook organised what is now regarded as the first packaged 'tour'; the first railway hotel was opened in York just before the 1840s railway mania; the first national railway timetable, Bradshaws, appeared in 1839; Cunard started the first ever Ocean steamship service; and Wells Fargo, the forerunner of American Express, began stagecoach services across the American west (Urry, 2007: 14). Also in 1840, Dr Arnold, the famous Headmaster of Rugby School, declared that 'Switzerland is to England … the general summer touring place' (quoted Ring, 2000: 25). 1840, then, is one of those remarkable moments when the world seems to shift and new patterns of relationships become irreversibly established.

Recent literature has, however, critiqued this notion of the 'tourist gaze' for reducing tourism to visual experiences – sight*seeing* – and neglecting other senses and bodily experiences involved in these doings of tourism. A so-called 'performance turn' within tourist studies highlights that tourists experience places in more multi-sensuous ways, touching, tasting, smelling, hearing and so on, as well as the materiality of objects and places and not just objects and places viewed as signs. With inspiration from Goffman's (1959) dramaturgical sociology and Thrift's (2008) non-representational theory, this performative turn conceptualises the corporeality of tourist bodies and the embodied actions of, and interactions between, tourist workers, tourists and locals. It has been suggested that it is necessary to choose between gazing and performing as *the* tourism paradigm (Perkins and Thorns, 2001). But *The Tourist Gaze 3.0* rethinks the concept of the tourist gaze as performative, embodied practices, highlighting how each gaze depends upon practices and material relations as upon discourses and signs. What is distinct is the emphasis upon embodied and 'hybrid' performances of gazing and photographing and the various materialities and technologies constituting each way of seeing (see particularly Chapters 8 and 9). Moreover, while sightseeing is crucial, seeing is not the only practice and sense that tourists engage in and activate. There are limits on how much vision can explain. And yet the tourist gaze is always present within tourism performances, as hiking, sunbathing, whitewater rafting and so on are of importance in part through their location within distinct visual environments. Also *The Tourist Gaze 3.0* illuminates some *darker* sides of the tourist gaze (Urry, 1992; Hollingshead, 1999; Morgan and Pritchard, 2005; Elliott and Urry, 2010). We subsequently discuss power relations between gazer and gazee within tourism performances, different forms of photographic surveillance and the changing climates that the global tourist gaze seems to generate.

For the moment, though, it is necessary to consider just what produces a distinct tourist gaze. Minimally, there must be certain aspects of the place to be visited which distinguish it from what is conventionally encountered in everyday life. Tourism results from a basic binary division between the ordinary/everyday and the extraordinary. Tourist experiences involve some aspect or element that induces pleasurable experiences which, by comparison with the everyday, are out of the ordinary. This is not to say that other elements of the production of the tourist experience will not make the typical tourist feel that he or she is 'home from home', not too much 'out of place'. But potential objects of the tourist gaze must be different in some way or other. They must be out of the ordinary. People must experience particularly distinct pleasures which involve different senses or are on a different scale from those typically encountered in everyday life. There are, however, many different ways in which such a division between the ordinary and the visually extraordinary become established and sustained.

First, there is seeing a unique object, such as the Forbidden City in Beijing, the Eiffel Tower, Ground Zero, Buckingham Palace, the Grand Canyon, or the spot in the tunnel in Paris where Princess Diana fatally crashed. These are absolutely distinct objects to be gazed upon which everyone knows about. They are famous for being famous, although such places may have lost the basis of their fame, such as the Empire State Building in New York. Most people living in the 'west' would hope to see some of these objects during their lifetime. They entail a kind of pilgrimage to a sacred centre, often a capital city, a major city or the site of a unique global event (Roche, 2000; Winter, Teo and Chang, 2009, on examples in the 'east').

Then there is the seeing of particular signs, such as the typical American skyscraper, Japanese garden, French château, Norwegian fjord and so on. This mode of gazing shows how tourists are in a way semioticians, reading the landscape for signifiers of certain pre-established notions or signs derived from discourses of travel and tourism (Culler, 1981: 128).

Third, there is seeing unfamiliar aspects of what had previously been thought of as familiar. One example is visiting museums which show representations of the lives of ordinary people, revealing their cultural artefacts. Often these are set out in a 'realistic' setting to demonstrate what houses, workshops and factories had been like. Visitors thus see unfamiliar elements of other people's lives which had been presumed familiar.

Then there is the seeing of ordinary aspects of social life being undertaken by people in unusual contexts. Some tourism in evidentially poor countries has been of this sort. Visitors have found it particularly interesting to gaze upon the carrying out of domestic tasks, and hence to see how the routines of life are surprisingly not that unfamiliar.

Finally, there is the seeing of particular signs that indicate that a certain other object is indeed extraordinary, even though it does not seem to be so. A good example is moon rock, which appears unremarkable. The attraction is not the object itself but the sign referring to it that marks it out as distinctive. Thus the marker becomes the distinctive sight (Culler, 1981: 139). A similar seeing occurs in art galleries when part of what is gazed at is the name of the artist, 'Rembrandt' say, as much as the painting itself which may be difficult for those with limited cultural capital to distinguish from others in the same gallery.

Heidegger captures something of the visual puzzlement involved in being a tourist, in his case while cruising down the Adriatic. He particularly emphasises the tourist *gaze*, that is how experiences of other places are transformed into 'an object ready-at-hand for the viewer' (Heidegger, 2005: 42). He goes on to complain, like countless other 'tourists' before and after, when his cabin 'did not offer much of a view, since it was blocked by the lifeboats' (2005: 7). But he subsequently gets a better view and gazes upon 'Greece'. Heidegger's problem then is that it does not look like 'Greece'. Is it really 'Greece'? He asks: 'Was this, though, already Greece? What I had sensed and expected did not appear.... Everything more looked like an Italian landscape' (2005: 8). He proceeds to worry that 'what was missing was the presence of that Greek element', again something that countless other tourists worry about when looking at the relatively unfamiliar, when it does not look as it should look (2005: 11). And when Heidegger gets to Olympia, the original place of festival of the ancient and modern Olympic Games, 'we found just a plain village disfigured even more by the unfinished new buildings [to become] hotels for the American tourists' (2005: 12). What should thus be gazed upon?

Thus there is no simple relationship between what is directly seen and what this signifies. We do not literally 'see' things. Particularly as tourists, we see objects and especially buildings in part constituted as signs. They stand for something else. When we gaze as tourists what we see are various signs or tourist clichés. Some such signs function metaphorically. A pretty English village can be read as representing the continuities and traditions of England from the Middle Ages to the present day. Other signs, such as lovers in Paris, function metonymically. Here what happens is the substitution of some feature or effect or cause of the phenomenon for the phenomenon itself. The ex-miner, now employed at the former coalmine to show tourists around, is a metonym for the structural change in the economy from one based on heavy industry to one based on tourist services. The development of the industrial museum in an old mill is a metonymic sign of the development of a post-industrial society (see Chapter 6).

MacCannell describes the complex relations involved in developing and reproducing 'attractions'. These relations occur over time between a 'marker', the 'sight' and the 'tourist' (1999: 41). Gazing is not merely seeing, but involves cognitive work of interpreting, evaluating, drawing comparisons and making mental connections between signs and their referents, and capturing signs photographically. Gazing is a set of practices. Individual performances of gazing at a particular sight are framed by cultural styles, circulating images and texts of this and other places, as well as personal experiences and memories. Moreover, gazing involves cultural skills of daydreaming and mind travelling (Löfgren, 1999). 'The extraordinary', as Rojek says, 'spontaneously invites speculation, reverie, mind-voyaging and a variety of other acts of imagination' (1997: 53).

The notion of the tourist gaze is not meant to account for why specific individuals are motivated to travel. Rather we emphasise the systematic and regularised nature of various gazes, each of which depends upon social discourses and practices, as well as aspects of building, design and restoration that foster the necessary 'look' of a place or an environment. Such gazes implicate both the gazer and the gazee in an ongoing and systematic set of social and physical relations.

These relations are discursively organised by many professionals: photographers, writers of travel books, blogs and guides, local councils, experts in the 'heritage industry', travel agents, hotel owners, designers, tour operators, TV travel programmes, tourism development officers, architects, planners, tourism academics and so on. In contemporary tourism, these technical, semiotic and organisational discourses are combined to 'construct' visitor *attractions*, or what Heidegger describes as an alien power which enforces 'its own commands and regulations', in his case over Greece on his attempted 'sojourn' (2005: 55–6).

Focusing on the gaze brings out how the organising sense in tourism is visual. And this mirrors the general privileging of the eye within the history of western societies. Sight was long viewed as the noblest of the senses, the most discriminating and reliable of the sensuous mediators between humans and their physical environment. This emphasis on sight is present within western epistemology, within religious and other symbolisms and within notions of how society should be visible, made transparent, to government (Urry, 2000: ch. 4).

At the same time as this visual proliferation, so the visual is commonly denigrated within many discourses of travel (Buzard, 1993) and more generally (Jay, 1993). The person who only lets the sense of sight have free rein is ridiculed. Such sightseers, especially with a camera draped around their neck, are conventionally taken to be superficial in their appreciation of environments, peoples and places. Martin Parr's photographic collection *Small Worlds* reveals and exposes such a denigration of the (normally male) camera-wearing tourist (1995; Osborne, 2000: ch. 7).

There can be an acute embarrassment about mere sightseeing. Sight may be viewed as the most superficial of the senses, getting in the way of real experiences that should involve other senses and necessitate long periods of time in order for proper immersion. Famously, Wordsworth argued that the Lake District demands a different eye, one that is not threatened or frightened by the relatively wild and untamed nature. It requires 'a slow and gradual process of culture' (Wordsworth, 1984: 193). This criticism of the mere sightseeing tourist is taken to the extreme with the critique of the 'hyper-real', simulated designed places that have the appearance of being more 'real' than the original (Baudrillard, 1983, 1988; see Chapter 5). With hyper-reality the sense of vision is said to be reduced to a limited array of visible features. It is then exaggerated and dominates the other senses. Hyper-real places are characterised by surface appearances. The sense of sight is condensed to the most immediate and visible aspects of the scene, such as the seductive façades of

Main Street in Disneyland or the ocean-liner environment at Manchester's Trafford Centre, although such places can of course be performed in different ways (see Chapters 6 and 8; Bryman, 1995; see also Fjellman, 1992, on Disney, the 'authentic' theme park!).

However, although the tourist gaze emerges in this general sense, there are different kinds of gaze authorised by various discourses. These discourses include *education*, as with the eighteenth-century European Grand Tour and with many current study-tour pro-grammes; *health*, as with tourism designed to 'restore' the individual to healthy functioning often through staying in particular sites of bodily restoration (such as the Swiss Alps or Rotarua in New Zealand); *group solidarity*, as with much Japanese or Taiwanese tour-ism (as at Niagara Falls: Shields, 1990); *pleasure and play*, as with 'ludic' tourism within all-inclusive Caribbean resorts only available for those who happen to be aged 18–30; *heritage and memory*, as with the development of indigenous histories, museums, re-created festi-vals, feasts, dances and so on (see Arellano, 2004, on Inca heritage); and *nation*, as with the increasingly profitable and autonomous notion of *Scotland – the brand* (McCrone et al., 1995).

Moreover, different discourses imply different socialities. With what we call the *romantic* gaze, solitude, privacy and a personal, semi-spiritual relationship with the object of the gaze are emphasised. In such cases, tourists expect to look at the object privately or at least only with 'significant others'. Large numbers of strangers visiting, as at the Taj Mahal, intrude upon and spoil that lonely contemplation desired by western visitors (famously seen in the Princess Diana shot at the Taj; Edensor, 1998: 121–3). The romantic gaze involves further quests for new objects of the solitary gaze, the deserted beach, the empty hilltop, the uninhabited forest, the uncontaminated mountain stream and so on. Notions of the romantic gaze are endlessly used in marketing and advertising tourist sites, especially within the 'west'.

By contrast, what we call the *collective* tourist gaze involves convivi-ality. Other people also viewing the site are necessary to give liveliness or a sense of carnival or movement. Large numbers of people indicate that this is *the* place to be. These moving, viewing others are obligatory for the collective consumption of place, as with Barcelona, Ibiza, Las Vegas, the Beijing Olympics, Hong Kong and so on. Baudelaire relat-edly describes the notion of *flânerie*: 'dwelling in the throng, in the ebb and flo, the bustle, the fleeting' (quoted in Tester, 1994: 2). Indian visitors to the Taj Mahal are implicated in a communal witnessing with family and friends of a national monument (Edensor, 1998: 126), whereas many seaside resorts in northern Europe and North America have lost the crowds necessary for the collective gaze – they have become sites of a kind of lost collective gaze (Walton, 2000).

Beyond these two forms of the gaze, various writers have shown other gazes, other ways in which places get visually consumed both while people are stationary and through movement. These vary in terms of the socialities involved, the lengths of time taken and the character of visual appreciation. Thus first, there is the *spectatorial* gaze that involves the collective glancing at and collecting of different signs that have been very briefly seen in passing at a glance. Examples of this would be the collecting of glances as from a tourist bus window (Larsen, 2001) or from Norwegian cruise ships or ferries that enable visitors to see 'Norway in a Nutshell'. Then there is the notion of the *reverential* gaze used to describe how, for example, Muslims spiritually consume the sacred site of the Taj Mahal. Muslim visitors stop to scan and to concentrate their attention upon the mosque, the tombs and the Koranic script (Edensor, 1998: 127–8). The *anthropological* gaze describes how individual visitors scan a variety of sights/sites and are able to locate them interpretatively within a historical array of meanings and symbols. Some tour guides may themselves provide accounts that interpret sights/sites historically and inter-culturally (as with Bali: see Bruner, 1995, on the anthropologist as tour guide).

Related to this is the *environmental* gaze. This involves a scholarly or NGO-authorised discourse of scanning various tourist practices to determine their footprint upon the 'environment'. On the basis of such reflexivity it is then possible to choose that with the smallest footprint and then recommend through various media to like-minded environmentalists (as with the UK-campaigning organisation Tourism Concern: Urry, 1995a: 191). Then there is the *mediatised* gaze. This is a collective gaze where particular sites famous for their 'mediated' nature are viewed. This is the gaze of so-called movie-induced tourism (see Chapter 5). Those gazing on the scene relive elements or aspects of the media event. Examples of such mediated gazes include locations in Santa Monica and Venice Beach where many Hollywood films are set, the village of Avoca in County Wicklow now overrun by *Ballykissangel* tourists and the Taj Mahal which is a setting for various 'masala' movies where particular scenes can be relived (Edensor, 1998: 127). Finally, there is the *family* gaze. Haldrup and Larsen suggest how much tourist photography revolves around producing loving family photographs set within distinct visual environments (2003; see Chapters 7 and 8).

As discussed in detail in Chapter 8, gazing is an embodied social practice that involves senses beyond sight. At times we refer to travel as *corporeal* travel. This is to emphasise something so obvious that it has often been forgotten (especially according to Veijola and Jokinen, 1994, by most male theorists!). It is that tourists moving from place to place comprise lumpy, fragile, aged, gendered, racialised bodies. Such bodies encounter other bodies, objects and the physical world multi-sensuously. Tourism involves *corporeal* movement and forms of pleasure and these are central to any study of diverse tourisms. In that sense, the tourist gaze involves relations between bodies that are themselves in at least intermittent movement.

This corporeality of movement produces intermittent moments of *physical proximity*, to be bodily in the same space as some landscape or townscape, or at a live event or with one's friends, family, colleagues, partner or indeed in the company of desired 'strangers' (all skiers, or all aged 18–30 and single, or all bridge players). Much travel results from a powerful 'compulsion to proximity' that makes the travel seem absolutely necessary (Boden and Molotch, 1994; Urry, 2007). Much work and social life entail travel because of the importance of connection, of needing to meet, to encourage others, to sustain one's networks (Larsen et al., 2006). To be there oneself is what is crucial in most tourism, whether this place occupies a key location within the global tourist industry or is merely somewhere that one has been told about by a friend. Places need to be seen 'for oneself' and experienced directly: to meet at a particular house of one's childhood or visit a particular restaurant or walk along a certain river valley or energetically climb a particular hill or capture a good photograph oneself. Co-presence, then, involves seeing or touching or hearing or smelling or tasting a particular place (see Rodaway, 1994; Urry, 2000, on the multiple senses involved).

A further kind of travel occurs where a 'live' event is to be seen, an event programmed to happen at a specific moment. Examples include political, artistic, celebratory and sporting occasions, the last are especially 'live' since the outcome (and even the length) may be unknown. Each of these generates intense moments of co-presence, whether for Princess Diana's funeral, the Shanghai World Expo, Glastonbury Festival, or the 2010 World Cup in South Africa. Each of these cannot be missed and they produce enormous movements of people at very specific moments in 'global cities' in order to 'catch' that particular live mega-event. Roche describes the planned mega-events as 'social spatio-temporal "hubs" and "switches" that … channel, mix and re-route global flows' (2000: 199). Such events are spatio-temporal moments of global condensation, involving the peculiarly intense 'localisation' of such global events within 'unique places due to the fact that they staged unique events'. These places therefore have the 'power to transform themselves from being mundane places … into being these special "host city" sites' that come to occupy distinct niches within global tourism (Roche, 2000: 224; see Chapter 6).

Such co-presence nearly always involves travel over, and beyond, other places, to get to those visually distinct sites to watch a live event, to climb a particular rock-face, to wander 'lonely as a cloud', to go white-water rafting, to bungee jump and so on. These corpore-ally defined practices are found in specific, specialised 'leisure spaces', geographically and ontologically distant from work and domestic sites. Indeed, part of the attraction of these places, where bodies can be corporeally alive, apparently 'natural' or rejuvenated, is that they are sensuously 'other' to everyday routines and places. Ring interestingly describes how during the nineteenth century the Alps were developed into such a specialised space where the English gentleman could apparently feel properly alive (2000).

Such places involve 'adventure', islands of life resulting from intense bodily arousal, from bodies in motion, finding their complex way in time and space (see Frisby and Featherstone, 1997; and Lewis, 2000, on the rock-climbing 'adventurer'). Some social practices involve bodily resistance where the body physicalises its relationship with the external world. In the late eighteenth-century development of walking as resistance, the 'freedom' of the road and the develop-ment of leisurely walking were modest acts of rebellion against estab-lished social hierarchy (Jarvis, 1997). Similarly, extreme 'adventure tourism' demonstrates forms of physical resistance to work and the everyday (Perkins and Thorns, 2001). The hedonistic desire to acquire a bronzed body developed through resistance to the Protestant Ethic, women's domesticity and 'rational recreation' (see Ahmed, 2000). A similar resistance to the embodiment of the 'Protestant Ethic' can be seen in the growth of health-spa travel where the body stays still and is subjected to exotic, pampered luxury treatments.

So far we have regarded the body from the viewpoint of the tour-ist. But tourism is often about the body-as-seen, displaying, perform-ing and seducing visitors with skill, charm, strength, sexuality and so on (see Chapter 4). Furthermore, we have so far considered the gaze from the perspective of the gazer. However, much tourism research concerns the consequences of being gazed upon, with working within a 'tourist honeypot' and subject to a gaze somewhat similar to being within a panopticon, for example (Urry, 1992). Staged authenticity may have the effect of keeping out what may be deemed the intrusive eye while providing visitors with what seems properly 'authenticated'. However, whether this is possible depends upon various determinants such as the relations of power within the 'host' community, the time-space characteristics of visitors and the kinds of gaze involved. For example, the least intrusive gaze may be the spectatorial since it is likely to be mobile and will soon pass by (although the endlessly anonymous traffic may itself be over-whelming). The anthropological gaze can be the most intrusive since tourists will insist on staying for lengthy periods within the host community in order to get to know it 'authentically'.

But tourists not only gaze but are also gazed upon by staff and 'locals'. Locals gaze upon tourists' practices, clothes, bodies and cameras and find them amusing, disgusting, curious or attractive. Maoz speaks of a 'mutual gaze' to highlight how tourists too can become the mad ones behind bars, watched by locals (2006; see Chapter 8).

Mobile Worlds

In 1990, when the first edition of this book was published, it was unclear how significant the processes we now call 'globalisation' would become. Indeed, the internet had only just been invented and there was no indication how it would transform countless aspects of social life, being taken up more rapidly than any previous technology. And no sooner had the internet appeared than another 'mobile technology', the mobile phone, transformed communications practices on the move. Overall the last two decades have seen remarkable 'time-space compression' as people across the globe have been brought closer through various technologically assisted developments. There is increasingly what Bauman describes as the shift from a solid, fixed modernity to a more fluid and speeded-up 'liquid modernity' (2000).

And part of this sense of compression of space has stemmed from the rapid flows of travellers and tourists physically moving from place to place, and especially from hub airport to hub airport. Elsewhere we distinguish between virtual travel through the internet, imaginative travel through phone, radio and TV, and corporeal travel along the infrastructures of the global travel industry (Urry, 2007; also see Cresswell, 2006). The amount of 'traffic' along all these has magnified over this last decade or so and there is no evidence that virtual and imaginative travel is replacing corporeal travel, but there are complex intersections between these different modes of travel that are increasingly de-differentiated from one another. As Microsoft asks, 'Where do you want to go today?' And there are many different ways of getting 'there'.

What we call corporeal travel has taken on immense dimensions and comprises the largest ever movement of people across national borders. Because of these liquidities the relations between almost all societies across the globe are mediated by flows of tourists, as place after place is reconfigured as a recipient of such flows. There is an omnivorous producing and 'consuming [of] places' around the globe (see Urry, 1995a). Core components of contemporary global culture now include the hotel buffet, the pool, the cocktail, the beach (Lencek and Bosker, 1998), the airport lounge (Cwerner, Kesselring and Urry, 2009) and the bronzed tan (Ahmed, 2000).

This omnivorousness presupposes the growth of 'tourism reflexivity', the set of disciplines, procedures and criteria that enable each (and every?) place to monitor, evaluate and develop its tourism potential within the emerging patterns of global tourism. This reflexivity is concerned with identifying a particular place's location within the contours of geography, history and culture that swirl the globe, and in particular identifying that place's actual and potential material and semiotic resources. One element in this 'tourism reflexivity' is the very institutionalisation of tourism studies, of new monographs, textbooks, exotic conferences, departments and journals (see *The Sage Handbook of Tourism Studies*: Jamal and Robinson, 2009). There are also many consultancy firms interlinked with local, national and international states, companies, voluntary associations and NGOs. The emergence of this 'tourism industry' is captured in the figure of Rupert Sheldrake, an anthropologist of tourism, in David Lodge's *Paradise News* (1991).

This reflexivity is not simply a matter of individuals and their life-possibilities but of sets of systematic, regularised and evaluative procedures that enable places to monitor, modify and maximise their location within the turbulent global order. Such procedures 'invent', produce, market and circulate, especially through global TV and the internet, new or different or repackaged or niche-dependent places and their corresponding visual images. And the circulating of such images develops further the very idea of the globe itself seen, as it were, from afar (see Franklin, Lury and Stacey, 2000).

Of course not all members of the world community are equal participants within global tourism. Side by side with global tourists and travellers within many of those 'empty meeting places' or 'non-places' of modernity, such as the airport lounge, the coach station, the railway terminus, the motorway service stations, docks and so on, are countless global exiles (Augé, 1995). Such exiles are fleeing from famine, war, changing climates, torture, persecution and genocide, as economic and social inequalities and the consequential displacements of population that have magnified in recent years and forced mobility upon many. The recent growth of 'people smuggling' has generated a multi-billion pound industry with millions in transit across the world at any time.

Significantly for the 'tourist gaze', many developments are taking 'tourism' from the margins of the global order, and indeed of the academy, to almost the centre of this emergent mobile world of 'liquid modernity'. First, tourism infrastructures have been constructed in what would have been thought of as the unlikeliest of places. While clearly most people across the world are not global tourists *qua* visitors, this does not mean that the places that they live in and the associated images of nature, nation, colonialism, sacrifice, community, heritage and so on are not powerful constituents of a rapacious global tourism. Some destinations that are now significantly included in the patterns of global tourism comprise Alaska, Antarctica, Nazi-occupation sites in the Channel Islands, extinct coal mines, Ground Zero, Iceland, Mongolia, Mount Everest, Northern Ireland, Northern Cyprus under Turkish 'occupation', Pearl Harbor, post-communist Russia, the Soweto township in South Africa (see Figure 1.2), outer space, the *Titanic*, Vietnam and so on.

In certain cases becoming a tourist destination is part of a reflexive process by which societies and places come to enter the global order, or to 're-enter' as in the cases of China after 1978 or Cuba during the 1990s, in part using pre-communist American cars in its place-marketing; see Figure 1.3.

Further, there are large increases in tourists emanating from many very different countries, especially those of the 'Orient', which once were places mainly visited and consumed by those from the west. Now rising incomes for an Asian middle class (as well as the student study tour and 'backpacker tourism') have generated a strong desire to see those places of the west that appear to define global culture. The development of a huge middle-class tourist demand from mainland China is a major new development. Hendry, however, describes how various theme parks full of exotic features of 'westernness' are established *within* various Asian countries (2000). She describes this as *The Orient Strikes Back*, the putting on display of many features of western culture for Asians to view, to wonder at and to exoticise, without leaving their home country (more generally, see Winter, Teo and Chang, on *Asia on Tour*, 2009).

Moreover, many types of work are now found within these circuits of global tourism and so it is difficult not to be implicated within, or

Figure 1.2   *Informal township, Soweto*

Figure 1.3   *1950s American cars re-forming the place-image of Cuba*

affected by, one or more of these circuits that increasingly overlap with a more general 'economy of signs' spreading across multiple spaces of consumption (Lash and Urry, 1994; see Chapter 4). Such forms of work include transportation, hospitality, travel, design and consultancy; the producing of 'images' of global tourist sites, global icons (the Eiffel Tower), iconic types (the global beach) and vernacular icons (Balinese dances); the mediatising and circulating of images through print, TV, news, internet and so on; and the organising through politics and protest campaigns for or against the construction or development of tourist infrastructures. And it involves the almost ubiquitous sex-tourism industries (Clift and Carter, 2000; see Chapter 3).

Also, increasingly, roaming the globe are powerful and ubiquitous global brands or logos (Klein, 2000). Their fluid-like power stems from how the most successful corporations over the last two decades have shifted from the manufacture of products to become brand producers, with enormous marketing, design, sponsorship, public relations and advertising expenditures. Such brand companies include many involved in travel and leisure: Nike, Gap, easyJet, Body Shop, Hilton, Virgin, Club Med, Sandals, Starbucks and so on produce 'concepts' or 'lifestyles'. They are 'liberated from the real-world burdens of stores and product manufacturing, these brands are free to soar, less as the dissemination of goods and services than as collective hallucinations' (Klein, 2000: 22). Klein brings out the importance in this of the 'global teen market', with about one billion young people disproportionately consuming similar consumer brands across the globe (2000: 118–21).

There are thus many ways in which huge numbers of people and places are caught up within the swirling vortex of global tourism. There are not two separate entities, the 'global' and 'tourism' bearing some external connections with each other. Rather they are part and parcel of the same set of complex and interconnected processes. Moreover, such assembled infrastructures, flows of images and of people, and the emerging practices of 'tourist reflexivity' should be conceptualised as a 'global hybrid' (Urry, 2003). It is hybrid because it is made up of an assemblage of technologies, texts, images, social practices and so on, that *together* enable it to expand and to reproduce itself across the globe. This is analogous to the mobilities of other global hybrids, such as the internet, automobility, global finance and so on, that spread across the globe and reshape and re-perform what is the 'global'.

For Bauman, the vagabond and the tourist are plausible metaphors for postmodern times: the vagabond, he says, is a pilgrim without a destination, a nomad without an itinerary; while the 'world is the tourist's oyster ... to be lived pleasurably' (Bauman, 1993: 241). Both vagabonds and tourists move through other people's spaces, they both separate physical closeness from moral proximity, and both set standards for happiness and the good life. According to Bauman, the good life has come to be thought of as akin to a 'continuous holiday' (1993: 243). There is thus no separate tourist gaze since, according to Bauman, this is simply how life is lived at least for the prosperous one-third within the new global order.

Feminist analysts criticise the masculinist character of these metaphors that imply that there really can be ungrounded and unbounded movement. Yet different people have very different access to being 'on the road', literally or metaphorically (Wolff, 1993). Moreover, Jokinen and Veijola demonstrate the deficiency of many nomadic metaphors that are 'masculinist' (1997). If these metaphors are re-coded as paparazzi, homeless drunk, sex-tourist and womaniser, then they lose the positive valuation that they enjoyed within masculinist nomadic theory. Indeed, the mobilities of some always presuppose the immobilities of others. The mobile tourist gaze presupposes immobile bodies (normally female) servicing and displaying their bodies for those who are mobile and passing by.

So Morris recommends the metaphor of the motel for the nature of contemporary mobile life (1988). The motel possesses no real lobby, it is tied into the network of highways, it functions to relay people rather than to provide settings for coherent human subjects, it is consecrated to circulation and movement, and it demolishes the particular sense of place and locale. Motels 'memorialize only movement, speed, and perpetual circulation' – they 'can never be a true *place*' and each is only distinguished from the other in 'a high-speed, *empiricist* flash' (Morris, 1988: 3, 5). The motel, like the airport transit lounge or the coach station, represents neither arrival nor departure. It represents the 'pause' before tourists move on to the next stopping-point along the extraordinary routeways of a 'liquid modernity', leaving behind of course those immobilised bodies subject to high-speed passing glances (such as the 50,000 employees at Chicago's O'Hare airport: Gottdiener, 2001: 23).

The analysis of globalisation has thus ushered in some momentous reconfigurations of the tourist gaze, both for the ever-mobile bodies intermittently pausing and for the immobilised bodies that meet in some of these 'strange encounters' of the new world order. Such encounters involve exceptional levels of 'non-interaction', or urban anonymity especially within the 'walled cities' or camps known as airports (Cwerner, Kesselring and Urry, 2009; Adey, 2006, 2010).

There has thus been a major shift from a limited range of tourist gazes in the nineteenth century to the proliferation of discourses, forms and embodiments of tourist gazes now. In a simple sense, we can talk of the globalising of the tourist gaze, as multiple gazes have become core to global culture sweeping up almost everywhere in their awesome wake. There is much less 'tourism' *per se* that occurs within specific and distinct kinds of time-space; there is the 'end of tourism' within the more general 'economy of signs'. There are countless mobilities, physical, imaginative and virtual, voluntary and coerced as well as increasing similarities between behaviours that are 'home' and 'away' (Shaw et al., 2000: 282; Urry, 2007; Haldrup and Larsen, 2010). Tourist sites proliferate across the globe as tourism has become massively mediatised, while everyday sites of activity get redesigned in 'tourist' mode, as with many themed environments. Mobility is increasingly central to the identities of many young people, to those who are members of diasporas and to relatively wealthy retired people who can live on the move or spend much time in their cottage or holiday flat (Urry, 2007). And 'tourism reflexivity' leads almost every place – however apparently boring – to develop some niche location within the swirling contours of the emergent order (see Martin Parr's collection of *Boring Postcards*, 1999).

Elsewhere it is seen how notions of chaos and complexity can help to illuminate the unexpected, far-from equilibrium movements of social and physical processes that rage across the globe (Urry, 2003). These movements have unpredictably elevated 'tourism', even as it de-differentiates from leisure, shopping, art, culture, history, the body, sport and so on, from the very margins to a central place within this emergent global order. And as it does so here and there pockets of disorder remain, of openings and gaps, memories and fantasies, movements and margins. (MacCannell, 2001, argues something similar in his notion of the 'second gaze'.) One thing that is sure about the emergent global order is that it is only at best a contingent and temporary ordering that generates its massive and complex disordering.

In the next chapter we go back to the origins of this mass mobile world and examine some of the processes that engendered the exceptionally distinct mass tourism by the sea for the first industrial working class, which developed in the north of England.

2

Mass Tourism

Introduction

The first example of mass tourism occurred among the industrial working class in Britain. The mass tourist gaze was initiated in the backstreets of the industrial towns and cities in the north of England. This chapter is devoted to examining why this industrial working class came to think that going away for short periods to other places was an appropriate form of social activity. Why did the tourist gaze develop among this industrial working class in the north of England? What revolution in experience, thinking and perception led to such novel and momentous modes of social practice?

The growth of such tourism represents a kind of 'democratisation' of travel. We have seen that travel had been enormously socially selective. It had been available for a relatively limited elite and was a marker of social status. But in the second half of the nineteenth century there was an extensive development in Europe of mass travel by train. Status distinctions then came to be drawn between different classes of traveller, but less between those who could and those who could not travel. We noted above how 1840 is one of those remarkable moments when the world seems to shift and new patterns of social relations become established. This is when the 'tourist gaze', that combining together of the means of collective travel, the desire for travel and the techniques of photographic reproduction, becomes a core component of western modernity.

We consider later how in the twentieth century the car and the aeroplane have further democratised geographical movement. As travel became democratised so extensive distinctions of taste came to be established between the different places to which people travelled, which became markers of social 'distinction'. The tourist gaze came to have a different importance in one place rather than another. A resort 'hierarchy' developed and certain places were viewed as embodiments of mass tourism, to be despised and ridiculed. Major differences of 'social tone' were established between otherwise similar places. And some such places, these new working-class resorts, quickly developed as symbols of 'mass tourism', as places of inferiority which stood for everything that dominant social classes held to be tasteless, common and vulgar.

Explanations of the tourist gaze, of the discourses which established and sustained mass tourism for the industrial working class in the nineteenth century, tend to be over-general. Such developments are normally explained in terms of 'nineteenth-century industrialisation' (Myerscough, 1974). In identifying more precisely those aspects of such industrialisation that were especially important, attention will be paid here to seaside resorts whose development was by no means inevitable. Their growth stemmed from certain features of nineteenth-century industrialisation in Britain and the growth of new modes by which pleasure was organised and structured in a society based upon an emergent, organised and large-scale working class. We examine their development because this was the first mass tourism to occur.

The Growth of the British Seaside Resort

Throughout Europe a number of spa towns developed in the eighteenth century. Their original purpose was medicinal: they provided mineral water used for bathing in and drinking. It is not clear exactly how and why people came to believe in these medicinal properties. The first spa in England appears to have been in Scarborough and dates from 1626 when a Mrs Farrow noticed a spring on the beach (see Hern, 1967: 2–3; Blackbourn, 2002). Within a few decades the medical profession began to advocate the desirable effects of taking the waters, or taking the 'Cure'. Various other spas developed, in Bath, Buxton, Harrogate, Tunbridge Wells and so on. An amazing range of disorders were supposedly improved by both swallowing the waters and by bathing in them.

Scarborough, though, was distinctive since it was not only a major spa but was also by the sea. A Dr Wittie began to advocate both drinking the sea water and bathing in the sea. During the eighteenth century there was a considerable increase in sea bathing as the developing merchant and professional classes began to believe in its medicinal properties as a general pick-me-up. At that stage it was advocated for adults and there was little association between seasides and children. Indeed, the point of bathing in the sea was to do one good and this was often done in winter, involving 'immersion' and not what is now understood as swimming (Hern, 1967: 21).

These dips in the sea were structured and ritualised and prescribed to treat serious medical conditions. Bathing was only to be undertaken 'after due preparation and advice' as the historian Gibbon put it (Shields, 1990), and was also normally undertaken naked. The beach was a place of 'medicine' rather than 'pleasure'.

Spa towns remained relatively socially restrictive. Access was only possible for those who could own or rent accommodation in the particular town. Younger summarises how: 'life in the seventeenth- and eighteenth-century watering-places resembled in many ways life on a cruise or in a small winter sports hotel, where the company is small and self-contained, rather than the modern seaside resort, where the individual is submerged in the crowd' (1973: 14–15).

However, as sea bathing became more popular it was harder for dominant social groups to control access. Conflicts were generated in Scarborough because of its dual function as both spa and resort by the seaside. In 1824 the spa property was fenced off and a toll gate opened so as to exclude the 'improper classes' (Hern, 1967: 16). Pimlott summarised the effects of the widespread development of specialised seaside resorts where this social restriction was not possible:

> The capacity of the seaside resorts, on the other hand, was unbounded. While social life at the spas was necessarily focussed on the pump-room and the baths, and there was no satisfactory alternative to living in public, the sea coast was large enough to absorb all comers and social homogeneity mattered less. (1947: 55)

One precondition, then, for the rapid growth of seaside resorts in the later eighteenth and especially in the nineteenth centuries was space. Britain possessed an extensive coastline which had few other uses apart from fishing, and which could not be privately controlled since ownership of the shoreline and beach between high and low tide was invested in the Crown (see Thompson, 1981: 14).

The development of these new resorts by the seaside was spectacular. In the first half of the nineteenth century coastal resorts showed faster rates of population increase than that of manufacturing towns: 2.56 per cent per annum compared with 2.38 per cent (Lickorish and Kershaw, 1975: 12). The population of Brighton increased from 7,000 to 65,000 in half a century, partly because the Prince Regent made it fashionable, a portion of the West End was *maritimized* (Shields, 1990). The population of the 48 leading seaside towns increased by nearly 100,000 between 1861 and 1871; their population had more than doubled by the end of the century.

By 1911 55 per cent of people in England and Wales took at least one trip to the seaside and 20 per cent stayed for a longer period each year (Myerscough, 1974: 143).

A complex of conditions produced the rapid growth of this new mass leisure activity and hence of these relatively specialised and unique concentrations of services in particular urban centres, concentrations designed to provide novel and what were at the time amazing objects of the tourist gaze.

First, there was some increase in the economic welfare of substantial parts of the working-class population. The real national income per head quadrupled over the nineteenth century (see Deane and Cole, 1962: 282). This enabled sections of the working class to accumulate savings from one holiday period to the next, given there were at the time few holidays with pay (Walton, 1981: 252).

In addition, there was rapid urbanisation, with many small towns growing incredibly rapidly. In 1801, 20 per cent of the population lived in towns; by 1901 80 per cent did. This produced extremely high levels of poverty and overcrowding. Moreover, these urban areas possessed almost no public spaces, such as parks or squares (Lash and Urry, 1987: ch. 3). Unlike older towns and cities, a marked degree of residential segregation by class developed. This was crucial for the emergence of the typical resort, which attracted particular social groupings from certain neighbourhoods of emerging industrial towns and cities. *The Economist* in 1857 summarised the typical urban pattern:

> Society is tending more and more to spread into classes – and not merely classes but localised classes, class colonies. … It is the disposition to associate with equals – in some measure with those who have similar practical *interests*, in still greater measure with those who have similar tastes and culture, most of all with those with whom we judge ourselves on a moral equality, whatever our real standard may be. (20 June 1857: 669; Johnson and Pooley, 1982)

One effect of the economic, demographic and spatial transformation of nineteenth-century towns was to produce self-regulating working-class communities, communities relatively autonomous of either the old or new institutions of the wider society. Such communities were important in developing forms of working-class leisure which were segregated, specialised and institutionalised (Thompson, 1967; Clarke and Critcher, 1985).

The growth of a more organised and routinised pattern of work led to attempts to develop a corresponding rationalisation of leisure:

'To a large extent this regularisation of the days of leisure came about because of a change in the daily hours of work and in the nature of work' (Cunningham, 1980: 147). Particularly in the newly emerging industrial workplaces and cities, work came to be organised as a relatively time-bound and space-bound activity, separated off from play, religion and festivity. Over the course of the eighteenth and nineteenth centuries work was increasingly valued for its own sake and not merely as a remedy for idleness. Some attempts were made to move from an orientation to task towards an orientation to time (see Thompson, 1967; Lash and Urry 1994: chs 9, 10).

Industrialists attempted to impose a rigorous discipline on their newly constructed workforce (Pollard, 1965). Tough and quite unfamiliar rules of attendance and punctuality were introduced, with various fines and punishments. Campaigns were mounted against drinking, blood sports, bad language and idleness (see Myerscough, 1974: 4–6; Cunningham, 1980: ch. 3 on 'rational recreation'). Many fairs were abandoned and Saints' Days and closing days at the Bank of England were dramatically reduced. From the 1860s onwards the idea of civilising the 'rough' working class through organised recreation became more widespread among employers, middle-class reformers and the state (see Rojek, 1993: ch. 2). The typical forms of preferred recreation were educational instruction, physical exercise, crafts, musical training and excursions. Country holidays for deprived city children, as well as the camps organised by the burgeoning youth movement (the Boys' Brigade, Scouts, Jewish Lads' Brigades and so on) were one element of the social engineering of the working class favoured by the rational recreation movement.

As work became in part rationalised, so the hours of working gradually reduced. Parliament introduced various pieces of protective legislation in the second half of the nineteenth century. Particularly important was the attainment of the half-day holiday, especially on Saturdays (see Cunningham, 1980: ch. 5). Phelps-Brown noted that: 'The achievement of a work-week not exceeding 54 hours and providing a half-holiday was unique in its time and was celebrated as "la semaine anglaise"' (1968, 173; Cunningham, 1980: 142–5).

The achievement of longer breaks, of week-long holidays, was pioneered in the north of England and especially in the cotton-textile areas of Lancashire (Walton, 1981, 1983, 1997, 2000). Factory owners began to acknowledge 'wakes weeks' as regularised periods of holiday which were in effect traded for much more regular attendance at work during the rest of the year: 'The total closure of a mill at a customary holiday was preferable to constant disruption throughout the summer, and there were advantages in channelling holiday observances into certain agreed periods' (Walton, 1981: 255).

Some employers thus began to view regular holidays as contributing to efficiency. However, the gradual extension of holidays from the mid-nineteenth century onwards mainly resulted from defensive pressure by the workforce itself, particularly the more affluent who saw such practices as ways of developing their own autonomous forms of recreation. The factory inspector Leonard Horner ascribed the survival of holidays to custom rather than to 'liberality on the part of the masters' (Walton, 1978: 35). A particularly significant feature of such holidaymaking was that it should be collective. As Walton argues, at wakes week 'as at Christmas, Easter and Whitsuntide, custom dictated that holidays should be taken *en masse* and celebrated by the whole community' (1978: 35). From the 1860s onwards, wakes weeks came mainly to involve trips by the whole neighbourhood to the seaside and away from people's normal places of work and living (Walton and Poole, 1982; Walton, 2000).

In the late eighteenth and early nineteenth centuries there was a shift in values connected with the developing Romantic movement. Emphasis was placed upon the intensity of emotion and sensation, on poetic mystery rather than intellectual clarity and on individual hedonistic expression (Feifer, 1985: ch. 5 on the 'Romantic' tourist). The high priests of Romanticism were the Shelleys, Byron, Coleridge, Keats and the Wordsworths (Bate, 1991). Romanticism suggested that one could feel emotions towards the natural world and scenery. Individual pleasures were to be derived from appreciating impressive physical sights. Romanticism implied that those living in newly emerging industrial towns would benefit from spending short periods away from them, viewing or experiencing nature. Romanticism not only led to the development of 'scenic tourism' and appreciation for magnificent stretches of the coastline. It also encouraged sea bathing. Considering the generally inclement weather and the fact that most bathers were naked since no suitable bathing attire had yet been designed by the early nineteenth century, some considerable development of a belief in the health-giving properties of 'nature' must have occurred. Much nineteenth-century tourism was based on the natural phenomenon of the sea and its presumed healthiness (Hern, 1967: ch. 2; Walton, 1983: ch. 2; Sprawson, 1992).

A further precondition for the growth of mass tourism was greatly improved transportation. In the late eighteenth century it took three days to travel from Birmingham to Blackpool. Even the trip from Manchester to Blackpool took a whole day. Only Brighton was reasonably well served by coach. By 1830, 48 coaches a day travelled between London and Brighton and the journey time was reduced to 4½ hours (see Walvin, 1978: 34). But there were two major problems with coach travel. First, many roads were in very poor condition. It was only in the 1830s that the turnpike trusts created a reasonable national network and journey times fell dramatically. Second, coach travel was very expensive, costing something like 2½d. to 3d. a mile. Richard Ayton noted of Blackpool visitors in 1813 that: 'Most of them come hither in carts, but some will walk in a single day from Manchester, distant more than forty miles' (Walvin, 1978: 35).

At first, the new railway companies in the 1830s did not realise the economic potential of the mass, low-income passenger market. They concentrated instead on both goods traffic and on transporting prosperous passengers. But Gladstone's Railway Act of 1844, an important piece of legislation, obliged the railway companies to make provision for the 'labouring classes' (Walvin, 1978: 37). Even before this, the opening of the railway lines between Preston and Fleetwood in 1840 produced an extraordinary influx of visitors to Fleetwood, many of whom then travelled down the coast to Blackpool. By 1848 over 100,000 trippers left Manchester by train for the coast during Whit week; by 1850 it was over 200,000 (Walvin, 1978: 38). The effect on the social tone of Blackpool in the middle of the century was noted at the time:

> Unless immediate steps are taken, Blackpool as a resort for respectable visitors will be ruined. … Unless the cheap trains are discontinued or some effective regulation made for the management of the thousands who visit the place, Blackpool property will be depreciated past recovery. (quoted in Walvin, 1978: 38)

Indeed, the 'social tone' of Blackpool appears to have fallen quickly, since 15 years earlier it was said to have been 'a favourite, salubrious and fashionable resort for "respectable families"' (Perkin, 1976: 181).

But the role of the railways should not be overemphasised. Generally, the railway companies found that the seasonal nature of the holiday meant it was not particularly profitable. It was only at the end of the century that they really set about promoting travel to different resorts by outlining the most attractive features of each resort (see Richards and MacKenzie, 1986: 174–9). And rarely, as in the case of Silloth in the north-west of England, did the railway companies try to construct a wholly new resort, Silloth, which in fact failed (Walton, 1979).

It has also been argued that railway development accounts for the differences in 'social tone' between the rapidly emerging seaside resorts in the mid-nineteenth century. On the face of it, a reasonable explanation of these differences would be that those resorts which were more accessible to the great cities and industrial towns were likely to be more popular and this would drive out visitors with higher social status. Thus Brighton and Southend were more popular and had a lower social tone than Bournemouth and Torquay, which were not in day-tripping range from London (Perkin, 1976: 182).

But such an explanation does not fully work. Scarborough and Skegness were practically the same distance from the West Riding, yet they developed different social tones. Although the railway obviously made a difference, its arrival does not fully explain the marked variations that emerged. Nor, Perkin argues, do the actions of local elites. There were in fact energetic campaigns in most of the places that became working-class resorts (such as Blackpool or Morecambe) to stop the local railway companies from running Sunday day trips because it was thought that the trippers would drive out the wealthier visitors that all resorts wanted to attract.

Perkin argues instead that the effect of the local elites on the respective 'social tones' of different resorts resulted from how land and buildings were locally owned and controlled. The factor determining each resort's social tone was the competition for domination of the resort between three fractions of capital: local, large capital, especially owners of the main hotels, concert halls, shops and so on; local, small capital, especially boarding-house keepers, owners of amusement arcades and so on; and large, externally owned, highly capitalised enterprises providing cheap mass entertainment (Perkin, 1976: 185). Particularly important was the prior ownership and control of land in each locality. Perkin shows this in the contrast between Blackpool and Southport, the latter being located nearer to large centres of population and possessing fine wide beaches. Both resorts began with the more or less spontaneous provision of sea-bathing accommodation by local innkeepers, farmers and fishermen. But in Southport land was unenclosed and various squatters who provided sea-bathing facilities soon became tenants of the joint lords of the manor who in turn laid out the spacious and elegant avenue, Lords Street. The landlords also prevented new industrial and much commercial development, with the result that Southport became a resort of large hotels, residential villas, large gardens and retirement homes for cotton magnates and the like (Walton, 1981: 251).

Blackpool, by contrast, began as a community of small freeholders. By 1838 there were only 24 holdings of land in the town over 25 acres and most of these were well away from the seafront. Even the larger holdings on the front were sold off and divided up into plots for seafront boarding houses. Walton notes that no large resort was so dominated by small lodging houses as Blackpool. This was because:

> There was no room for a planned, high-class estate to grow up on the landowner's own terms, for Blackpool's small freeholders were understandably more concerned with taking the maximum profit from a cramped parcel of land than with improving the amenities of the resort as a whole. (Walton, 1978: 63)

Land in Blackpool was thus developed at high densities from the first, and few restrictions were placed on developers by landowners, for the fragmented pattern of landownership meant that there was always competition to sell and for building.

As a result, the whole central area became an ill-planned mass of smaller properties, boarding houses, amusement arcades, small shops and the like, with no space for the grand public buildings, broad avenues and gardens found in Southport. Although local small capital attempted to appeal to the rapidly expanding middle-class tourist market, Blackpool did not possess the attractions necessary to appeal to this market, and simultaneously it was proving immensely popular, because of its cheapness, with the industrial working class. This included both trippers and those staying overnight. The numbers of visitors increased greatly during the 1870s and 1880s, by which time, the *Morning Post* declared, in Blackpool 'more fun could be found, for less money, than anywhere else in the world' (24 August 1887). Efforts by the Corporation to exclude traders selling cheap goods and services failed, and by the 1890s enough local ratepayers had acquired an interest in catering for the working-class holidaymaker for Blackpool's 'social tone' to be firmly set (Perkin, 1976: 187). The main exception to this pattern was to be found in the area known as the North Shore where the Blackpool Land, Building and Hotel Company acquired control of three-quarters of a mile of seafront and carefully planned a socially select and coherent development (see Walton, 1978: 70–1). During the nineteenth century Southport in fact prospered more than Blackpool, with a larger population even as late as 1901 (Perkin, 1976: 186).

So differences in the social tone of resorts (the 'resort hierarchy') are explicable in terms of the intersection between land ownership patterns and scenic attractiveness. Those places which ended up as working-class resorts, or what might be described as 'manufacturing resorts' linked into a particular industrial city, were those which generally had highly fragmented land ownership in the mid-nineteenth century and a relatively undesired scenic landscape. Such resorts developed as fairly cheap places to visit, with the resulting tourist infrastructure to cater for a mass working-class market normally derived from a specific industrial town or city. As the market developed, so wealthier holidaymakers went elsewhere looking for superior accommodation, social tone and tourist gaze. Holidaymaking is a form of conspicuous consumption in which status attributions are made on the basis of *where* one has stayed and that depends in part upon what the other people are like who also stay there. The attractiveness of a place and hence its location within a resort hierarchy also depends upon *how many* other people are staying in the same place, and especially how many other people there are like oneself.

There were some interesting differences in the nineteenth century between popular holidaymaking in the south of Britain and the north (Walton, 1981). In the south, day excursions were more popular and they tended to be organised by the railway companies, national interest groups like the National Sunday League, or commercial firms like Thomas Cook (see Farrant, 1987, on the development of south-coast resorts, of 'London-by-the-Sea'). Thomas Cook was founded in 1841 when Cook chartered a train from Leicester to Loughborough for a temperance meeting (Brendon, 1991). His first pleasure excursion was in 1844 and the 'package' included a guide to recommended shops and places of historic interest upon which to 'gaze'. Cook wrote eloquently of the desirability of mass tourism and the democratisation of travel:

> But it is too late in this day of progress to talk such exclusive nonsense … railways and steamboats are the results of the common light of science, and are for the people. … The best of men, and the noblest of minds, rejoice to see the people follow in their foretrod routes of pleasure. (quoted in Feifer, 1985: 168–9)

Interestingly, among those undertaking Cook's 'packages' to the continent, women considerably outnumbered men. In restrictive Victorian Britain Thomas Cook provided a remarkable opportunity for (often single) women to travel unchaperoned around Europe.

The immense organisational and sociological significance of Thomas Cook is well summarised by Younger: 'His originality lay in his methods, his almost infinite capacity for taking trouble, his acute sense of the needs of his clients. … He invented the now universal coupon system, and by 1864, more than a million passengers had passed through his hands' (1973: 21; Urry, 2007).

In northern England voluntary associations were important in developing the holiday movement. Pubs, churches and clubs often hired an excursion or holiday train and provided saving schemes for their members. The proximity of friends, neighbours and local leaders provided security and social control. Large numbers of quite poor people were thereby enabled to go on holiday, spending nights away from home. The pattern was soon established of holidaymakers returning again and again to the same accommodation within the same resort. Blackpool, with its high proportion of Lancashire-born landladies, enjoyed a considerable advantage in this respect. Holiday clubs became common in many places in industrial Lancashire, although they remained a rarity elsewhere. Walton well summarises late nineteenth-century developments in industrial Lancashire:

> The factory communities, after early prompting by employers and agencies of self-improvement, thus created their own grassroots system of holiday organisation in the later nineteenth century. Each family was enabled to finance its own holiday without assistance from above. The unique Lancashire holiday system was thus based on working-class solidarity in retaining and extending the customary holidays, and by cooperation and mutual assistance to make the fullest use of them. … Only in Lancashire … was a balance struck between the survival of traditional holidays and the discipline of industrial labour. Only here did whole towns go on holiday, and find resorts able to look after their needs. (1978: 39)

This pattern was particularly found in the cotton-textile industry, partly because of the high employment of women. This meant higher family incomes and a greater interest in forms of leisure that were less male-based and more family/household-based (see Walton, 1981: 253). Elsewhere, Walton maintains, 'too great an attachment to customary holidays and ways of working retarded the development of the working class seaside holiday over much of industrial England' (1981: 263).

Indeed, this was a period in which many other leisure events came to be organised – there was a plethora of traditions invented between 1870 and 1914, often promoted and rendered sacred by royal patronage. Examples included the Royal Tournament in 1888, the first Varsity match in 1872, the first Henry Wood Promenade Concert in 1895, the Highland Games (first made royal in 1852) and so on. As Rojek argues, in the late Victorian/Edwardian period there was a restructured system of moral regulation, which involved not the denial of pleasures but their cultivation. In this process national spectacles played a key role, most spectacularly through the 'Trooping the Colour' on Horse Guards Parade (see Rojek 1993: ch. 2; McCrone, 1998). Participating at least once in these leisure events came to be an important part of the emergent sense of Britishness in the late nineteenth century, a sense increasingly derived from people's *leisure* activities.

In the inter-war period many developments affected the development of the tourist gaze within Britain. First, there was the growth of car ownership to over two million by 1939, as well as the widespread development of coach travel and the idea of touring the countryside (Light, 1991).

Second, there was the considerable development of air transport, with over 200 million miles flown in 1938. This was partly the result of the systematic encouraging of what Adey terms 'air-mindedness' (2006).

Third, various new organisations developed, such as the Cyclists' Touring Club, the Cooperative Holidays Association, Sir Henry Lunn's, the Touring Club of France, the International Union of Official Organizations for Tourist Propaganda, the Youth Hostels Association, the Camping Club of Great Britain and so on.

Fourth, there was the early development of holiday camps, beginning with Joseph Cunningham's Isle of Man camp in 1908 and culminating in Billy Butlin's luxury Skegness camp that opened in 1936 (Ward and Hardy, 1986).

Fifth, there was increasing attraction of travelling by liner and especially of pleasure cruising on what were at the time sumptuous consumption and leisure palaces on the sea (Walton, 2000; Stanley, 2005).

Finally, there was a strong growth of the holidays-with-pay movement, culminating in the Holidays Act of 1938, although much of this only came into effect after 1945 (Walvin, 1978: ch. 6). Sir Walter Citrine, giving evidence to the Select Committee for the Trades Union Cogress (TUC), declared that going on holiday 'is an increasing factor in working-class life. I think most people now are appreciating the necessity for a complete change of surroundings' (quoted in Brunner, 1945: 9).

Overall, Brunner maintained that nevertheless the seaside resort remained the Mecca for the vast majority of British holidaymakers throughout this period. Indeed, she claimed that such resorts are: 'essentially native to this country, more numerous and more highly specialised in their function as resorts than those of any other land' (1945: 8). Seaside holidays were still the predominant form of holiday in Britain up to the Second World War and expanded faster than other type of holiday in the inter-war period (see Walvin, 1978: 116–18; Walton, 2000). Thus by the Second World War there was widespread acceptance of the view that going on holiday was good for one, that it was the basis of personal replenishment. Holidays had become almost a marker of citizenship, a right to pleasure. And around that right had developed in Britain an extensive infrastructure providing specialist services, particularly in these resorts. Everyone had become entitled to the pleasures of the 'tourist gaze' by the seaside.

The next section details how that gaze came to be organised in various resorts, beginning with one 'working-class resort', Morecambe, in the top north-west corner of England just south of the Lake District. It will be shown that different resorts came to specialise in providing the tourist gaze and related services to distinct groups in the social hierarchy.

'Bradford-by-the-Sea', Beaches and Bungalows

Up to the mid-nineteenth century almost all the largest seaside resorts had been located in the south of England, close to middle-class patrons and sources of finance (King, 1984: 70–4). Only these resorts could attract visitors from a 'national' market. Resorts away from the south coast had to rely on a local or regional market. But by the beginning of the twentieth century this had dramatically changed. It was in the north of England, and especially in the Lancashire textile towns, that working-class holidays were pioneered in the late nineteenth century:

> It was here that the seaside holiday, as opposed to the day excursion, became a mass experience during the last quarter of the nineteenth century. Elsewhere, even in London, the process was slower and patchier. But working-class demand became the most important generator of resort growth in northern England in late Victorian times. (Walton, 1983: 30–1)

A number of major resorts developed in the north of England. By 1911 Blackpool had become the fifth-largest resort in the country while Lytham, Morecambe, Southport and St Anne's all showed significant population growth. This was therefore a period which 'saw the swift and emphatic rise of the specialized working-class resort' (Walton, 1983: 67). Compared with the previous period, the fastest-growing resorts were more widely dispersed throughout Britain.

'Morecambe … tried to become a select resort and commuter terminus for West Riding business men, but became instead the Yorkshireman's Blackpool' (Perkin, 1976: 104; Quick, 1962). A condition essential to the growth of the working-class holiday resort was the strong ties of community found in the industrial centres in the north of England (Walton, 1978: 32). But Morecambe could not compete with Blackpool for the bulk of the holiday trade from Lancashire because Blackpool had established a more substantial tourist infrastructure much earlier. It was considerably nearer the rapidly expanding towns and cities in south and east Lancashire and therefore attracted huge numbers of day-trippers. Once a resort had established a pull over its 'industrial hinterland' its position was unlikely to be challenged, since visits to that resort became part of the 'tradition' or 'path dependency' of holidaymaking. Resorts that developed later, such as Bournemouth or Skegness, were able to do so because they had no obvious or similar rivals close by (Walvin, 1978: 161).

In the case of Morecambe it was clear by the second half of the nineteenth century that it could not compete with Blackpool for Lancashire holidaymakers. The Wigan coal-owner and alderman Ralph Darlington declared to a Commons Committee in 1884 that: 'Morecambe does not stand in estimation with us as a watering place. I should say it is not one at all' (quoted in Grass, 1972: 6). Likewise Thomas Baxter, chairman of the Morecambe Board of Health in 1889, observed that: 'there was no doubt that Blackpool had always had the pull all over Lancashire' (*Observer*, 11 October 1889).

Morecambe's inability to compete for the Lancashire holiday market, combined with the rail link to the Yorkshire woollen towns, meant that many visitors came from Leeds and Bradford. This was because the connections with Yorkshire extended not only to the holiday trade but also to patterns of migration. Many people from Yorkshire, both workers and employers, came to live in Morecambe, some of whom commuted to Bradford or Halifax daily (Perkin, 1976: 190). The first mayor of the new Corporation, Alderman E. Barnsbee, was a Bradford man who retired to Morecambe. In addition, Morecambe was not the only holiday destination for those living in the West Riding. It had to face considerable competition from the resorts on the east coast, in both Yorkshire and Lincolnshire. Yet it did become increasingly popular. A *Daily Telegraph* correspondent wrote in 1891: 'as Margate is to the average Cockney, so is Morecambe to the stalwart and health-loving Yorkshireman. For it is allowed on all sides that Morecambe is true Yorkshire to the backbone. ... Yorkshiremen, Yorkshire lads, and Yorkshire lasses have selected to colonise and to popularise this breezy, rainy, wind-swept, and health-giving watering-place' (quoted in Grass, 1972: 10). Furthermore, in the inter-war period a Lord Mayor of Bradford proclaimed that 'most of the citizens of Bradford, to say nothing of the children, have enjoyed spending some of their leisure time in this wonderful health resort' (*Visitor*, July 1935, Diamond Jubilee Souvenir).

Morecambe, however, did not attract as many middle-class visitors that were hoped for. Partly this was because the town leaders could not prevent the growth of many day-trippers, described by the *Lancaster Guardian* as a 'disorderly and riotous mob' (22 August 1868), and partly because very many relatively small houses (often 'back houses') made it impossible to stop the establishment of new boarding houses and small hotels which provided accommodation for less well-off visitors, especially from west Yorkshire. There was a considerable debate between the champions of 'respectability', who were organised through the Board of Health until 1894 and the Urban District Council after then, and the providers of 'mass holiday consumption', such as the large entertainment companies. In an editorial in 1901, the *Visitor* supported the latter group on the grounds that in a town with 'no public band, no public parks, no pier supported from the rates', they had 'done their work catering for the visitors admirably this season' (2 October 1901). As early as the late 1890s the advocates of commercial development had won the day and attempts by the Urban District Council to maintain 'respectability' had failed. The *Daily Telegraph* summed up Morecambe in 1891: 'It may be that, to the fastidious, rough honest-hearted Morecambe is a little primitive, and slightly tinged with vulgarity. But it is never dull' (quoted in Perkin, 1976: 191).

In the later years of the century there were a number of developments: a rapid rate of population increase (over 10 per cent per annum); much growth of capital expenditure, especially on major facilities including a revolving tower; and an extensive growth of lodging-house and hotel accommodation (see Denison-Edson, 1967).

But its prosperity was dependent upon the level of prosperity in west Yorkshire. When Bradford, and especially the woollen industry, was doing well, then Morecambe seemed to prosper. As the *Observer* noted in 1883: 'when the Bradford trade has been at a low ebb it has not been at all plain sailing for "Bradford-by-the-Sea"' (25 May). Also, Morecambe remained the prisoner of the railway companies and the quality and quantity of the train services they provided.

In the inter-war period Morecambe was successful, partly because there was an extensive growth of paid holidays for those in work, and partly because most holidays were still taken at the seaside and family-households were transported there by rail and to a lesser extent by coach. Spokesmen from Morecambe advocated that all workers should receive a week's holiday with pay (*Visitor*, 22 January 1930). By 1925 there were two holiday camps in Heysham, part of the same borough. Morecambe experienced considerable annual growth in population, 3.8 per cent during the 1930s (Denison-Edson, 1967: 28). The 1930s and 1940s were particularly prosperous, with the town council investing heavily in new objects for the tourist gaze, an example of how a Conservative council could engage in 'municipal conservatism'.

We now briefly describe two other resorts by way of comparison: Brighton, on the south coast, and Birchington, in Kent. Each was the first to develop new objects of the tourist gaze at the seaside, Brighton with the first beach devoted to 'pleasure' and Birchington with the first bungalow houses.

We already noted the early and extensive development of Brighton during the eighteenth century. The beach was viewed as a site for medical treatment and was regulated by 'dippers', the women responsible for immersion (see Shields, 1990: ch. 2). In the mid-nineteenth century this medicalised beach was replaced by a pleasure beach, which Shields characterises as a liminal zone, a built-in escape from the patterns and rhythms of everyday life. Such a zone had a further characteristic, of carnival, as the beach became noisy and crowded, full of unpredictable social mixing, and involving the inversion of social hierarchies and moral codes. In the classic medieval carnival, the grotesque body was counterposed to the disciplined body of propriety and authority; in the nineteenth-century holiday carnival, the grotesque body was shamefully uncovered and open to the gaze of others. Literally, grotesque bodies became increasingly removed from actual view and were gazed upon through commercialised representations, especially the vulgar picture postcard. Shields summarises the carnival of the beach rendered appropriate for pleasure:

> It is this foolish, impudent, undisciplined body which is the most poignant symbol of the carnivalesque – the unclosed body of convexities and

orifices, intruding onto and into others' body-space, [which] threatens to escape, transgress, and transcend the circumscriptions of the body. (1990: 95)

Brighton was the first resort in which the beach became constructed as a site for pleasure, for social mixing, for status reversals, for carnival. This is one reason why in the first few decades of the twentieth century Brighton developed a reputation for sexual excess and particularly for the 'dirty weekend'. This became part of the place-image of Brighton, although the beach no longer so functions as a site of the carnivalesque.

Whereas Brighton's class associations were with royalty and the aristocracy, the resorts in Kent in the mid-nineteenth century were associated with the new middle class (King, 1984: 72–8). The developing professional middle class increasingly stayed in Cliftonville and Westgate. In the latter, all the roads were private and only detached houses were allowed. The first bungalows in Britain were built in 1869–70 in Westgate and more extensively in Birchington in 1870–3, just next door (King, 1984: 74). Until this development there was no specialist house building by the seaside. Indeed, in the earlier fishing villages houses were often built with their backs to the sea, as at Ravenglass on the edge of the Lake District. The sea was there for fishing, not for gazing on. Nineteenth-century resorts were public places with some distinctive public buildings, such as assembly rooms, promenades, public gardens, dance halls and so on. Residential provision was similar to that found in inland towns and was not distinct.

By contrast, the development of the bungalow as a specialised form of housing by the seaside resulted from the heightened attraction of visiting the seaside not for strictly medical reasons but for the bracing air and fine views; the increasing demand from sections of the middle class for accommodation well away from other people, for being able to gaze at the sea in relative solitude; and the rising popularity of swimming as opposed to dipping and hence the perceived need for semi-private access for the whole family and especially for children. Birchington ideally met these conditions. There were no public facilities, there was an attractive coastline for building, the first bungalows were 'rural looking' and offered attractive contrasts with the urban, and tunnels could be built linking each bungalow directly with the beach. In the twentieth century there has been an extensive 'bungaloid growth' at the seaside so that in some sense in the twentieth century the bungalow *is* the English seaside. And as it has become the housing of the lower middle class, so its earlier fashionability and bohemianism evaporated and indeed it became an object of considerable status hostility (see King, 1984: ch. 5). This further brings out how seaside resorts are places of contested social tone and fights over cultural capital.

Conclusion

So we have examined in this chapter the nineteenth-century origins of English seaside resorts. We tried to bring out just how distinct this development was. They were the first places where the rapidly growing industrial working class in Europe would go away for leisure and pleasure, generally with others from the same class neighbourhood. They left behind, if only for a day or a week, industrial towns and cities, places of backbreaking labour, water and airborne pollution, rampant ill-health and a lack of visual stimulation. The resorts offered some remarkable contrasts as the collective tourist gaze took improbable root in these places by the sea. These places came then to be re-made and re-seen as places of visual enticement, places 'on the margin' but increasingly central to the growing 'economy of signs' of an industrial economy.

The twentieth century then ushered in some striking further transformations of the tourist gaze. Places by the sea emerged all over the world, modelling themselves on these early mass resorts but developing many new features and characteristics to gaze upon, as we examine in the rest of this book. In some cases, these early resorts came to seem dated and very much left-behind in the slow lane, as competition between places to be gazed upon became first nationalised and then internationalised.

3

Economies

Introduction

The relations between the tourist gaze and those industries that develop to meet that gaze are complex. Most tourist services are delivered at the time and place at which they are produced, although there are a few exceptions to this. Thus the quality of the social interaction between the provider of the service, such as the waiter, flight attendant, tour rep or hotel receptionist, and the consumers is part of the 'product' purchased by tourists. If aspects of that social interaction are unsatisfactory (the off-hand waiter, the unsmiling flight attendant, or the rude receptionist), then what is purchased is in effect a different service product. One major problem results from how the production of such consumer services is not entirely carried out backstage, away from the gaze of tourists who cannot help seeing some aspects of the industry which is attempting to serve them. But furthermore, tourists tend to have high expectations of what they should receive since 'going away' is normally endowed with significance and anticipated through advertising and marketing undertaken by tourist organizations. People are looking for the extraordinary and hence will be critical of services appearing to undermine such quality. These expectations of service quality are especially pronounced in the case of international business travellers (see Beaverstock et al., 2010).

One consequence of this is that services cannot be provided anywhere; they have to be produced and consumed within specific places. Part of what is consumed is, in effect, the place in which the service producers are located. If the particular place does not convey appropriate cultural meanings and display memorable visual features, the quality of the specific service may be tarnished. There is therefore a crucial 'spatial fixity' about tourist services. In recent years there has been enormously heightened competition to attract tourists. So while the producers are to a significant extent spatially fixed, in that they have to provide particular services in particular places, consumers are mobile, able to consume tourist services to some degree on a global basis. The industry is inevitably competitive since almost every place in the world could well act as an object of the tourist gaze. There is also a crucial temporal fix to some services. Many services (such as a hot meal) need to arrive at a very specific time, and each service encounter is always a 'moment of truth'. Services are performances of the here-and-now (see Chapter 4). A service that does not arrive at the right time is very likely to be perceived as a poor service. And yet services have an unpredictable 'afterlife'; bad and good services can stick in the memory and 'travel the world' through travel talk and reviews on the internet. Any moment of poor service may come back to haunt that place in the future.

The emphasis on the quality of the social interaction between producers and consumers of tourist services means that tourist developments are not simply explicable in terms of 'economic' determinants. As shown later it is also necessary to examine a range of social and cultural changes which transform people's expectations about what they wish to gaze upon, what significance should be attached to that gaze, and what effects this has upon the providers of relevant tourist services. This industry has normally necessitated considerable levels of public involvement and investment, and in recent years this has increased as all sorts of places attempt to construct or reinforce their position as favoured objects of the tourist gaze. The economics of tourism cannot be understood separately from the analysis of cultural, management and policy developments found later in this book, just as work in tourist industries cannot be understood separately from the social expectations that surround the complex delivery of services. Work relationships in tourist industries are significantly socially defined.

In this chapter attention will be directed to some developments in the changing political and cultural economy of the tourism. We trace a shift from Fordism to post-Fordism during the last decades and then exemplify this through recent discussions of the related notions of the 'Experience Economy', 'McDonaldization', and 'Disneyfication'.

Fordism and Post-Fordism

We begin with Campbell's classic analysis of the character of consumption (1987). He argues that covert daydreaming and anticipation are central to modern consumerism. Individuals do not seek satisfaction simply from products, from their selection, purchase and actual use. Rather, satisfaction stems from anticipation, from imaginative pleasure-seeking. People's basic motivation for consumption is not simply materialistic. Rather, people seek to experience 'in reality' the pleasurable dramas they have already experienced in their imagination. However, since 'reality' rarely provides the perfected pleasures encountered in daydreams, each purchase leads to disillusionment and to the longing for ever-new products and services. There is a dialectic of novelty and insatiability at the very heart of contemporary consumerism.

Campbell seems to view 'imaginative hedonism' as a relatively autonomous characteristic of modern societies and separate from specific institutional arrangements, such as advertising or particular modes of social emulation (1987: 88–95). Both claims, though, are dubious in general but particularly so with regard to tourism. It is hard to envisage the nature of contemporary tourism without seeing how such activities are constructed in people's imagination through advertising and the media, and through competition between different social groups employing different kinds of capital (see Selwyn, 1996, on tourism images). If Campbell is right in arguing that contemporary consumerism involves imaginative pleasure-seeking, then tourism is surely the paradigm case. Tourism necessarily involves daydreaming and anticipation of new or different experiences from those normally encountered in everyday life. But such daydreams are not autonomous; they involve working over advertising and other media-generated sets of signs, many of which relate to complex processes of social emulation, as we show later.

One further problem in Campbell's otherwise useful analysis is that he treats modern consumerism as though it is historically fixed. He thus fails to address the changing character of consumption and the possible parallel transformations in the nature of capitalist production (consumption is used here in the sense of 'purchase' and does not imply there is no 'production' within households). However, many writers argue that a sea-change took place within contemporary societies, involving the shift from organised to disorganised capitalism (Lash and Urry, 1987, 1994). Other writers have characterised this as a move from Fordism to post-Fordism, and in particular from mass consumption to more individuated patterns of consumption (Piore and Sabel, 1984; Harvey, 1989; Poon, 1989, 1993).

But this consumption side of the analysis is undeveloped, indicating the 'productivist' bias of much literature here. In order to deal with this we now set out two ideal types of Fordist mass consumption and post-Fordist differentiated consumption.

Mass consumption: this involves the purchase of commodities produced under conditions of mass production; a high and growing rate of expenditure on consumer products; individual producers tending to dominate particular industrial markets; producers rather than consumers as dominant; commodities being little differentiated from each other by fashion, season and specific market segments; and relatively limited choice – what there is tends to reflect producer interests whether private or public. Such a system was set in motion by Thomas Cook, who historically popularised tourism through mass consumption, or what we might term Cookism rather than Fordism. Thomas Cook realised that 'mass tourism' had to be *socially* and *materially* invented and organised through producer expertise. As a result of various system innovations, Cook turned expensive, risky, unpredictable and time-consuming individual travel into a highly organised, systematised and predictable social activity for the masses, based upon expert knowledge. Cook's early innovations included systems of ticketing, guiding, conducted tours, block bookings, the railway coupon and the organised collection and delivery of luggage (Brendon, 1991).

Post-Fordist consumption: this involves consumption rather than production as dominant with consumer expenditure increasing as a proportion of national income; new forms of credit permitting consumer expenditure to rise with high levels of indebtedness; very many aspects of social life are commodified; much greater differentiation of purchasing patterns by different market segments; more volatility of consumer preferences; the growth of a consumer movement and the 'politicising' of consumption; the reaction of consumers against being part of a 'mass' and the need for producers to be more consumer-driven, especially in the case of service industries; developing more products, each having a shorter life; new kinds of commodity which are more specialised and based upon non-mass forms of production ('natural' products, for example); and much attention paid to developing sign-value and 'branding'.

Although some consumption patterns cross-cut this division, western societies have been broadly moving from the former ideal type to the latter. This shift is reflected in the changing character of contemporary tourism (see Poon, 1993; Urry, 1995a). For example, in Britain the holiday camp was the quintessential example of Fordist holidaymaking. In the move to post-Fordism such camps have been renamed 'centres' or 'holiday-worlds' and now present themselves as places of 'choice', 'independence' and 'freedom'. We show in later chapters how many other changes are occurring in contemporary holidaymaking of a broadly 'post-Fordist' sort. These changes have been characterised by Poon as the shift from 'old tourism', which involves packaging and standardisation, to 'new tourism', which is segmented, flexible and customised (1993). Some such changes are also transforming relations *between* tourism and other cultural practices. In Chapter 5 we consider 'postmodernism', a significant feature of which is the importance placed on play, pleasure and theming. Later in this chapter we consider how 'globalisation' produces further shifts in the production and consumption of tourism sites – especially through the emergence of global brands and the Web 2.0 revolution of the internet.

First, though, we discuss two influential contemporary theories of post-industrial production and consumption: the experience economy (Pine and Gilmore, 1999) and Disneyization (Bryman, 2004). Both concepts highlight how extraordinary personalised experiences are key in the post-Fordist consumption economy.

The distinctive feature of the experience economy is that services need to be more than just mere 'services', which can seem boring to the increasingly thrill-seeking consumer. Services need to be somehow pleasurable and memorable; they must be 'experiences', 'revealed over a duration'. Pine and Gilmore coined the term 'experience economy' in 1999 and argued that the service economy is turning into an experience economy. Revenue derives from staging and enacting memorable, exciting and engaging experiences, rather than providing services on demand as cheaply as possible. This is a largely consumer-driven transformation as consumers are said to desire extraordinary services. In a post-Fordist economy businesses need to think of themselves as 'theatres' with their staff as performing artists in order to engage with consumers (Pine and Gilmore, 1999: 104). Places of service encounters need to be imagined and staged as affective venues of atmosphere and eventness where memorable experiences come to be 'revealed over time'. Service producers must thus learn to perform, play, enact and stage – not unlike actors in a theatre. They are no longer providers of benefits but stagers of sensations.

Pine and Gilmore interestingly introduce theatre metaphors to management and design as well as arguing that the rest of the economy ought to learn from Walt Disney and other entertainment businesses where experiences have always been at their heart (1999: 98). In a fully-fledged experience economy, customers fly with, eat and shop at, and book into with those businesses that not only meet basic needs and functions in the here-and-now, but turn them into personal and memorable experiences that remain in the memory (Pine and Gilmore, 1999: 99).

Pine and Gilmore's ideas have rapidly spread into policy and commercial fields as part of a wider interest in developing a new 'cultural economy' (Löfgren, 2003; Gibson and Kong, 2005; O'Dell and Billing, 2005). Policy makers, urban planners and architects, who are seeking to revitalise decaying places and commercialise cultural institutions such as theatres and museums, increasingly turn into 'experience-scapes' (Hayes and MacLeod, 2007). Tourism and hospitality managers also adopt Pine and Gilmore's ideas so as to develop innovative approaches to service performance (Landry, 2006; Bell, 2007).

The notion of Disneyization has similarities with the experience economy. This is because Disney theme parks are the metaphor and lead model within the notion of an experience economy. According to Bryman, 'Disneyization connects with a post-Fordist world of variety and choice in which consumers reign supreme' (2004: 5). This is an economy where consumer variety and choice is delivered through the spectacular 'theming' of servicescapes and by turning service encounters into events where performative workers simultaneously entertain and treat consumers as 'kings'. Disneyization is a strategy through which businesses seek to increase the value of goods and services by transforming them into differentiated experiences, 'magically' making the ordinary extraordinary.

This notion of Disneyization differs from Ritzer's McDonaldization thesis (2008). The latter emphasises how consumption is homogenised and standardised across the world, that is, Fordist. McDonaldization suggests that tourists crave for experiences and services that are predictable, standardised, risk-free and calculable – just like the Big Mac no matter where it is served. According to Bryman, 'Disneyization seeks to create variety and difference, where McDonaldization wreaks likeness and similarity. It exchanges the mundane blandness of homogenised consumption experiences with frequently spectacular experiences' (2004: 4; see Chapter 4 on Disney parks).

However, Bryman also brings out that some services and leisure spaces contain elements of both McDonaldization and Disneyization. Many tourism sites, such as all-inclusive resort hotels (Edensor, 1998), package tours (Haldrup and Larsen, 2010), cruises (Weaver, 2005) and theme parks (Lukacs, 2008), combine the predictable and standardised together with the personal and experiential. Moreover, a more general McDonaldization of the wider society has made the need to McDonaldize holidays less important. Thus if we consider standardized meals:

> In the past, one reason that tour operators had to offer standardized meals was that the food available at any given tourist site was like to prove too unusual and unpredictable and therefore unpalatable for

many tourists. However, now tourists can safely be left on their own at most locales since those that want standardized meals can almost undoubtedly find them readily available at a local McDonald's, or at an outlet of some other international chain of fast-food restaurants. (Ritzer and Liska, 1997: 98)

Globalisation

The English seaside resort examined in the previous chapter went into at least relative decline in the mid-1960s, at the moment when mass tourism, at least in Europe, started to internationalise. This internationalisation means that tourist patterns in a particular society cannot be explained without examining developments taking place in most other countries. Through internationalisation, tourist sites can be compared with those located at home and abroad, especially via the internet. So when people visit somewhere in their own country they are in effect choosing not to visit somewhere abroad. All potential objects of the tourist gaze can be located on a scale and compared with each other, often now more or less instantaneously via television and the internet.

One consequence of such globalisation is that different countries, or different places within a country, come to specialise in providing particular kinds of objects to be gazed upon. An international division of tourist sites has emerged in the last two or three decades. Britain came to specialise in history and heritage, and this affects both what overseas visitors expect to gaze upon and what attracts British residents to spend time holidaymaking within Britain. Moreover, this internationalisation is more developed in Britain than in some other countries. This is partly because of the early and innovative development of the package or inclusive holiday in Britain, and partly because there were already many historical sites to attract significant numbers of overseas tourists. Just as the UK economy in general is an open economy, so this is also true of tourism.

Tour operators based in Britain have sold their inclusive or package holidays at cheaper prices than comparable European countries. In the 1980s, in most hotels in Spain, Portugal and Greece, it was the British-based tour operators that offered the lowest price; British-based companies were effective at reducing unit costs and generating a huge market for international travel in the UK. There are now about 19 million package holidays sold each year (compared with 8 million in 1983; www.telegraph.co.uk/travel/budgettravel/5130485/Return-of-the-package-holiday.html; accessed 31.03.10). Inclusive holidays had such an impact in Britain because of the early emergence of integrated companies, the tour operators, who combined together the developing technologies of jet transport and computerised booking systems from the 1960s onwards.

With the formation of a single European market, tour operators in Europe increasingly operate in each of the major countries. This has increased competition and reduced the level of concentration within a single country, as well as increasing cross-border takeovers and mergers. This has also raised the level of vertical integration, with the operators also owning travel agencies, hotels and airlines (Chandler, 2000: D5–9).

It seems that with increased leisure time people, especially young people, are increasingly moving away from the standardised package holiday and seeking many more forms of leisure activity, including independent travel (Desforges, 1998). There has been a marked increase in seats-only flights, partly because of the demand for more flexibility and partly because of the growth in overseas property ownership (until the Great Crash of 2008 with its decline in holiday-making and some rise, it seems, in packaged holidays). Only about one-tenth of overseas visitors to Britain are on inclusive holidays.

Barrett also suggests that some switching to independent travel 'is partly a reaction to the "naffness" of package holidays', that indeed even in the 1980s they were no longer viewed as fashionable or smart (1989b). Between 2003 and 2007, independently booked holidays rose from 21.7 million to 27.2 million, while package holidays stagnated at around the 19 million mark (www.telegraph.co.uk/travel/budgettravel/5130485/Return-of-the-package-holiday.html; accessed 31.03.10). This has been further developed by the popularity of low-budget airlines such as Ryanair and easyJet operating with a different business model, as discussed below.

Furthermore, new technologies, in particular ICTs, are especially important because of the immense informational and communication problems involved in planning and coordinating actions at a distance. We now consider the major impact the internet has upon the political economy of tourism, particularly with so-called Web 2.0. Since the early days of the internet, tourism industries, travel agencies, tour operators and airlines used the internet for internal and external management, planning, logistics and communication, on the one hand, and issuing tickets, promoting destinations, developing appropriate tourist gazes and place myths on websites to tourists, on the other (Buhalis and Law, 2008). While 'shopping' on the internet is not yet widespread, except for specific products such as books, booking hotels and air tickets is now commonly undertaken online (Pan and Fesenmaier, 2006; Xiang and Gretzel, 2009). Over half of Danes surveyed in 2008 regularly buy air tickets and/or book hotel rooms online (www.dst.dk/nytudg/14530; accessed 04.05.10).

Schmallegger and Carson highlight how the internet is significant for tourism within promotion, product distribution, communication, management and research (2008). Overall, the internet makes possible a 'networked economy' where tourism suppliers can more easily operate on a global scale, are less reliant on traditional intermediaries such as travel agents, tour operators and check-in staff, and can make the tourism 'product' more individual and flexible.

The exceptional growth of cheap airlines illustrates these processes. Such companies cut flight prices through online booking on their websites and thereby selling directly to passengers without the expense of travel agents. Budget airlines provide financial incentives for self-booking online and do not issue paper tickets (like most other airlines now). At one time, playing on the British Airways' slogan 'the world's favourite airline', easyJet branded itself 'the web's favourite airline'. In 2001 Ryanair's website handled 75 per cent of all their bookings. Today 97 per cent of Ryanair's passengers book online and 75 per cent use the internet to check in and Ryanair closed all its airport check-in desks on the 1st October 2009 (http://news.bbc.co.uk/2/hi/business/7903656.stm; accessed 31.03.10). In airport terminals tourists are increasingly interacting with faceless 'internet screens' rather than the more or less human faces of the tourism industry. Much service provision is increasingly becoming, we can say, 'face-to-interface' rather than 'face-to-face'.

A further indicator of the networked nature of tourism economies is the proliferation of international internet-based reservation websites, such as Hotels.com, Expedia.com and Cheapflights.com. These are very visible on the internet when browsing for cheap air tickets or hotels around the world. Such 'search engines have become a powerful interface that serves as the "gateway" to travel-related information as well as an important marketing channel through which destinations and tourism enterprises can reach and persuade potential visitors' (Xiang and Gretzel, 2009: 179). Hotels.com is an American-based Hotel Reservations Network (HRN) offering consumers discounted hotel rooms in major cities around the world. At Expedia.com it is possible to compare prices for airline tickets, hotel reservations, car rentals, cruises, vacation packages and various attractions at particular destinations across much of the world. As Expedia.com says:

Expedia delivers consumers everything they need for researching, planning, and purchasing a whole trip. The company provides direct access to one of the broadest selections of travel products and services through its North American Web site, localized versions throughout Europe, and extensive partnerships in Asia. Serving many different consumer segments – from families booking a summer vacation to individuals arranging a quick weekend getaway, Expedia provides travelers with the ability to research, plan, and book their comprehensive travel needs. Expedia-branded Web sites feature airline tickets, hotel reservations, car rental, cruises, and many other in-destination services from a broad selection of partners. (www.expedia.com/default.asp; accessed 02.05.10)

At Hotels.com and Expedia.com travellers purchase the service directly through the websites without having contact with the actual provider of the service. At Cheapflights.com the site redirects costumers to the websites of the service providers themselves. While tourism industries are less dependent upon traditional intermediaries, the power and presence of these virtual reservation networks mean that hotels and airlines have to be linked up to such hubs. There is a new widespread dependence upon all-pervasive technical intermediaries or systems that are themselves very significant global internet brands.

 Consumers find such sites attractive. First, they are time-effective if they work, since costumers only need to consult one such 'site' (hub) rather than Google-ing for and visiting several sites. Second, they create transparency, comparability and informed choice in a virtual world of many choices and disparate sites, something that has characterised the internet since its inception. Each search for a given service (say, a hotel in Warsaw at a particular weekend) will produce a list of available hotels, listing amenities and including photographs, the specific price for those nights, and a star ranking based upon both 'traditional stars' and customer reviews. Third, they allow for more flexible and individualised travel patterns. Systems affected through the internet permit customers to 'self-serve' themselves with airline tickets and other standardised products. Consumers can put together more flexible packages, a kind of holiday 'mix 'n' match' or what the industry terms 'Free and Independent Travel' or FITs. Expert systems developments enable the prospective traveller to provide some parameters of intended travel and then allow the computer to generate related consumer products.

Until recently the tourism industries largely controlled information flows since tourists could not interact with this information or contribute their own content. This changed with Web 2.0 as the internet became in some ways more open, collaborative and participatory. It affords an open online participatory culture where connected individuals not only surf but can make things through editing, updating, blogging, remixing, posting, responding, sharing, exhibiting, tagging and so on. Web 2.0 highlights how consumers have become part of the production process. Perhaps the key defining feature of Web 2.0 is that users are involved in processes of production and consumption as they generate and browse online content, as they tag and blog, post and share. This has seen the 'consumer' taking a more active role in the 'production' of commodities. Indeed, it is the mundane personal details posted on profiles and the connections made with online 'friends' that become *the* commodities of Web 2.0. It is the profile, the informational archive of everyday lives, that draws people into the network and encourages individuals to make 'friends' (Beer and Burrows, 2007: 3.3).

Web 2.0 also impacts upon tourism businesses and how tourists plan their journeys. They not only 'post' 'travel tales' to significant others, but also to 'strangers' in user-generated social networking sites (e.g. Facebook, Myspace), photo communities (e.g. Flickr, Photobucket) and travel communities (e.g. Virtualtourist, Tripadvisor). Users produce web content as well as consuming it. Web 2.0 provides tourists with opportunities to publish their recommendations, reviews and photographs on reservation websites (such as Hotels.com and Expedia.com) and travel websites (such as Tripadvisor.com and Virtualtourist.com) to other tourists who can thus plan their journeys without necessarily consulting the tourism industry's brochures and home pages.

These travel-community websites featuring user-contributed travel reviews are conceived as being more sincere than the always glossy brochures and home pages of the tourism industry. Tripadvisor.com claims to host 'more than 30 million trusted traveler reviews and opinions'. Such 'reviews and opinions' from other tourists who have experienced the service of a particular hotel can powerfully debunk an expensive four or five star hotel or upgrade a cheaper two or three star hotel. This is a new economy where tourism services are continually 'shamed' or 'recommended' on a global virtual stage with millions of daily visitors. While word-of-mouth recommendations always have been a crucial factor in triggering journeys to particular places, they were traditionally confined to a small world of friends, family members and co-workers. 'Electronic word-of-mouth' does not know such a restricted world since it is global in scope (albeit highly unequal around the world). Given that tourists rely more on such search engines to locate and compare travel information, it is unsurprising that research shows that favourable recommendations, or electronic word-of-mouth, are good for business, whereas bad recommendations can have fatal consequences, especially for smaller or less known companies or brands (Litvin et al., 2008).

Thus, such travel community websites are 'powerful' in that they can support or harm, be in line with or out of touch with, for instance, a city's official brand or a hotel's assigned stars (see Pan et al., 2007; Ek et al., 2008). Place branding and star-reviewing is no longer in the hands of the tourism industries; tourists are now part of that place-making and experience evaluating process. This also means that a moment of poor service at one moment in time can haunt that place if the tourist goes on to share that experience.

The sincerity of user-generated material is also recognised by many tourist organisations. For instance, VisitBritain, the official website for travel and tourism in the UK, asks tourists to upload comments, photos and videos: 'This is your chance to share what you love about Britain with the world! Browse the reviews to see what other travellers remember about their holiday in England, London, Scotland or Wales and check out photos, videos and comments' (www.visitorreview.com/visitbritain; accessed 31.03.10). So user-generated content not only creates problems for tourism managers. It also affords new ways of communicating directly with costumers, the cheap and specialised promotion of places and services, insight into the rating of one's own and competitors' services and so on (Schmallegger and Carson, 2008). It helps to extend and 'democratise' the tourist gaze.

In the next section we consider the organisation of the tourist industry more generally through examining some aspects of the social relations between hosts and guests.

Social Relations

We saw in Chapter 1 how there can be complex relationships between tourists and the local populations of those places where tourists gaze. There are various determinants of the social relations between such 'hosts' *and* 'guests', as Smith (1989) and others elaborate. These determinants are set out and developed below:

1 The *number* of tourists visiting a place in relationship to the size of the host population and to the scale of the objects being gazed upon. For example, the geographical size of New Zealand would permit more tourists to visit without environmental damage (except for climate change) or undesirable social effects. By contrast the physical smallness of Singapore means that extra tourists cannot easily be accommodated except by even more hotel building which would only be possible by demolishing the remaining few Chinese shophouses which are one of the main objects of the tourist gaze. Similarly, the medieval city of Dubrovnik has an absolute physical carrying capacity determined both by the city walls and the population of over 4,000 people currently living within its walls.

2 The predominant *object* of the tourist gaze, whether it is a landscape, a townscape, an ethnic group, a lifestyle, historical artefacts or buildings, or simply sand, sun and sea. Those tourist practices that involve the observation of physical objects are less intrusive than those that involve observing individuals and groups. Moreover, within the latter, the observation of the private lives of host groups will produce the greatest social conflict. Examples here include Eskimos or the Masai, who responded to the gaze by charging a '£ for car' for visits to their huts. By contrast, where what is observed is more of a public ritual then social conflict will be less pronounced and wider participation may be positively favoured, as in various Balinese rituals (see Smith, 1989: 7; see Chapter 8 below).

3 The *character* of the gaze involved and the resulting spatial and temporal 'packing' of visitors. For example, the gaze may be something that can take place more or less instantaneously (seeing/photographing New Zealand's highest mountain, Mount Cook), or it may require prolonged exposure (seeing/experiencing the 'romance' of Paris). In the case of the former, Japanese tourists can be flown in for a visit lasting just a few hours, while the romance of Paris necessitates a longer and 'deeper' immersion.

4 The *organisation* of the industry that develops to service the mass gaze: whether it is private or publicly owned and financed; whether it is locally owned or involves significant overseas interests; whether the capital involved is predominantly small- or large-scale; whether the staff is local or from elsewhere; and whether there are conflicts between the local population and the emergent tourist industry. Such conflicts can occur around many issues: conservation as opposed to commercial development, the wages to be paid to locally and non-locally recruited employees, the effects of development on local customs and family life, what one might call the 'trinketisation' of local crafts, and how to compensate for the seasonality of work available. Moreover, 'hosts' are not a uniform group since those benefiting from tourism financially are less critical of 'guests' than those that do not, such as Venetian residents (Quinn, 2007).

5   The effects of tourism upon the *pre-existing agricultural and industrial activities*. These may range from the destruction of those activities (much agriculture in Corfu); to their gradual undermining as labour and capital are drawn into tourism (much of Spain); to their preservation as efforts are made to save pre-existing activities as further objects to be gazed upon (cattle farming and gazing upon grazing in the Norfolk Broads).

6   The economic, social and ethnic *differences between visitors and most hosts*. In northern Europe and North America, tourism creates fewer social conflicts since many 'hosts' will themselves be 'guests' on other occasions. It may be that in a rather inchoate way tourism develops 'international understanding' or a cosmopolitan attitude (Szerszynski and Urry, 2002, 2006; Verstraete, 2010). Elsewhere, however, there are usually large inequalities between the visitors and the indigenous population, most of whom could not envisage having the income or time to be tourists themselves. These inequalities are even more marked when visitors are international business travellers (Beaverstock et al., 2010). Such differences can be reinforced in many developing countries by the nature of tourist development, which appears exceptionally opulent and highly capitalised, as with many hotels and resorts in India, China, Singapore and North Africa, partly because there are few service facilities otherwise available to visitors let alone to the host population.

7   The degree to which the mass of *visitors demand particular standards of accommodation and service*, that they should be enclosed in an environmental bubble to provide protection from many features of the host society (Edensor, 1998; see Chapter 6). This demand is most marked among international business travellers and inclusive tour visitors, who not only expect western standards of accommodation and food, but also bilingual staff and well-orchestrated arrangements. Many tourists rarely leave the security of the western tourist bubble and to some degree are treated as dependent 'children' by tourist professionals (Smith, 1989: 10–11; Edensor, 1998). In some cases, the culture actually is dangerous, as in some major cities, global slums and areas of warlordism and terrorism. This expectation is less pronounced among individual exploring 'travellers', repeat tourists, poorer tourists such as students, and those visitors for whom 'roughing it' and 'danger' is part of the 'experience' (see Edensor, 1998, on backpacker tourism; Freire-Medeiros, 2011, on favela tourism).

8   The degree to which tourists *demand the right to gaze at hosts*, to use and move through their everyday spaces and gaze upon them with curiosity and to photograph them close hand or secretly at a distance. One study of an American folk community shows that 75 per cent of the locals regard tourist photography as having a 'negative impact' upon their life (Chhabra, 2010: 10). This can create feelings of being constantly watched, being objectified by the tourist gaze and living

within a tourist honey pot (Maoz; 2006; Quinn, 2007; see Chapter 8). Jordan and Aitchison show how many female tourists (especially those on their own) are subject to the sexualised and controlling gaze of local men (2008). Bodies themselves are especially subject to the gaze, especially with the marked racial and gender inequalities that are involved. McClintock describes the extraordinary intertwining of male power with both colonised nature and the female body in the history of travel into and across the 'virgin' territories of Empire (1995).

9   The degree to which the *state* in a given country actively promotes tourism or tries to prevent it. There are countless examples of the former, where large numbers of tourists are part of the 'scenery' (Smith, 1989). By contrast, some oil states had for moral and social reasons explicitly restricted tourism (Saudi Arabia), although Dubai has turned itself into one of the most exceptional tourist destinations since its oil began to run out some decades back (Elliott and Urry, 2010; see Chapter 9). During the Cultural Revolution in China in the late 1960s the state sought to prevent the growth of tourism. When this changed in the mid-1970s, western visitors were so unusual that they were often applauded as celebrities. But by 2020 China is forecasted to be the world's leading tourist destination and tourist-generating country.

10 The extent to which *tourists can be identified and scapegoated* for supposedly undesirable economic, social and cultural developments. This is more common when visitors are economically and/or culturally and/or ethnically distinct from the host population (see Saldanha, 2002, for frictions between 'raving tourists' and locals in Goa, India). It is also more common when the host population is experiencing rapid economic and social change. It is also common in places where tourists more or less outnumber locals and invade their everyday spaces. Venetian residents blame tourists for overcrowding public transport, slowing down their everyday mobility, increasing prices for goods and services, generating waste, and so on (Quinn, 2007: 467–9). However, such change is often not simply the outcome of 'tourism'. And it is much easier to blame the 'nameless, faceless foreigner' for local problems of economic and social inequality (Smith, 1989). Moreover, some objections to tourism are objections to 'modernity' itself: to mobility and change, to new kinds of personal relationships, to a reduced role of family and tradition, and to different cultural configurations (see the 'Global Code of Ethics for Tourism': www.tourismpartners.org/globalcode.html; accessed 22.03.10).

11 The *relational gazes of hosts and guests*. The tourist gaze is 'mutual' where the eyes of guests and hosts intersect, however briefly, each time the tourist gaze is performed (see Chapter 8). While much research stresses the power of guests in objectifying hosts as scenery (or eyesores) and treating places as their 'oyster', hosts also exercise power and objectify through what the 'local gaze' (Maoz, 2006; see also Cheong and Miller, 2000; Chan, 2006).

The social impact of tourism practices thus depends upon the intersection of many processes. We stress throughout this book that distinctions between hosts and guests are increasingly fluid in mobile societies where there is much travel for work and pleasure, and places are globally connected with wide-reaching cultural, social and economic networks. Tourist places are not unique, bounded and fixed 'islands' that are subject to external forces producing impacts. They come into existence through relationships. Places float around within mobile, transnational networks of humans, technologies, objects, risks and images that continuously connect and disconnect them to other places (Urry, 2007: 42). Massey says that what gives a place its specificity is not some long history but how it is constructed out of the 'constellation of relations articulated together at a particular locus' (1994: 217).

We briefly examine a few such places to demonstrate how some of these processes intersect. First, there is the Mediterranean basin where the growth of tourism has been one of the most significant economic and social developments. Tourism is a striking symbol of post-war reconstruction, generating the world's largest destination with more than 275 million international tourists a year, accounting for around 30 per cent of international tourist arrivals (www.planbleu. org/publications/SoED2009_EN.pdf, p. 100; accessed 19.03.10; see Pons et al., 2008). As incomes grew in post-war West Germany, France, Scandinavia, the Low Countries and Britain, so there was a more than corresponding increase in demand for overseas travel. In response, southern Europe developed enormous tourist industries. And those industries have been particularly cost-effective, which in turn lowered the real cost of overseas travel and led to further expansion. Spain was the first and has remained the largest Mediterranean destination. Other major destinations are France (the world's most visited country), Italy, Greece, Portugal, Malta, Cyprus and Turkey. Overall, tourism generates a net distribution of wealth from northern to southern Europe.

Some of the effects of extensive tourist practices in parts of these countries are well known. These stem from the huge number of tourists and their seasonal demand for services, the deleterious social effects particularly resulting from the gendered work, the geographical concentration of visitors, the lack of concerted policy response, the cultural differences between hosts and guests, and the demand by some visitors to be enclosed in expensive 'environmental bubbles'.

One place said to be 'overrun' by tourists is Florence, where the resident population of some 400,000 accommodates 7 million visitors each year. This led to the 1980s plan to remove the city's academic, commercial and industrial functions from the centre and to turn Florence entirely over to tourism. It would have meant, according to critics, the 'Disneyfication of Florence' (Vulliamy, 1988: 25).

Robert Graves similarly decried the tourist transformation of Majorca, an island which many consider has exceeded its carrying capacity:

> the old Palma has long ceased to exist; its centre eaten away by restaurants, bars, souvenir shops, travel agencies and the like. ... Huge new conurbations have sprung up along the neighbouring coast. ... The main use of olive trees seems to be their conversion into ... salad bowls and boxes for sale to the tourists. But, as a Majorcan wag remarked, once they are all cut down we will have to erect plastic ones for the tourists to admire from their bus windows. (1965: 51; see Heidegger, 2005: 56, on how tourism is obliterating the possibility of the 'sojourn')

Turkey is a more recent country to develop as a major destination. The immediate attraction for local investors in Turkey is that most revenue comes in the form of foreign exchange. Turkish tourism has so far involved the ongoing proliferation of some ugly unplanned developments of large-scale hotels and holiday apartments, such as those in Bodrum, Marmara and Alanya, which may indeed be demolished. As early as 1988, one specialist operator, Simply Turkey, withdrew from selling holidays in Gumbet because it was 'No longer small and pretty, it is a sprawling building site, noisy and dusty, with a beach not large enough to cater for its rapid development' (quoted in Whitaker, 1988: 15). The impact of rapid tourism growth is particularly contested because south-west Turkey has attracted considerable numbers of individual 'travellers' seeking out its antiquities. Turkey is hence poised between the conflicting interests of mass tourism and a more socially select tourism, between collective and romantic tourist gazes (see Haldrup and Larsen, 2010, on the Danish tourist invasion of Alanya in Turkey).

Many argue that there is a very serious environmental threat to the Mediterranean and especially the coastline, where most tourists visit and increasingly where much of the population live. It is suggested that the number of visitors to the Mediterranean could increase from what was around 100 million in the 1980s to 637 million by 2025 (www.watermonitoringalliance.net/index.php?id=2052&L=2%2F%2 Finclude; accessed 19.03.10). This will place a huge strain upon food, water and human resources, and have major implications for climate change. There is an increasing development of 'desertification', with 30 per cent of Greece and 60 per cent of Portugal facing a moderate risk. Some consider that there is a long-term possibility of the Sahara desert extending north of the Mediterranean if climates continue to change.

The second most important area of tourism is that of North America. Developments are different from Europe in that the car, the highway, the view through the windscreen and the commercial strip are central. Jäkle talks of how, in the post-war period, cities, towns and rural areas were all remade in the 'universal highway order' (1985: ch. 9). There was a rapid improvement of the quality of the road system, to engender faster travel and higher traffic volumes. In post-war USA certain landscapes were substantially altered so as to produce a gaze: '*pleasing* to the motorist … using the land in a way that would "make an attractive *picture* from the Parkway"' (Wilson, 1988, 1992: 35, our italics). The state, according to Wilson, turned nature into something 'to be appreciated by the eyes alone' (1992: 37). The view through the car windscreen means that: 'the faster we drive, the flatter the earth looks' (Wilson, 1992: 33).

More generally, Baudrillard suggests that deserts in the USA constitute a metaphor of endless futurity, the obliteration of the past and the triumph of instantaneous time (1988: 6). Driving across the desert involves leaving one's past behind, driving on and on and seeing the ever-disappearing emptiness framed through the shape of the windscreen (Kaplan, 1996: 68–85). These empty landscapes of the desert are experienced through driving huge distances, travel involving a 'line of flight' into the disappearing future. Roads came to be built for the convenience of driving, not for the patterns of human life that might be engendered. The ubiquity of the radio and CD players and to some extent of air conditioning in American cars insulates passengers from most aspects of the environment except the mobile tourist glance through the windscreen (Larsen, 2001; Urry, 2007). And this view reveals almost nothing because townscapes consist of commercial strips, the casual eradication of distinctive places and the generation of a standardised landscape. Jäkle terms this the production of 'commonplaceness' (1985) while Augé speaks of non-places (1995). The commercial strips lack the ambiguities and complexities that generally make places interesting. They are 'unifunctional landscapes' which became even more uniform in appearance as large corporations operate chains of look-alike and standardised establishments (McDonald's, Howard Johnson, KFC, Holiday Inn and so on). The automobile journey has become an icon of post-war America, reflected in Kerouac's *On the Road* (1957) or the film *Easy Rider* (1969). While in *Lolita* (1962) Humbert Humbert concludes: 'We have been everywhere. We have seen nothing' (quoted in Jäkle, 1985: 198).

One exemplary tourist site in North America is Niagara Falls. Reaction to it has always involved superlatives, framed within discourses of the sublime (see Shields, 1990). Observers reported themselves lost for words. It was an exotic wonder; it had an immense aura. Thus in the eighteenth century the Falls were an object of intense natural aura; in the nineteenth century they functioned as a liminal zone gazed upon and experienced by courting couples; but in the later twentieth century they became another 'place' collected by the mobile visitor for whom the gaze at the Falls stands for spectacle, sex and commerce. All the emphasis at the Falls is placed on the props, on honeymoon suites and heart-shaped 'luv tubs'. The Falls now stand for kitsch, sex and commercial spectacle. It is as though the Falls are no longer there as such and can only be seen as spectacle. Thus the same entity in a physical sense has been transformed by various tourism interests.

Related to this is the growth of 'sex-tourism', bodies as objects of the tourist gaze in certain south-east Asian societies as well as in most major cities throughout the world (Oppermann, 1999). In South Korea this has been specifically encouraged by the state. Its main form consists of the kisaeng tour specifically geared to Japanese businessmen (Mitter, 1986: 64–7). Many Japanese companies reward their outstanding male staff with all-expenses tours of kisaeng brothels and parties, and many Japanese tourist agencies have encouraged and provided such sex services (Leheny, 1995: 375). South Korean ministers have congratulated the 'girls' for their contribution to their country's economic development.

Other countries with a similarly developed sex industry are the Philippines and Thailand. In the case of the former the state encourages the use of 'hospitality girls' in tourism, and the Ministry of Tourism recommends various brothels (Mitter, 1986: 65). Package tours organised with a Manila agent include pre-selected 'hospitality girls'. Of the money earned, only about 7–8 per cent is retained by the women sex-workers. These social practices have been generated by exceptionally strong patriarchal practices which cast women as either 'madonna/virgin' or 'whore'; the belief among men from affluent countries that women of colour are sexually available, submissive and willing to be bought; the high rate of incest and domestic violence by fathers/husbands in some such societies; rural depopulation which draws people into the cities looking for any possible work; and the growth of 'specialist' tour companies and websites devoted to facilitating travel for groups of male 'sex-tourists' (see Enloe, 1989, on attempts to organise to protect prostitutes; Leheny, 1995; Clift and Carter, 1999). Since the mid-1990s the Thai government has tried to restrain the sex industry and promote other forms of tourism. This is in part because of the growing threat of AIDS and in part because new types of tourists, including women and young families, find offensive such sexualised gazes and bodies (Leheny, 1995).

But there is more to sex-tourism than prostitution. First, the tourism industry has long made use of 'sex' in its marketing (Cohen, 1995; Dann, 1996b; Pritchard and Morgan, 2000a, 2000b, 2000c). Idealised and attractive female bodies are endlessly exhibited in brochures and on postcards. The following is how the Jamaican Tourist Board scripts the Caribbean Island of Negril as a male, heterosexual and white Garden of Eden:

> Rugged cliffs give way to pure white beaches, making a luscious mixture of seductiveness and innocence. The sun is so warm it's almost sinful. As it melts into the tranquil Caribbean sea, tempting sunsets appear as girls with cinnamon-coloured skin walk the beach wearing bikinis the size of butterflies. This is your Eden. Welcome to the Negril. (Quoted in Morgan and Pritchard, 2000a: 127)

Thus sexualised 'place-myths' are inscribed into those places especially where the sun holds sway.

Second, sexual desire energises *much* tourism. Littlewood shows that the unofficial story of the noble 'Grand Tour' was a long string of sexual adventures, although 'letters home commonly tell of the churches visited, not the brothels' (2001: 4). He argues that sexual fantasies are an integral part of *cultural* tourism as such, not a perverted deviation from it (2001; see also Ryan and Hall, 2001). Hot sun and sexual pleasure go hand in hand according to Littlewood (2001: 1–7). In the northern imagination, (semi-)exposed bodies and 'sultry climates' stimulate sexual desire and practice. Oscar Wilde, the champion of hedonism, said: 'I no longer want to worship anything but the sun. Have you noticed that the sun detests thought' (quoted in Littlewood, 2001: 190). When white tourists strip off their clothes within liminal spaces such as pools and beaches, they simultaneously disrobe their workaday selves and perform in order to be gazed upon by other tourists. Moreover, getting a tan inscribes a kind of 'savage' sexuality on to the body. The bronzed body is still a powerful sexualised sign, reflecting a western tradition of equating sexual potency and availability with 'dark skin'. The sensuous experience

"exoticism"

of the sun *touching* one's naked, sweating skin can in itself be sensual, having 'sex with the sun', as Littlewood puts it (2001: 194).

Third, a further important sexualised space is the hotel:

> Hotels occupy a fascinating place in the social imagination of the West, in many ways they are synonymous with sex, romance and adventure – linked in popular culture with clandestine meetings of spies and lovers, with wedding nights, honeymoons and illicit or transistory assignations. (Pritchard and Morgan, 2006: 765)

It is no coincidence that red-light districts largely comprise hotels and in-migrating prostitutes and strippers that 'service' tourists, and in particular those visitors who are doing business in financial services (Elliott and Urry, 2010: ch. 6).

We now examine further some ways in which tourism services and experiences are divided by class, gender and ethnicity. In Chapter 2 we emphasised the importance of social-class divisions in structuring how tourist developments occurred in different ways in different places. The effects include the resulting respective social tone of different resorts and the patterns of landholding; the importance of the aristocratic connection in constructing the fashionability of certain places; the growth of the middle-class family holiday and the development of the bungalow as a specialised building form by the seaside; the importance of the 'romantic gaze' and its role in constructing nature as an absolutely central positional good; the character of the 'collective' gaze and the role of others like oneself in constituting the attraction of certain places; and in Chapter 5 we discuss the enhanced cultural capital of the service class and its heightening of the appeal of rural and industrial heritage and of the postmodern.

But gazing is also inflected by divisions of gender and ethnicity. These interconnections are important in forming the preferences that different social groupings develop about where to visit and in structuring the effects of such visits upon host populations and the fashionability of different sites. There are two key issues here: the social composition of fellow tourists and the social composition of those who are living in the places visited. These are important because most tourist practices involve movement into and through various sorts of public space – such as theme parks, shopping malls, beaches, restaurants, hotels, pump rooms, promenades, airports, swimming pools and squares. In such spaces people both gaze at and are gazed upon by others (and are photographed and photograph others). Complex preferences have come to develop for the range of appropriate others that different social groups expect to look at and photograph in different places; and in turn different expectations are held by different social groups about who are appropriate others to gaze at oneself. Part of what is involved in tourism is the purchase of a particular themed experience, and this depends upon a specifiable composition of the others with whom that experience is being shared (see discussion in Chapter 8).

The combination of gender and ethnic subordination in south-east Asia has colluded to construct young Asian women as objects of a tourist/sexual gaze for male visitors from other societies, visitors who are ethnically dominant. We have seen how the resulting tourist patterns cannot be analysed separately from relations of gender and racial subordination (Hall, 1994; Kinnaird and Hall, 1994).

The importance of gender inequalities can be seen in another way. In almost all societies men have enjoyed a higher standard of living and 'leisure freedom' than women. This relates in an important way to the development of holidays. Until the nineteenth century access to travel was largely the preserve of men. But this changed a little with the development of 'Victorian lady travellers', some of whom visited countries considered at the time 'uncivilised' and 'uncharted', especially for women (Enloe, 1989: ch. 2). Other women took advantage of Cook's tours. As one woman wrote: 'We would venture anywhere with such a guide and guardian as Mr Cook' (quoted in Enloe, 1989: 29). From then onwards access to holidays has been less unequally distributed as compared with some other forms of leisure.

The early forms of mass tourism were based around heterosexual couples. Indeed, during the course of the nineteenth century the holiday unit increasingly comprised such a couple plus their children (as recorded in innumerable photographs; see Chapter 7). And by the inter-war period in much of Europe the family holiday had become much more child-centred. This was given a significant boost by the development of the holiday camp in the 1930s, in which child-based activities were central. From that time on much tourism revolves around performing a loving family life within an extraordinary place. Tourism is not only a way of practising or consuming (new) places, but also an emotional geography of sociability, of being together with close friends and family members away from home (Larsen, 2008b).

Most holidaymaking marketing involves a 'compulsory heterosexuality' with pictures of actual couples, with or without children, or potential couples. In the brochures produced by tour operators there are three predominant images. These are the 'family holiday', a couple with two or three healthy school-age children; the 'romantic holiday', that is, a heterosexual couple on their own gazing at the sunset (indeed, the sunset is a signifier for romance); and the 'fun holiday', that is same-sex groups each looking for other-sex partners for 'fun'. There is also, as we have noted, the 'sex holiday' for men. Social groups that do not fall into any of these particular visual categories are poorly served by the tourist industry. Many criticisms have been made of how difficult holidaymaking is for single people, single-parent families, those who are disabled and until recently gay couples or groups. Recently, however, the growth of some 'gay tourism' is said to be one 'of the fastest growing niche markets in the international travel industry' (Casey, 2009: 158). In the UK, for example, the Visit Britain Tourist Board has undertaken a campaign to target gay and lesbian tourists from overseas.

Another social group often excluded from conventional holiday-making and marketing material are non-white social groups such as black Britons. The advertising material produced by holiday companies shows that tourists are white; there are few black faces among the holiday-makers. Indeed, if there are any non-white faces in the photographs it would be presumed that they are the 'exotic natives' who are being gazed upon. The same process would seem to occur in those areas in Britain that attract large numbers of foreign tourists. If black or Asian people are seen there, it would be presumed that they were visitors from overseas, or service workers, but not British residents themselves on holiday. The countryside is particularly constructed as 'white', as Taylor shows with regard to typically dominant photographic images (1994; see also Winter et al., 2009, on the tanned body within Asia).

An interesting issue is whether members of ethnic minorities undertake western-type holidays. Aspects of the western holiday, in which one travels elsewhere because of the sun, hotel or scenery, form a cultural practice that is idiosyncratic at least to some recent migrants to Britain (see Ahmed, 2000, on the ambiguities of the sun tan). Some migrants at least would consider that travel should have a more serious purpose than this: to look for work, to join the rest of one's family, to visit relatives, or to participate in diasporic travel.

There has been, more generally, a recent increase in such VFR-tourism (visiting friends and relatives). In 2007 there were almost as many visitors coming to the UK to visit friends and relatives as for conventional holidays (www.statistics.gov.uk/STATBASE/Product. asp?vlnk=1391; accessed 10.10.06). This increase in VFR trips stems from what Boden and Molotch call a 'compulsion to proximity', the desire to be physically co-present with other people even if this involves significant inconvenient travel (1994).

Various research shows how migration and tourism are complexly folded into each other (Larsen et al., 2006) 'The migration process appears to require a return, a journey back to the point of departure' (Goulborne, 1999: 193). This is particularly the case with members of diasporas. While these traditionally entail a desire for a permanent return, today's migrants can fulfil their compulsion to proximity with their homeland and heritage through occasional visits. Mason demonstrates how British people with Pakistani ancestors regularly visit Pakistan to be co-present with their kin, to keep their family networks 'alive' and to show their children their 'origins' (2004). Moreover, for many cultures much travel entails crossing national frontiers. Households in developing countries develop extensive mobility patterns when their incomes increase. The proliferation of 'global diasporas' extends the range, extent and significance of all forms of travel for far-flung families and households. It is said in Trinidad that one can really only be a 'Trini' by going abroad. Around 60 per cent of nuclear families have at least one member living abroad (Miller and Slater, 2000: 12, 36). Ong and Nonini also show the importance of mobility across borders in the case of the massive Chinese diaspora that is thought to be between 25 million and 45 million in size (1997). Clifford summarises how:

> Dispersed peoples, once separated from homelands by vast oceans and political barriers, increasingly find themselves in border relations with the old country thanks to a to-and-fro made possible by modern technologies of transport, communication, and labour migration. Airplanes, telephones, tape cassettes, camcorders, and mobile job markets reduce distances and facilitate two-way traffic, legal and illegal, between the world's places. (1997: 247)

Such diasporic travel is also rather open-ended in terms of its temporality. Unlike conventional tourism that is based upon a clear distinction of periods of 'home' and of 'away', the diasporic traveller often has no clear temporal boundaries as one activity tends to flow into the other, as Cwerner shows in the case of Brazilians living in London for quite indeterminate periods of time (2001).

Yet many tourist developments will exclude many ethnic groups, such as the heritage industry discussed in Chapter 6. Here we note that white faces overwhelmingly populate such a heritage. Ethnic groups are important in the British tourist industry, though, and in some respects play a key role. They are employed in those enterprises concerned with servicing visitors, especially in major cities. We return to this issue in the next chapter.

Furthermore, certain ethnic groups have come to be constructed as part of the 'attraction' or 'theme' of some places. This is most common in the case of Asian groups. In Manchester this occurred around its collection of Chinese restaurants in a small area, and resulted from the internationalisation of British culinary taste in the post-war period (see Frieden and Sagalyn, 1989: 199–201). By the 1980s city planners were committed to a new vision of 'Chinatown', reconstructed and conserved as a now desirable object of the tourist gaze. Further analysis of this would need to explore the social effects for those of Asian origin becoming constructed as an exotic object and whether this distorts patterns of economic and political development. It would also be interesting to consider the effects on the white population of coming to view those of Asian origin as not so much threatening or even inferior but as exotic, as curiously different and possessing a rich and in part attractive culture. Such debates are developing in the context of many cultures taken to be exotically different, as such cultures become themed, photographed and displayed around the world.

Tourism as Strategy

The effects of tourism are complex and contradictory. There has been much discussion about the desirability of tourism as a strategy for economic development in so-called developing societies. This raises various difficult issues.

The growth of tourism in developing countries, such as 'game tourism' in Kenya, 'ethnic tourism' in Mexico, gambling in Macao and so on, does not derive from processes only internal to those societies. Such development results from external transformations: technological changes such as cheap air travel and internet booking systems; developments in capital, including the growth of worldwide hotel groups (Ramada), travel agencies (Thomas Cook) and personal finance organisations such as credit cards (American Express); the widespread growth of the 'romantic' gaze so that more people wish to isolate themselves from existing patterns of mass tourism; the increased fascination of the developed world with the cultural practices of less developed societies; the development of tourists as a 'collector' of places often gazed upon and experienced on the surface; and the emergence of a powerful interests promoting the view that tourism has major development potential. The last of these is most dramatically seen in China over the past thirty years which has gone from hugely restricted internal migration and tourism to becoming, in a way, the world's most significant centre of global tourism in this new century (see Nyíri, 2010).

However, the benefits from tourism are often less than anticipated. Much tourist investment is undertaken by large-scale companies based in North America or western Europe, and the bulk of tourist expenditure is retained by the transnational companies involved; often only 20–60 per cent of the price remains in the host country. Most of the foreign exchange earned from tourism is repatriated to companies based elsewhere. This repatriation is more likely with the high level of vertical integration in the industry in poorer societies.

A further problem occurs where tourism accounts for an exceptionally high proportion of the national income of the country. Some Caribbean islands experience this (Sheller, 2003). It means that if anything undermines tourist demand, an enormous loss of national income results. This happened in Fiji in 1987 following military coups (see Lea, 1988: 32–6, on advertising needed to restore consumer confidence).

It must also be asked: development *for whom?* Many of the facilities (airports, golf courses, luxury hotels and so on) will be of little benefit to most of the local population. Likewise much indigenous wealth generated will be highly unequally distributed and so most of the population will gain little benefit. This does of course depend on patterns of local ownership. Finally, much employment generated in tourist-related services is relatively low-skilled and may reproduce the servile character of previous colonial regimes, what one critic termed 'flunkey training' (quoted in Crick, 1988: 46).

However, it should also be asked whether many developing countries have much alternative to tourism as a development strategy. Although there are serious economic costs, as well as social costs we have not fully considered here, it is difficult in the absence of viable alternatives to see that developing societies have a great deal of choice but to develop their attractiveness as objects of the tourist gaze, particularly for visitors from North America, western Europe and increasingly from parts of Asia and especially the Chinese middle class.

4

Working under the Gaze

Introduction

We have analysed various aspects of the tourist gaze and noted that the gaze can take different forms, relating to the kinds of organisation possible of the tourist-related industries that develop to meet such different gazes. In this chapter we consider in detail the complex relationship between two elements involved in the provision of tourist services. On the one hand, there are the practices of tourism, which are highly structured by distinctions of taste. Such practices lead people to want to be in certain places, gazing at particular objects, in the company of specific other types of people. On the other hand, many services are provided and performed for such tourists, mainly under conditions of profit maximisation. And as we saw in the last chapter, huge international industries have developed so that services are provided at a cost which permits large segmented markets to develop and be profitably sustained.

Various contradictions may develop between the practices and the industries that have emerged. Such industries of transport, hotels, property development, catering and entertainment are all concerned with the provision of consumer *services* and are sometimes known as the 'hospitality' industry. Such provision is often highly complex, even to the extent that it is often unclear just what the product is that is being consumed. Furthermore, the tourist gaze is structured by culturally specific notions of what is extraordinary and therefore worth viewing. This means that services provided, which may of course be incidental to the gaze itself, must take a form which does not contradict or undermine the quality of the gaze, and ideally should enhance it. This in turn poses, as we shall see, immense problems of managing such industries, to ensure the service provided by the often relatively poorly paid service workers is appropriate to the almost sacred quality of the visitors' gaze on some longed-for and remarkable tourist site.

Such tourist-related services have to be provided in, or at least near to, the objects of the tourist gaze; they cannot be provided anywhere. Tourist services develop in particular places and cannot be shifted elsewhere. They normally have a particular 'spatial fix'. Further, much service production involves close spatial proximity between the producers and the consumers of the services. This results from the nature of many service products provided for tourists, such as a meal, a drink, a ride at the funfair and so on. Such consumer services involve a close connectedness or proximity between producers and consumers who often have to perform to ensure the enacted services are exciting and memorable to the tourists consuming them. In this chapter we discuss how in post-Fordist experience economies such performances of service are crucial for the tourist gaze.

Performing a 'Service'

With manufactured goods it is normally clear what the product consists of (even though they have both sign and use value). In many service industries this is not so straightforward (Bagguley et al., 1990: ch. 3). Mars and Nicod describe the problem of specifying the boundary of a given service:

> 'service' as we use it, refers to an action or material thing that is more than one might normally expect. In a transport cafe it can mean no more than passing the sauce bottle with a smile. In the Savoy it might mean making prodigious efforts to supply a rare delicacy or indulging a customer's particular preference or foible. ... The more people actually pay for service, the more exacting will be their demand for better *and more individual* service. (1984: 28)

Expenditure of labour is central to service work, whether this labour consists of passing the sauce or of some more extensive and discriminating activity. Tourist-related services are often labour-intensive and hence labour costs are a significant proportion of total costs. Moreover, since in manufacturing technical change can more radically reduce unit costs, services will over time be relatively more expensive. Employers in the various service sectors will seek to monitor and, where possible, minimise costs.

As noted, labour is to varying degrees implicated in the delivery or enactment of many tourist-related services. This occurs as the outcome of a necessarily *social* and embodied process in which some interaction occurs between one or more producers and one or more consumers. The quality of the social interaction is itself part of the service purchased (Bryman, 2004; Boon, 2007). To buy the service is to buy a particular kind of social experience. Sasser and Arbeit, for example, suggest that: 'Even if the hamburger is succulent, if the employee is surly, the customer will probably not return' (1976: 63). Many services are high-contact systems in which there is considerable involvement of customers in the service, as O'Dell shows in the case of spas (2007). As a result it is may be difficult to rationalise the system (Pine, 1987: 64–5).

Services normally necessitate some social interaction between producers and consumers at the point of production. Unless the service can be more or less entirely materialised, then there has to be some geographical or spatial proximity between one or more of the service producers and consumers. Second, a distinction may be made between two classes of employee: those back-stage workers who have minimal contact with the service consumers and those front-stage workers who have high face-to-face contact with tourists (Boon, 2007). The front-stage workers literally work under the tourist gaze. As we will discuss later, such front-stage workers undertake performative work. In the case of the former, employers will seek technical change and the extensive rationalisation of labour; with the latter employees would be recruited and trained on the basis of interpersonal attributes and public relations skills (Pine, 1987: 65).

But there are difficulties in employing such a divisive strategy: there can be unproductive resentment between the two groups, such as between chefs and waiters; the maintenance of the distinction between the groups may be hard to sustain where customers cannot be spatially confined to very restricted areas, as in hotels or spas; and the variability in demand for many services means that a considerable premium is placed on the flexible use of labour, something difficult to organise if there is a strong demarcation between these different groups of employees.

Furthermore, the social composition of the producers, at least those who are serving in the front line, may be part of what is in fact 'sold' to the customer. In other words, the 'service' partly consists of a process of production which is infused with particular social characteristics, of gender, age, race, educational background and so on. When the individual buys a given service, what is purchased is a particular social composition of the service producers. In some cases what is also bought is the social composition of the other service *consumers*. Examples of this are especially found in tourism/transport and resorts where people spend considerable periods of time consuming the service in close proximity to others and hence part of what is being bought is the social and bodily characteristics of those other consumers (hence the appeal of Club Class or an up-market cruise).

We now examine the significance of 'performative labour' for delivering services. As labour is itself part of the service product, this poses particular issues for management. These are especially significant, the longer the delivery takes, the more intimate the service and the greater the importance of 'quality' for consumers. In some cases employees' speech, appearance and personality are treated as legitimate areas of intervention and control by management.

Gabriel discusses the services provided by a gentlemen's club in London (1988: ch. 4). For its members, the club provides them far more than traditional English meals. It also offers:

> a whole range of *intangible products*, a place where important contacts can be made, where guests can be offered hospitality, where information can be exchanged, where certain rituals can be preserved and daily re-enacted. The very anachronistic nature of the club is part of this appeal; it is the appeal of the old. (1988: 141)

Gabriel goes on to say that the only way of assessing their success is through 'providing those "intangible" services which cannot be rationalized and incorporated in the catering machinery' (1988: 141). The staff provide an intangible ambience which could be lost if the catering were rationalised.

Such services require what is called emotional work (Hochschild, 1983), or aesthetic labour (Warhurst et al., 2000) or performative work (Bryman, 2004). What these concepts share is the recognition that servicing is increasingly a performative *doing*, a bodily performance that needs to please, seduce or entertain, especially visually. These authors all argue that there is a theatre-like character to front-stage service encounters and that 'good' service requires managerial scripting and skills of 'acting', both by following a script and through improvisation.

In her classic study of airline cabin crew, Hochschild coined the term 'emotional work'. By this she refers to the products 'in which the emotional style of offering the service is part of the service itself, in a way that loving or hating wallpaper is not part of producing wallpaper' (Hochschild, 1983: 5–6). Drawing upon Goffman's notion of 'impression management', Hochschild argues that service work requires the 'management of feeling to create a publicly observable facial and bodily display' (1983: 7). What is required of good flight attendants are the emotional skills of showing positive emotions even when faced with rude customers and situations of stress. They need to sound and especially to *look* happy. This involves smiling in a pleasant, friendly and involved way to consumers. They need to be able manage, suppress and disguise their own feelings behind an ever-present *smile*. And they must wear that smile gently and effortlessly: 'for the flight attendant, the smiles are part of her work, a part that requires her to coordinate self and feeling so that the work seems to be effortless' (Hochschild, 1983: 8). Crucial to many consumer services is this 'emotional work' of a public and recognisable sort. In the case of flight attendants specific training brings this about, resulting in a commercialisation of human feeling. Flight attendants are taught how to smile and they are instructed to do so constantly when subject to the gaze of passengers.

Hochschild argues that this emotional work was made more difficult for flight attendants with the intensification of labour on American airlines since neo-liberal deregulation from the mid-1970s onwards: 'The workers respond to the speed-up with a slowdown: they smile less broadly, with a quick release and no sparkle in the eyes, thus dimming the company's message to the people. It is a war of smiles' (1983: 127). Such a decline in quality is exceptionally hard for management to monitor and control, even if they are well aware that attendants are no longer providing the complete service that passengers expect.

Yet among KLM aircrews a more complex picture emerges (Wouters, 1989). What seems to have happened more recently is that the demands made by the company with regard to sex, age, weight, jewellery, make-up, shoes, smile, behaviour and so on have become rather looser, particularly with the increased diversity of contemporary air travellers. Wouters explains this as follows:

> an aeroplane now has become a melting-pot, not only of nationalities but also of social classes. Behaviour in contacts between flight attendants and passengers correspondingly had to become less uniform or standardized and more varied and flexible ... in each contact there is a need to attune one's behaviour to the style of emotion management of the individual passenger. (1989: 113)

The 'choreographed smile' typifies the ever-smiling 'smile factories' of Disney parks (Van Maanen, 1991; Bryman, 2004). The Disney Institute instructs their staff to: 'Start and end every Guest contact and communication with direct eye contact'; while Walt told staff always 'to smile' and 'turn the cheek to everybody, even the nasty ones'. Or to cite one Disney member of staff: 'We get daily abuse from costumers but you have to keep on smiling. We're supposed to make eye contact, greet each and every guest for eight hours. If you don't you get reprimanded' (quoted in Bryman, 2004: 108, 109). The smiling body doing emotional work is a docile unemotional face (at least at face-value). So 'smiling staff' are aware of being objects of the gaze of tourists and potentially managers. The leading role of the smile and positive body language more broadly signals the power of the tourist gaze in orchestrating service encounters. In addition, Disney staff are told always to use 'friendly phrases', exchange pleasantries with customers and exhibit appropriate behaviour. The 'smiling body' is a disciplined, docile body fighting for costumer satisfaction within a battle of 'smile wars': 'the power of the smile can only be co-produced with the client; it requires a satisfied customer' (Veijola and Valtonen, 2007: 19).

In Disney theme parks (and experience economies more broadly) 'emotional work' becomes explicitly performative, discursively and spatially organised as if undertaken in a Goffmanesque theatre (see Chapter 8 for discussion of Goffman):

> By performative labour, then, I simply mean the rendering of work by managements and employees alike as akin to a theatrical performance. In the Disney Theme parks, the metaphor of the theatrical performance is explicit with references to 'cast members', 'auditioning', 'onstage' and 'backstage'. (Bryman, 2004: 103)

The language of Disney speaks of guests rather than customers, cast members rather than employees, host(ess) rather than frontline employees, onstage rather than public areas, backstage rather than restricted areas, casting rather than hiring for a job, role rather than job, costume rather than uniform, audition rather than job interview, audience rather than crowd, pre-entertainment area rather than queue, imaginer rather than attraction designer and so on (Bryman, 2004: 11). The production side of the tourism economy (and the service economy more broadly) is increasingly theatrical and performative; they resemble real theatres as workers are 'cast members' wearing costumes and trained to enact scripts and roles that fit in with a theatrical, themed environment.

Not all such emotional or performative work is fully pre-scripted and repetitive. Even the Disney Institute admits that 'smiling, greeting, and thanking guests are all well and good, but if these actions are restricted to rote, mechanistic behaviors, their effectiveness is severely limited' (quoted in Bryman, 2004: 108). The smile needs to appear authentic with the competent service performer smiling personally. This requires that one cares for the 'corporate brand', knows how to 'charm' through improvisation and enjoys servicing others, and this in part involves accepting that one is 'inferior' to the guest and never damaging the face of the guest. They need to exhibit a will to please within what Veijola and Valtonen term a 'servient economy' (2007: 17). While service encounters are scripted by power relations, we also need to explore how service workers have to cope with and indeed bend scripts so as to restore some autonomy and critique.

Some emotional work is little scripted by management. Indeed, the emphasis may be more on establishing a more 'genuine' emotional relationship between producers and consumers (as in a 'local' restaurant) rather than one contrived or artificial (James, 1989). In one restaurant: 'Staff were constantly encouraged to "cater for" the customers: to smile, exchange pleasantries, and, if there was time, longer conversations' (Marshall, 1986: 41). The 'emotional work' undertaken by tour reps is also little scripted and supervised: 'Reps were given considerable autonomy. Reps were responsible for scripting their own commentary on the coach from the airport and were only given general guidelines as to what to include in the "welcome meeting". Supervision at the resort was limited, with only very occasional visits from their immediate manager' (Guerrier and Adib, 2003: 1405; Wong and Wang, 2009). And yet, even emotional work conducted without much direct supervision will be scripted by 'absent' or invisible cultural codes, norms and etiquettes of behaviour in service encounters between hosts and guests. Service performances can never be 'for the first time' because they require rehearsal, imitation of other performances and adjustment to norms and expectations.

Moreover, not all situations can be dealt with in circumscribed fashion. Mars and Nicod note more generally the distinction between routines and emergencies (1984: 34–5). There is a chronic tension between service receivers who regard all sorts of issues as an emergency (such as an overcooked steak) and service producers who have to learn to deal with such incidents as routine. This tension is most marked in highly prestigious hotels where customers pay for and expect very high levels of personal service and where such problems cannot be treated as purely matters of routine. By contrast, in less prestigious and cheaper hotels staff develop techniques to suggest that everything is under control even if there are 'normal' emergencies because of the intensity of work that has to be undertaken.

We have seen that performing tourist work requires skills of wearing a smile lightly, some expressive, theatrical skills, the ability to deal with stress and emergencies, and more or less tacit knowledge of and willingness to follow norms as to appropriate social behaviour. But such skills are seldom sufficient if one lacks what we might term 'bodily capital'. This refers to the appearance, movement and tone of the 'servicing body', which often happens to be female. This ties into Warhurst et al.'s notion of 'aesthetic labour', which refers to the skills of looking, conversing and behaving in a manner appropriate upon the specific stage where it is enacted (2000). Often, a nice smile is not enough if the body that gives it is perceived to be too old, over-weight, deformed, scruffy, boring, clumsy, ethnic, out of style or speaking in the wrong tone. As Hochschild says in relation to age: '"Smile-lines" are not seen as the accumulated evidence of personal character but as an occupational hazard, an undesirable sign of age incurred in the line of duty on a job that devalues age' (1983: 22).

'Stigmatised bodies' seldom find a job on the front-stage of the service economy, especially with regard to those jobs (e.g. tour reps and air cabin crew) or businesses (e.g. the trendy bar) that have a certain aura of 'coolness' or 'glamour' (despite often being low-pay jobs). The tourism and hospitality industry prefer those who live up to their customers' standards of aesthetically pleasing bodies, both when it comes to appearance and manners. While different leisure and tourism settings obviously hold different notions of appropriate or desirable bodies of aesthetic labour (say, between the posh, old-styled country hotel and the hip urban café), the general trend is a liking for and front-staging of bodies that appear young, beautiful and articulate, while less attractive bodies are kept backstage or excluded if the labour supply allows this.

Many performances are provided by women, youngish people and increasingly foreigners, with both legal and illegal status. Often the actual delivery is provided by relatively low-level workers who are badly paid (at least relatively) and who may have little involvement or engagement with the overall enterprise. And the service encounter is always an asymmetrical power relationship. There is an implicit promise from the subordinate to the superior that they will treat the latter in a dignified fashion and as a respectable person; anything else will be 'morally' wrong (Dillard et al., 2000). And since tips and provisions from the sale of optional tours and services are crucial to much service, 'disrespectfulness' may be costly. These relatively low-level workers are normally female and implicit in some work relations is the 'sexual' servicing of customers or, indeed, management (Adkins, 1995; Baum, 2007; Veijola and Valtonen, 2007). Overlying the interaction, the 'service', are assumptions and notions of gender-specific forms of appropriate behaviour and bodily display, often defined by a 'male gaze'. Both emotional work and aesthetic labour are inscribed with supposedly feminine values of servicing and looking good at the same time.

Desmond, indeed, notes that live performance and bodily display are very common within tourism (1999). The moving body is often what gets gazed upon, as a 'spectacular corporeality' increasingly characterises global tourism. The performed body in dance has become common, such as Maori war-dances, Balinese dance ceremonies, Brazilian samba and Hula dancing in Hawaii. These examples involve what MacCannell terms a 'reconstructed ethnicity' and a 'staged authenticity' (1973). In some cases, these dances are such powerful signifiers that performances are the dominant signifier of the culture in question. Thus with Maori and Hawaiian cultures the dance *is* the culture, swamping all other signifiers and being recognisable across the globe. Desmond has outlined the racial and gender history of the making of the female Hula dancer, from the early years of the last century to the current point where six million visitors a year are attracted to a naturalistic Eden signified by bodily displays of 'natural' female Hula dancers, a place-image globally recognised and endlessly re-circulated (Desmond, 1999: Part 1).

Much service work might well be said to be difficult and demanding, under-recognised and relatively under-rewarded. There can be a high emotional price to pay for emotional labour, such as alienation from one's true feelings and identity (Hochschild, 1983; Veijola and Valtonen, 2007). In a study of tour reps, one respondent stated:

> We pretend to be cheerful, pleasant, earnest, energetic, and so forth throughout the journey even though those emotions are unfelt in most cases. Furthermore, we also depress our anger, hate, or disgust when facing difficult guys. We are also not allowed to manifest worry or fear even if we are indeed in some serious trouble. I don't want people to lose confidence in my ability (Karen, female, 32 years old, a tour leader for 7 years). (Wong and Wang, 2009: 255)

Yet, this idea that service work is necessarily alienating is too one-sided. Reflecting upon his time working as a waiter, Crang argues: 'it never felt to me as if I was being alienated from my emotions, my manners, or my leisure practices. I always felt that "I" was still there: I genuinely liked people who tipped me; I genuinely wanted to help; I genuinely had fun' (1994: 698). Other studies indicate that one pleasure of service work is the fluid boundaries between work and leisure (Weaver, 2005: 10). This blurring is particularly evident with regard to tour reps that work in the consumption spaces of tourists and they need to enact fun and to party: 'the rep will have failed if she or he does seem to be having fun and helping the holidaymaker having fun' (Guerrier and Adib, 2003: 1402). Moreover, some service work and places of service are considered 'cool', while others are 'uncool', so they are looked down upon and valued less:

> As in other areas of work, it is clear that polarisation is taken place within tourism work, but the criteria of distinction relates to the branding and image of the work rather than to its technical or pressional status. 'Cool' work is equated with style, fashion and consumer branding (bars, night clubs, boutique hotels, creative venues) while 'uncool' includes the work of drudgery in the sector (cleaning, popular service) and also some glamour from the past, airline cabin crew, particularly with some newer, low-cost airlines. (Baum, 2007: 1396)

We argued that for many consumers what is actually consumed as a service *is* the particular moment of delivery by the relatively low-level service deliverers: the smile on the flight attendant's face, the pleasantness of the manner of the waitress, the sympathy in the eyes of the tour rep and so on. The problem for management is how to ensure that these moments do in fact work out appropriately, while minimising the cost of an undesirably intrusive (and hence resented) system of management/supervision, as well as reducing friction with other more highly paid, often male, workers backstage (see the classic Whyte, 1948).

Jan Carlzon, former President of the Scandinavian airline SAS, terms these 'moments of truth' for any organisation (1987). He suggests that in SAS there are something like 50 million moments of truth each year, each of which lasts perhaps 15 seconds when a customer comes into contact with an employee. It is these moments of truth that determine whether or not SAS succeeds or fails. As Goffman once noticed: 'life may not be much of a gamble, but interaction is' (1959: 243). Thus any 'moment of truth' is a gamble since even the most fleeting misconduct is likely to be noticed and disturbing to the interaction order. Carlzon argues that the importance of such moments means that organisations have to be reorganised, towards service to the customer as the primary objective. As a consequence, the actual service deliverers, the company's 'foot soldiers' who know most about the 'front line' operations, have to be given more responsibility to respond effectively, quickly and courteously to the particular needs of the customer. This in turn means that the efforts of the front-line employees need to be more highly valued. Since they are the providers of the 'moments of truth' their motivation and commitment are crucial. Carlzon argues that in such a service-oriented organisation individual decisions should be made at the point of responsibility and not higher up the hierarchy. The service deliverers have themselves to be the 'managers' and more consumer-oriented.

One example of this can be seen in the management literature relating to hotels. What makes some visitors return again and again to the same hotel (Greene, 1982)? This has little to do with a hotel's physical features but rather results from two-way recognition between staff and the hotel's guests. Greene argues that there is nothing more satisfying than walking into a hotel and seeing a familiar face, and then in turn being greeted by name and not by one's room number. He proposes a number of techniques by which hotel staff are reminded of guests' names so that they can be used at each 'moment of truth'. This strategy was carried to considerable lengths by the Porterhouse Restaurant Group, which devised a scheme to motivate its staff to identify as many customers as possible by name. Those who could identify 100 or more became members of the '100 Club', those who could identify 250, members of the '250 Club' and so on. One manageress achieved a UK record of being able to recognise an amazing 2,000 visitors (Lunn, 1989).

The importance of remembering and greeting guests by name is also seen in a Goffman-inspired study of impression management at the Ritz-Carlton (Dillard et al., 2000). At this high-class hotel, front-stage staff are taught dramaturgical discipline so that they foster the right impression and follow the moral standards that the hotel strives for. One aspect of this 'scripting' is 'the three steps of service: (a) A warm and sincere greeting. Use the guest name, if and when possible; (b) Anticipation and compliance with guest needs; (c) Fond farewell. Give them a warm good-bye and use their names when possible' (Dillard et al., 2000: 408). So one 'moment of truth' is whether the front-line staff can convey a *personal* service by greeting the guest by name or remembering their specific needs and preferences: 'A steak, you can get everywhere. But your table, with your favorite glass of wine, and whatever kind of service it is that you prefer, whether it's a lot of schmoozing or whether it's invisible service, these are things that you as a business person in a market segment, are willing to pay for, and find it very difficult to get' (Dillard et al., 2000: 408). Other 'moments of truth' are whether the staff succeeds in complying with the guest's idiosyncratic needs (especially when dramaturgical contingencies arise) and deliver 'deep enough apologies for disruptive events'.

Four concluding points should be noted about these services. First, the production of many services is *context* dependent; they depend for their successful production upon aspects of the social and physical setting within which they occur. Examples include the style of furnishings in a travel agent's reflecting an appropriate corporate image, the apparently safe interior of an aeroplane, the antique furniture in the country hotel, the quality of the sound and lighting in an Ibiza club, a historically interesting set of buildings in a resort, the themed environment of many theme parks, amusement parks, restaurants, pubs and shopping malls, and so on. In other words, the delivery of many services is interconnected with aspects of the built environment and especially the nature of design and brand architecture within the experience economy (see Chapter 6). In certain cases the service cannot be received in an inappropriate physical and social context – part of the 'service', part of what is consumed, is in effect the context (Urry, 1995a).

Second, there are very considerable variations in the expectations held by different sets of consumers. For instance, Mars and Nicod suggest that in cheaper hotels people expect a fast service but are not particularly bothered about its more general character (1984: 37). In top-quality hotels customers expect a wide range of idiosyncratic requests to be met, and indeed that staff are almost able to anticipate such requests in advance. Mars and Nicod suggest that particular difficulties are caused in middle-ranking establishments where the level and forms of service to be provided are less clear and can be contested. There are considerable differences between the perceived quality of service in different societies.

Third, the quality of many services is *contested* in contemporary societies. This is for a number of reasons: they meet an increasingly wide range of people's practical and emotional needs; their consumption normally involves spending considerable amounts of time since consumption occurs serially and not simultaneously; the consumers movement has encouraged people to be more critical and inquisitive about the quality of services being received; and consumers are increasingly choosy, eclectic and fickle. Service providers thus have all sorts of difficulties to face when confronted with the essentially contested character of 'services' in contemporary societies.

Fourth, the service product is predominantly *intangible*. So although there are certain tangible elements, such as the food or journey or drink, the crucial elements are intangible. This is shown in a study of small country hotels: 'service is not concerned with the product itself, but with the way in which the product is created and handled, with the manner, knowledge and attitude of the people who deliver it and with the environment in which it is delivered … in general terms quality is manifestly incapable of measurement' (Callan, 1989: 245). The service product is thus intangible because part of what are consumed are performances of hospitality affected through performative work, emotional and aesthetic labour. While service performances are taught, learned and regulated, service encounters cannot be completely predetermined and identical. There is always some element of unpredictability and fluidity to each 'moment of truth'. Cuthill maintains that: 'Service cultures are fluid and performed. They alter and shift with different customer groups and performances at different times of the day, week, or year, so that although a core service culture is created, it mutates with different performances' (2007: 68; see O'Dell, 2007, on services in spas).

These general points about services will now be applied to performing one particular type of service central to tourism: namely, eating and drinking.

Catering for the Customer

The development of the catering industry has been long and complex. Catering has become publicly available. Restaurants, bars and cafés are part of the *public* space of contemporary societies. This is in marked contrast to say nineteenth-century London, when the best places to eat were private or semi-private (Mennell, 1985: ch. 6). There were two forms: the private London clubs, which, grew more numerous from the 1820s onwards, and private hotels, where meals were served in the private suites of rooms and there were no 'public dining rooms'. This changed in the 1880s and 1890s with the opening of many grand hotels, stemming from increased mobility brought about by the railways. The new hotels were no longer private. Their public dining rooms were open at least to the wealthy 'public' and rapidly became fashionable. Their exclusiveness now stemmed not from semi-private association with a particular social circle, but more from their expense. Such hotels were no longer solely the preserve of men. They were public, or perhaps semi-public, spaces for wealthy men and women, to see and to be seen in, to enter the public sphere in a particular mannered fashion (Finkelstein, 1989).

The new hotels entailed innovative forms of organisation, particularly because the new clientele demanded the faster preparation of meals. The key figure in this rationalisation of the kitchen was Escoffier. Traditionally, the kitchen had been divided into a number of distinct sections, each responsible to a chef and for a particular category of dishes, and in which each chef worked independently of the others. Escoffier, by contrast, organised his kitchen into five sections, based not on the type of dish to be prepared but on the kind of operation to be undertaken (such as the *rotisseur* who did roasts, grilled and fried dishes, the *saucier* who made sauces and so on). These different sections were highly interdependent so that any particular dish resulted from the work carried out by chefs working in a number of different sections. The effect of this reform was to break down traditional craft demarcations and generate a new more complex division of labour based upon novel specialisation and a new interdependence of activities (Mennell, 1985: 155–9).

Subsequently, other features of catering work developed. One is that of *ad hoc* management. Because the level of demand for such services is highly volatile and unpredictable, management has to develop *ad hoc* ways of responding to varying demands and unanticipated crises. To cope with this unpredictability, managements largely try to avoid collective contracts and favour individual contract-making. Each employee will negotiate separate arrangements with management. What is of most significance to such employees is the total reward system, which includes not only basic pay, but also formalised perks such as accommodation, semi-formalised perks such as tips, and non-formal opportunities for perks and pilferage (Mars and Nicod, 1984). There is also the distinction between core and peripheral workers with the former benefiting most from the informal reward system.

These features derive from the key characteristic of restaurants identified in Whyte's classic study, namely, the combination of production *and* service (1948: 17). A restaurant thus differs from a factory, which is a unit of production, and it differs from a shop, which is a unit of service:

> The restaurant operator produces a perishable product for immediate sale within his establishment. Success in such a business requires a delicate adjustment of supply to demand and skilful coordination of production and service. ... This situation puts a premium upon the skilful handling of personnel. ... The restaurant must provide a satisfactory way of life for the people who do the work or else it cannot provide the satisfactions sought by its customers. (Whyte, 1948: 17–18)

There are important implications of how restaurants involve both production and service. Because employees are dealing with a perishable product, the tempo of work is highly variable; it is difficult to generate a rhythm by which to work and it also means that there are immense problems of coordination (Whyte, 1948: 18–19). The restaurant worker has two bosses, the supervisor/employer *and* the customer. The total reward depends upon satisfactory relationships with both. Moreover, low-status employees, such as waiters and waitresses, are able to demand prompt action from their status superiors, the chefs and cooks. But this is something that often generates resentment and a slowdown to demonstrate status superiority. Mars and Nicod suggest that these conflicts are likely to be less significant in very high-class hotels and restaurants where there is a common commitment to quality and less pressure on time (1984: 43–7), although, based upon his TV work, this is not the case with celebrity chef Gordon Ramsay's top restaurants. Whyte discusses various means of overcoming such problems, that is, to preserve communication between the kitchen and the waiters while limiting face-to-face interaction and hence the possibilities of friction.

A further aspect of the catering industry is when staff and customers meet there is a complex intertwining of labour and leisure. Marshall argues that had Whyte: 'investigated the staff-customer relationship with similar resolve he would have realised that the proximate culture of restaurant employees is only in part that of the "workplace"' (1986: 34). Marshall explores the contradiction between the poor conditions of work in the restaurant and the lack of resentment about them among the workforce. The pay was bad, the hours worked were exceptionally long and all staff had to demonstrate complete job flexibility. And yet there was little discontent about the work or about the wealth of the owner. There was more or less no unionisation, as with most of the rest of the industry (see Mars and Nicod, 1984: 109). There was also, rather unusually, little turnover of staff.

Marshall presumed that the employer's paternalism, combined with the material and symbolic significance of the total reward system, were sufficient to explain the apparent loyalty of the workforce. However, through participant observation, Marshall concluded that these 'employees were convinced that they weren't really "working" for their pay packets at all' (1986: 40). The staff rarely used the language of work. They did not say they were going to work, or were going home from work. The business after all involved the provision of leisure. Many of the customers were friends or relatives of the employees and, at least during slack times, the staff were encouraged to talk to and even participate in the leisure activities going on around them. Little attention was paid to punctuality and the staff were given freedom to organise their own routines of work. Moreover, much of the employee's leisure time was in fact also spent at the restaurant drinking in the bars. Thus many symbolic boundaries between work and leisure did not really operate. The daily round of activities (that is, of what was formally 'work' and what was formally 'leisure') were more a way of life. Other workplaces may have rather similar features, especially where leisure or tourist-related services are provided (fast-food outlets do not demonstrate such characteristics).

Some features of the work culture and situation of the cook made it unlikely that there will be active trade unionism and class consciousness among cooks and chefs. Chefs and cooks, particularly in private hotels and restaurants, typically have an orientation to the idea of service. There is the dedication to task because of the belief that the work they do is skilled, interesting and offers extensive scope for expressing their craft-like abilities. There are status differences between 'chefs' and 'cooks' in that the former view themselves as an elite serving an upper-class clientele in 'high-quality' establishments. Such status differences with deep historical roots undermine the perception of a homogeneous 'occupation'. This led to the perception among cooks of a distinct career structure through which they could progress upwards and come to run their own establishment.

Extensive technical change occurred among chefs and cooks in the 1970s. This was partly because of the introduction of electrical devices which replaced many routine hand operations, but mainly because of the widespread development of 'convenience foods'. In research in a cook-freeze kitchen, Gabriel shows that it is possible to transform a kitchen into a production line. One employee said: 'This is not a kitchen, it is a production line, but we don't get production money' (Gabriel, 1988: 57). But in relationship to cooking it is often difficult to establish just what skilled work really amounts to since it involves tacit skills not learnt through formal apprenticeships. It involves judgement and intelligence, sensitivity and subjectivity, as now revealed (sometimes in their absence!) on the ubiquitous TV programmes featuring celebrity and other chefs.

In the 1980s and 1990s there was extensive investment in the fast-food industry and what Levitt terms the 'industrialisation of service' (1981; Ritzer, 2008, on 'McDonaldization'). Such 'industrialised' food is produced in predictable, calculable, routinised and standardised environments, even where there is franchising. These fast-food companies have developed global networks with few 'failings' so that an African McDonald's will be every bit as 'good' as an American McDonald's. Such networks of control depend upon allocating a very large proportion of resources to the system, to branding, advertising, quality control, staff training and the internalisation of the corporate image.

McDonald's has generated new 'food' products such as Big Macs or the simulated Chicken McNuggets which alter people's eating habits and generate new social habits worldwide, such as eating standardised fast food bought from take-away restaurants. It promotes easy accessibility and flexible consumption at more or less any time ('grazing'). Fast food has broken down the tyranny of fixed mealtimes and the rigid timetabling of the day, especially while travelling and away from home.

Further, McDonaldization produces new kinds of low-skilled standardised jobs, especially for young people who may themselves be travelling the world via multiple McJobs. The employment effect has been to increase the proportion of the catering workforce under age 21. Working in fast food has been the most common choice of first-time job in Britain. A fast-food manager explained the recruiting policy: 'We just have to recruit young people because of the pace of work. Older people couldn't stand the pace … this job, with its clean, dynamic image, appeals to younger people' (quoted in Gabriel, 1988: 97).

In these restaurants the young staff have to learn how to present themselves in programmed ways to customers. There are stereotyped forms of address, sometimes printed on the back of the menu. Staff must also learn the company smile. A fast-food worker nevertheless explained: 'It's all artificial. Pretending to offer personal service with a smile when in reality no one means it. We know this, management knows this, even the customers know this, but we keep pretending' (Ritzer, 2008). Yet, although almost everything in the fast-food business is rule-bound, these rules are often broken in order to meet the demand at particular times of the day and to break the drudgery of work. Management regularly turns a blind eye to the ways in which employees maintain a measure of autonomy and put their mark on work they would otherwise find monotonous.

We have so far assumed that the same processes apply in each country. However, Mennell shows the differences between French and English experiences. There has been a long-standing dominance in England of the job of 'management', particularly of large hotels, and a corresponding disdain until recently for the occupations of chef and cook (1985: 195; hence the interesting growth in celebrity chefs). France, by contrast, saw the development of the chef as a professional. The *chef-patron* enjoyed immensely high status in French society. Mennell suggests that the situation in England facilitated more extensive implementation of de-skilling compared with France.

Crang pursues some of these issues of informality and style in a study of a 'themed' restaurant in Cambridge (1994, 1997). He notes how service encounters possess a rather complex *performative* character. One can think of this workplace as a stage, involving a mix of mental, manual and emotional labour. Staff are chosen because they possess the right sort of cultural and aesthetic capital, they have to be informal, young, friendly, with the right sort of body and skills to produce appropriate emotional performances during the course of each evening. The self is key here since the performances have to be 'authentically' fun-loving, informal and sociable.

Staff demonstrate various 'social and emotional' skills as they adjust their performances through cultural readings and interactions with a wide variety of customers. In some ways they have to be amateur social scientists, 'reading' each group of diners and predicting the kind of 'experience' they are expecting. The restaurant is described by the staff as a place of emotions, they talk of 'getting in the mood' at the beginning of the evening, allowing the emotions to flow. The staff, and especially the young female waitressing staff, operate of course under the gaze of customers and are expected to perform in accordance with gender-specific notions (see Adkins, 1995). So Crang shows how waiting work in a dinner-style restaurant is a form of conscious acting that is simultaneously scripted and creative, taking place before the dining audience. Due to a subtle combination of training and detailed in-house scripts for appropriate waitering, on the one hand, and pre-scripted, personal skills of improvising, on the other, a Goffmanesque universe of eagerness to please and friendliness is mostly enacted.

Haldrup and Larsen provide an ethnography of the tourist 'restaurant scene' in Alanya in Turkey, a hugely popular destination for Scandinavian package tourists and second-home owners (2010: ch. 6). 'Tourist restaurants' are recognisible by large images and multilingual menucards, a mixture of global and Turkish dishes, bright colours, national flags on the tables, international football T-shirts on the walls, international pop-tunes, large outdoor serving areas, international football matches on large TV-screens, insistent Turkish waiters on the street, location on the main streets or tourist sideways and the presence of tourists and *no* locals. The restaurant scene in Alanya is visibly divided and very few tourists eat where the locals go; eating and drinking tourists rub shoulders only with fellow tourists.

A 'banal nationalism' permeates these restaurants in Alanya. Their fronts are covered in national flags and restaurants are named *Sunset Copenhagen*, *Scandinavia* and *The Viking* ('Vikingen'). Tourists are continually reminded of their citizenship and nationality in such ways as being asked where they are from by waiters who try to lure them into their restaurant. Once the tourist exposes his nationality (say Danish) waiters begin to charm them in Danish and highlighting how the place is popular among Danes, cold Carlsberg beer is served, a forthcoming Danish football match is shown or a Danish football shirt is pointed out on the wall. And once inside the restaurant, one's national flag is placed at your table. Football jerseys, whether of the national team or Danish clubs, decorate the walls of many bars and restaurants, and they function as markers of national identity. For instance, the restaurant *Sunset Copenhagen* has the jerseys of rival Danish football clubs on display, while *Oscar's Scandinavian Restaurant*, on the other side of the street, is ornamented with the football jerseys of Norwegian teams. Both restaurants advertise on the street that they show Danish and Norwegian matches and have – as with many other restaurants and bars in Alanya – centrally placed TV-screens where they show 'not-to-be-missed' football matches and other sports events announced on the street. Thanks to global satellite TV, Danes can follow their local football team abroad.

One interesting finding is that such 'Scandinavian' restaurants tend to be owned by and employ Danes of Turkish origin or Turks living in Denmark outside the summer season. It is those restaurants with 'Danish Turkish' staff where Danish-ness is especially staged and performed. This highlights the mobilities of tourism staff. With reference to staff, we now examine the 'flexible' nature of the hospitality labour force.

'Flexible' and 'Mobile'

Restructuring through the flexible use of labour is something that has characterised many tourist-related services for decades, and the understanding of such services necessitates a careful examination of the changing gender relations in such industries, since particular kinds of labour flexibility presuppose a certain gendering of the labour force. Atkinson identified four forms of flexibility (1984). First, there is *numerical flexibility*, where firms vary the level of labour input in response to changes in the level of output. This may involve the use of part-time, temporary, short-term contract and casual workers. Second, there is *functional flexibility*, which refers to the ability of employers to move employees between different functional tasks according to changes in the work load. Third, there is the strategy of *distancing*, which involves the displacing of internal employment relations by commercial market relations through subcontracting and similar arrangements. Fourth, there is *pay flexibility*, whereby employers attempt to reward individual employees who have, for example, become 'multiskilled' and functionally flexible employees. These management strategies have the effect of restructuring employment in firms into 'core' and 'peripheral' workers.

The flexibility thesis was mostly discussed with respect to the 1980s restructuring of manufacturing industry. However, the service industry has for much longer been characterised by forms of flexibility. In tourist-related services we noted the use of pay flexibility, something related to the low levels of unionisation even in large hotels, and the relative absence of industrial disputes (Johnson and Mignot, 1982; Baum, 2007). Furthermore, both functional and numerical flexibility have been clear management goals in the hotel and catering industry from the 1960s onwards.

There is also a distinct gender division in the form and extent of these various flexible working practices (Bagguley, 1991; Baum, 2007). It seems that it was much more common for men to have jobs which involved functional flexibility. The 'operative positions', waiting and bar staff, kitchen hands, domestic staff and cleaners, are mainly undertaken by women, with chefs as the main exception. Moreover, it is in these positions that such women employees tend to work part-time, demonstrating 'numerical flexibility'. Such numerically flexible workers are also usually the least functionally flexible. Most part-time employees (mostly women) do not have the opportunity to develop a wide range of skills and experience to become functionally flexible as full-time employees, who are more likely to be male. Thus the gender of the employee seems to determine which form of flexible working is likely to be experienced.

The development of flexible forms of employment is affected by various factors. The fact that most tourist-related services are provided when the tourist gaze is present over the 'summer season' increases the use of temporary, part-time and functionally flexible workers. Baum states that around half of tourism staff in larger UK cities and elsewhere are students (2007: 1390). In many tourist-related services there is an exceptional variety of functions which have to be met – food production, food service, entertainment, accommodation, bars and so on – and this provides many opportunities for task flexibility. The industrial relations climate in these firms needs to be taken into account. Lack of extensive unionisation and employees' organisations based on occupational groups means there is little formally organised opposition to new working practices.

So far, then, flexible working practices have for some time been a key feature of tourist-related industries. With such staff demonstrating high turnover it may be difficult to sustain adequate skill levels and develop appropriate training programmes. Often companies use 'numerical flexibility' instead of developing the multiple skills of their core staff. Indeed, more generally there appears to be a paucity of career paths in tourist-related services except for those in managerial and chef positions. Metcalf summarised the situation for many workers in the hospitality industry: 'Very few career jobs were identified. ... Most jobs were characterised by young recruits, no promotion and high turnover. And leavers went into a variety of unskilled jobs' (1988: 89).

In addition to gender there are ethnic and mobility dimensions. Many tourism businesses are culturally diverse workplaces comprising many nationalities and people born elsewhere. Especially in major 'global' cities but increasingly also peripheral areas, hotels and restaurants make great use of mobile, transient staff (Duncan et al., 2009). For instance, some 25 per cent of the workforce in the Irish tourism and hospitality industry are non-Irish nationals (Baum, 2007). These mobile tourism workers are heterogeneous. On the one hand, there are migrants and refugees that undertake often low-entry but poorly paid back-stage region jobs such as cleaning and catering in hotels and restaurants. They fulfil such jobs since they have few other opportunities. And to this group we might add the many more or less trafficked women exploited in strip clubs, brothels, lap-dancing clubs, casinos and street corners in most tourist destinations around the world. For instance, in the red-light district of Copenhagen, hip locals, hotels, tourists, porn shops, drug addicts and prostitutes exist side by side. The sex industry, with which the tourism industry is heavily intertwined, is mainly constituted by more or less trafficked women from Eastern Europe and Africa. Trafficking and mobile sex workers are an integral part of the mobilities of hospitality work and tourism more generally. This is one dark affect of the (embodied) tourist gaze, causing pain and danger for many poor young women around the world (Jeffreys, 1999).

On the other hand, a different group of mobile service workers are younger tourists (often 'backpackers') that undertake temporary service work as part of their travel experience (Bianchi, 2000; Duncan et al., 2009). And one consequence of such 'mobilities of hospitality work' is that the distinctions between host and guest become porous and fluid. More and more often, tourists are served by staff who are guests too (and perhaps gone tomorrow too), so it is not only because of tourists that hotels, restaurants and resorts signify multiculturalism as much as nationality or localness. More generally, the categories of host and guest less frequently hold up in the field. Germann Molz and Gibson summarise how many researchers 'have challenged the binary opposition between host and guest by refining these categories in more pluralistic and heterogeneous terms' (2007a: 7; see Bell, 2007).

Conclusion

We have thus examined many aspects of the so-called 'hospitality industry'. Indeed, we have seen that there are ambiguities and anomalies in the notion of being 'hospitable' in a world of mass movement, intense commercialisation and likely exploitation (see Germann Molz and Gibson, 2007b). Hospitality presupposes various kinds of economies, politics and ethics as the tourist gaze extends around the world and draws into its warm embrace countless social relations between hosts and guests. These relations typically indicate strange combinations of hospitality *and* hostility as the world's largest industry has utterly industrialised, commercialised and scripted what once we might have valued as the pure act of giving unconditional hospitality to others (see Derrida, 2000, more generally).

While we have examined human performances of service work we end by noting how animals also work under the tourist gaze as part of a broader drift towards a society of spectacle. Zoos have long been tourist attractions. Here animals are literally the mad behind the bars, living on a stage where they are constantly watched, sometimes trained and applauded when performing their 'natural' instincts as part of what Franklin (1999) calls the 'zoological gaze' and Beardsworth and Bryman (2001) the 'Disneyization of Zoos'. Desmond shows how animals are required to perform a 'fiction of themselves as wild' as part of a theatrical staging: 'We can be overwhelmed by the scale of powerful jumps by the killer whales, for instance, while forgetting the frame of the show as a show during that moment. The spectacle of bodies in motion stands in for wildness and uncontrollability, not subject to the constraints of culture' (1999: 151; Cloke and Perkins, 2005).

We turn now to examine some broader transformations of tourist cultures which in turn affect the kinds of work that gets undertaken under the gaze.

5

Changing Tourist Cultures

Introduction

We have so far conceptualised the tourist gaze as being distinct from other social activities and occurring at particular places for specific periods of time. This viewpoint was reinforced by analysis in Chapters 3 and 4 of some salient characteristics of tourism. Although it is difficult to demarcate just what is and is not part of that industry, we presume a reasonably tight specification. In Chapter 4, for example, we discussed the specific character of service performances in the hospitality and experience economies. But in this chapter we consider how changes in the nature of especially western societies over the past few decades are undermining such a precise notion. We argue that there has been a reversal of the long-term process of structural differentiation by which relatively distinct social institutions came to specialise in particular tasks or functions. Part of this reversal is that 'culture' as an economy of signs is more central in the organisation of present-day societies. There has been a dissolving of the boundaries, not only between high and low cultures, but also between different cultural forms, such as tourism, art, education, photography, television, music, sport, shopping and architecture. In addition, mass communications have transformed the tourist gaze which is increasingly bound up with, and is partly indistinguishable from, all sorts of other social and cultural practices. This has the effect, as 'tourism' *per se* declines in specificity, of generalising the tourist gaze – people are much of the time 'tourists' whether they like it or know it. The tourist gaze is intrinsically part of contemporary experience but the tourist practices to which it gives rise are experiencing rapid and significant change. Such change cannot be separated from more wide-ranging structural and cultural developments within contemporary societies.

The Modern and the Postmodern

In the 1980s and 1990s it became common to understand some of these shifts through the distinction between modern and postmodern cultures, a distinction we will draw upon in this chapter.

The modern involves 'structural differentiation', the separate development of a number of institutional and normative spheres, of the economy, the family, the state, science, morality, and an aesthetic realm. Each of these becomes subject to self-legislation (see Lash, 1990: 8–9). Each sphere develops its own conventions and mode of valuation. Value within the cultural spheres is dependent upon how well a cultural object measures up to the norms appropriate to that sphere. This is 'horizontal differentiation'.

But a further aspect needs to be considered, 'vertical differentiation'. As each sphere becomes horizontally separated, so important vertical differentiations also develop. Within the cultural sphere this consists of a number of distinctions: between culture and life, between high and low culture, between scholarly or auratic art and popular pleasures, and between elite and mass forms of consumption. Within building design there is the distinction between 'architecture' (which obviously takes many different styles) and various vernacular forms of building. Modernism, then, is to be understood as a process of differentiation, especially as we have seen here, of the differentiation between the various cultural spheres both horizontally and vertically.

Postmodernism, by contrast, involves de-differentiation (Lash, 1990: ch. 1). There are various interconnected aspects. First, there is a breakdown in the distinctiveness of each of these spheres of activities, especially the cultural. Each implodes into the other, and most involve visual spectacle and play. This is seen most clearly in so-called multi-media events but much cultural production, especially via the central role of TV and now the internet, is difficult to categorise and place within any particular sphere.

Further, such cultural spheres are no longer auratic, in Benjamin's terms (1973). To say that a cultural phenomenon had aura was to say that it was radically separated from the social, it proclaimed its own originality, uniqueness and singularity, and it was based in a discourse of formal organic unity and artistic creativity. Postmodernist culture by contrast is anti-auratic. Such forms do not proclaim their uniqueness but are mechanically, electronically and digitally reproduced and distributed. There is a denial of the separation of the aesthetic from the social and of the contention that art is of a different order from life.

The value placed on the unity of the artistic work is challenged through an emphasis on pastiche, collage, allegory and so on. Postmodern cultural forms are not consumed in a state of contemplation (as at the classical concert) but of distraction. Postmodern culture affects the audience via its immediate impact, through what it does for one, through regimes of pleasure and affect, and not through the formal properties of the aesthetic material. And this serves to undermine any strong distinction between a high culture, enjoyed by an elite knowledgeable about the aesthetics of a given sphere (painting, music, literature), and the popular or low culture of the masses. Postmodernism is anti-hierarchical, opposed to such vertical differentiations.

There is also de-differentiation of 'cultural economy'. One aspect of this is the breakdown of some of the differences between the cultural object and the audience so that there is an active encouragement of audience participation, especially through SMS voting. Examples include the 'living theatre', TV game shows or confessional TV where anyone can be famous for 15 minutes (recent examples include *Big Brother*, *X-Factor* and *Pop Idol*). Another aspect is the dissolving of the boundaries between artistic production and the commercial. Developments here include the growth of 'free' artistic music videos to sell CDs, of 'downloads' and concert tickets, of songs appearing first within advertisements, of major artistic talents employed within the production of adverts, and of the use of 'art' to sell products via sponsorship. Commerce and culture are utterly intertwined in the postmodern.

There is also the problematising of the distinction between 'representations' and 'reality'. Signification is increasingly figural or visual and so there is a closer, more intimate, relationship between the representation and the reality than where signification takes place through words or music (without film, TV, video, pop video and so on). Further, an increasing proportion of the referents of signification, the 'reality', are themselves representations. Or as Baudrillard famously argued, what we increasingly consume are signs or representations (1983, 1985). Social identities are constructed through the exchange of sign-values. But these are accepted in a spirit of spectacle. People know that the media, for example, are a simulation, and they in turn simulate the media. This world of sign and spectacle is one in which there is no real originality, only what Eco terms 'travels in hyperreality' (1986). Everything is a copy, or a text upon a text, where what is fake can often seem more real than the real. This is a depthless world or a 'new flimsiness of reality' (Lash, 1990: 15). Lash summarises this argument: 'modernism conceives of representations as being problematic whereas postmodernism problematises reality' (1990: 13).

Interestingly, though, many tourist places and practices, even in the past, prefigure some postmodern characteristics. Resorts competed with each other to provide visitors with the grandest ballroom, the longest pier, the highest tower, the most modern amusement park, the most stylish holiday camp, the most spectacular illuminations, the most beautiful gardens, the most elegant promenade and so on. Because of the importance of the visual, of the gaze, tourism has always been concerned with spectacle and with cultural practices which partly implode into each other. Much tourist activity has been thoroughly anti-auratic. It has been based on mechanical and electronic reproduction (beginning with 'What the butler saw' machines, through spectacular illuminations, to *son et lumière* and laser shows); it has been based on popular pleasures, on an anti-elitism with little separation of art from social life; it has typically involved not contemplation but high levels of audience participation; and there has been much emphasis on pastiche, or what others might call kitsch (as in the Hawaiian ballroom at Maplin's holiday camp on the BBC TV programme *Hi-de-Hi!*).

What we have been describing are some characteristics of the collective and mediatised gaze. But in previous chapters we also discussed the 'romantic gaze', which is much more obviously auratic, concerned with the more elitist – and solitary – appreciation of magnificent scenery, an appreciation which requires considerable cultural capital, especially if particular objects also signify literary texts (as with the English Lakeland poets, for example). The 'romantic gaze' can also be said to involve de-differentiation. Historically, the 'romantic gaze' developed with the formation of picturesque tourism in late eighteenth-century England. The hybridised picturesque eye of skilled connoisseurship and Claude glasses derived pleasure from landscapes features that possessed resemblance to works of writing and painting. Visitors searched for and valued: 'that kind of beauty which would look well in a picture' (Ousby, 1990: 154). North European tourists consumed and pictured places through imported landscape images, and the distinction between nature and art dissolved into a circularity. Landscape became a reduplication of the picture that preceded it. An illustrative example of the conventions of picturesque sightseeing is provided in Thomas West's guidebook to the Lake District, highly influential in the late eighteenth century:

By this course the lake lies in order more pleasing to the eye, and grateful to the imagination. The change of scenes is from what is *pleasing* to what is surprising, from the delicate and elegant touches of *Claude*, to the noble scenes of *Poussin*, and, from these, to the stupendous, romantic ideas of *Salvator Rosa*. (Quoted in Andrews, 1989: 159)

West's much-loved route in the Lake District imitates the Italian landscape paintings of Claude, Poussin and Rosa. In so doing, West 'engaged in an act of translation, recuperating the specificity of this place to a series of places on the tourist circuit in Europe' (Duncan, 1999: 155). The landscape of Lake District is the product of mobility. The first visitors 'discovered' its sublime nature through 'imported' landscape models: it is indissolubly related to *other* tourist places. The tourist gaze, even the romantic gaze, implies that tourists are folded into a world of texts, images and representational technologies when gazing upon landscapes (see Larsen, 2006b, for a similar study of the making of the Danish island of Bornholm).

Much of what is appreciated is not directly experienced reality but representations, particularly through the medium of photography (Taylor, 1994). What people 'gaze upon' are ideal representations of the view in question which they internalise from various mobile representations. And even when they cannot in fact 'see' the natural wonder in question, they can still sense it, see it in their mind. And even when the object fails to live up to its representation, it is the latter which will stay in people's minds, as what they have really 'seen' (see Crawshaw and Urry, 1997; and Chapter 7 below).

Thus there is a cultural paradigm of de-differentiation; and various tourist places and practices historically prefigured this paradigm (see Chapter 6 for a discussion of related architectures). Yet there is an important sense in which much tourism has also been partially modernist. This sense is revealed through the term 'mass tourism', which is how much tourist activity was structured until recently. We noted in Chapter 3 aspects of this attempt to treat people in the same manner and not to set up differentiations between people who are consumers of the same holiday camp or hotel or restaurant. Central to the modern is the view of the public as a homogeneous mass and that there is a realm of values serving to unify the mass. Within tourism, the idea of the modern is reflected in the attempt to treat people *within* a socially differentiated site as similar to each other, with common tastes and characteristics, albeit with those being determined by the providers of the service in question. In the next section we consider how one key characteristic of postmodernism, like post-Fordism, is people's refusal to accept being treated as an undifferentiated mass. Part of postmodernism's hostility to authority is the opposition felt by many to mass treatment. Rather, people appear to want to be treated in a more differentiated manner and this has given rise to much lifestyle research by the advertising industry, seeking ever more finely distinguished categories of visitor (see Poon, 1993).

We have so far talked of different cultural paradigms without regard to the social forces that underlie them. The weakened collective powers of the working class and the heightened powers of the service and other middle classes have generated a widespread audience for new cultural forms and particularly for what some term 'post-tourism'.

Our argument here loosely derives from Bourdieu's classic text *Distinction* (1984). A number of its features are especially relevant to analysing the impacts of the cultural practices of one class upon another. Bourdieu brings out that the powers of different social classes (and by implication other social agents) are as much symbolic as economic or political. Such symbolic goods are subject to a distinct economy, a 'cultural economy', characterised by competition, monopolisation, inflation and different forms of capital, including especially cultural capital. Different social classes are engaged in a series of struggles with each other, to increase the volume of capital they possess *vis-à-vis* other classes, and to increase the valuation placed on the particular forms of capital they happen to possess. Each social class possesses a habitus, the system of classification which operates below the level of individual consciousness and which is inscribed within people's orienting practices, bodily dispositions and tastes and distastes. Classes in competition with each other attempt to impose their own system of classification upon other classes and to exert dominance. In such struggles a central role is played by cultural institutions, especially education and the media. The cultural realm has its own logic, currency and rate of convertibility into economic capital. Cultural capital is not just a matter of abstract theoretical knowledge but of the symbolic competence necessary to appreciate works of 'art' or 'anti-art' or 'place'. Differential access to the means of arts consumption is crucial to the reproduction of class and the processes of class and broader social conflict. This differential cultural consumption both results from the class system and is a mechanism by which classes and other social forces seek to establish dominance within a society (Bourdieu, 1984; Devine et al., 2005).

In particular, the service class is significant here. It consists of that set of places within the social division of labour whose occupants do not own capital or land to any substantial degree; is located within a set of interlocking social institutions which collectively 'service' capital; enjoys superior work and market situations generally resulting from the existence of well-defined careers, either within or between organisations; and has its entry regulated by the differential possession of educational credentials. These serve to demarcate the service class from more general white-collar workers and generate distinctions of cultural capital and taste (Butler and Savage, 1995; Savage et al., 1992).

The service class is discussed by Bourdieu. In talking of 'intellectuals', he contrasts their preference for 'aesthetic-asceticism' with the bourgeois preference for sumptuous interiors. This is reflected in liking modernist-style interiors among 'intellectuals'. Of their leisure patterns, Bourdieu writes: 'the most ascetic form of the aesthetic disposition and the culturally most legitimate and economically cheapest practices, e.g., museum-going, or, in sport, mountain-climbing or walking, are likely to occur particularly frequently among the fractions (relatively) poorest in economic capital' (1984: 267). Interestingly, Bourdieu talks of the symbolic subversion by intellectuals of the rituals of the bourgeois order through 'ostentatious poverty'. This is reflected in the tendency to dress casually when at work, to favour bare wood interiors, and to engage in mountaineering, hiking and walking, which represent their taste for 'natural, wild nature' (1984: 220). Intellectuals have a propensity to exhibit the 'romantic gaze'. The bourgeois, by contrast, is said to prefer 'organized, signposted cultivated nature' (Bourdieu, 1984: 220; Savage, Barlow, Dickens and Fielding, 1992; see Munt, 1994, on the tourism implications).

What we have referred to as the service class and other white-collar workers would also include those whose work is predominately symbolic. Much work of both is symbolic – in the media, new media, advertising, design, acting as cultural intermediaries. Such groups have a strong commitment to fashion, to the rapid and playful transformations of style (see Featherstone, 1987: 27; Lash and Urry, 1994). Such groups are not necessarily accepted by the intellectuals and the old cultural-capital establishment. So there is here a challenge to established culture, to high culture, while at the same time the emergence of celebrity intellectuals has demystified traditional sources of cultural capital: 'This interchange, the alertness of intellectuals to new popular styles and the marketability of "the new", creates conditions in which styles travel faster, both from the avant-garde to the popular, the popular to the avant-garde, and the popular to the jet-set' (Featherstone 1987: 27; Savage et al., 1992).

As a result, there comes to be generated a kind of stylistic melting-pot, of the old and the new, of the nostalgic and the futuristic, of the 'natural' and the 'artificial', of the youthful and the mature, of high culture and low, and of modernism and the postmodern. Martin summarises how the growth of these middle-class groups has upset pre-existing cultural patterns: 'The contemporary culture market muddles together the elite and the vulgar, yesterday's shock and today's joke in one gloriously trivial *bricolage*. Style is everything and anything can become style' (1982: 236–7).

Furthermore, Bourdieu argues, these groups also have a quite different approach to pleasure. The old *petit bourgeoisie* bases its life on a morality of duty, with 'a fear of pleasure … a relation to the body made up of "reserve", "modesty" and "restraint", and associates every satisfaction of the forbidden impulses with guilt' (Bourdieu, 1984: 367). By contrast, the new middle-classes urge

> a morality of pleasure as a duty. This doctrine makes it a failure, a threat to self-esteem, not to 'have fun'. … Pleasure is not only permitted but demanded, on ethical as much as on scientific grounds. The fear of not getting enough pleasure … is combined with the search for self-expression and 'bodily expression' and for communication with others. (1984: 367; see Elliott and Urry, 2010, on pleasure as duty)

This last argument needs some clarification. Capitalist societies are characterised by a strong emphasis upon consumption based upon the romantic ethic. Campbell argues that romanticism has provided that philosophy of 'recreation' necessary for a dynamic consumerism in which the search for pleasure is viewed as desirable in and of itself (1987: 201). Romanticism produced the widespread taste for novelty which ensured the ethical support for continuously changing patterns of consumption. Various middle-class groupings are in a transformed situation and have significant effects upon the wider society. These groups demonstrate the central significance of symbolic work; the increase in the importance of the media and of their contemporary role in structuring fashion and taste; the greater freedom and incentive of such groups to devise new cultural patterns; the heightened prestige that accrues for the middle classes not from respectability but from fashionability; the greater significance of cultural capital to such groups and the continuous need to augment it; and a reduced functional need to maintain their economic capital intact (Lash and Urry, 1994). Various 'postmodern' landscapes of gentrification and inner-city arts-led regeneration show how the design of gentrified areas reflects the cultural capital of such a class (Zukin, 1991).

In all these changes, the media and new media are significant in reducing the importance of separate and distinct systems of information and pleasure. People from different social groups are exposed to more generally available systems of information, and each group can now see representations of the private spaces of other social groups (Meyrowitz, 1985). The media provide an enormously increased circulation of other people's lives, including elite groups and 'celebrities' (see Richards et al., 1999; Rojek, 2004). This institutionalised voyeurism in turn enables many to adopt the styles of other groups, to transgress boundaries between different social groupings as supposedly embodying particular values such as high culture, low culture, artistic, tasteful, tasteless. The media have also undermined what is to be thought of as properly backstage, as what should be kept private and what can be made public (especially with the massive growth of confessional 'reality' TV and social networking sites). What Bourdieu calls the new *petit bourgeoisie* live for the moment: 'untrammelled by constraints and brakes imposed by collective memories and expectations' (1984: 317). They often feel guilt about being middle class since 'they see themselves as unclassifiable, 'excluded' … anything rather than categorized, assigned to a class, a determinate place in social space … freed from the temporal structures imposed by domestic units, with their own life-cycle, their long-term planning, sometimes over several generations, and their collective defences against the impact of the market' (Bourdieu, 1984: 370–1).

Martin similarly describes a destructured habitus amongst middle-class youth, especially from the 1960s onwards (1982). This she attributes to an immensely extended liminal zone derived from the decline in parental authority and the extension of the period when one is neither child nor adult. A particularly extended period of liminality develops in the new middle class in that it has a destructured habitus not only in youth but in many occupations, especially the media (Wittel, 2001). Likewise, Jameson analyses the growth of pastiche rather than parody of the original real historical referent. Pastiche fragments time into a series of 'perpetual presents' (Jameson, 1985: 118). People's lives in 'the new era of pastiche and nostalgia' are experienced as a succession of discontinuous events (Edgar,

1987). Although the individual blocks may be calculated and rational, the overall pattern is irrational. Spreading out from parts of the middle class is said to be a 'calculating hedonism' (Featherstone, 1987). People's sense of history has been lost since according to Frampton: '[W]e live in a paradoxical moment when, while we are perhaps more obsessed with history than ever before, we have, simultaneously, the feeling that a certain historical trajectory, or even for some, history itself, is coming to an end' (1988: 51). This is explored further in the next chapter when we encounter various debates over themed spaces and the 'heritage industry'.

This loss of historical sense has also been associated with another characteristic of contemporary media, that people increasingly live in a three-minute culture. TV viewers keep switching from channel to channel unable to concentrate on any topic or theme for longer than a few minutes; the instant search culture of the internet takes this to more of a three-second culture. Cultural conservatives argue that people no longer live their lives through identities imbued with the consciousness that they are the children of their parents who were in turn children of their parents, and so on. Even within generations the fascination with immediate consumption purchased through credit (often now online) rather than saving means that lifelong projects such as marriage become more a succession of marriages, 'serial monogamy' or affairs (Lawson and Samson, 1988; Giddens, 1992; Beck and Beck Gernsheim, 1995; Bauman, 2003).

In the next section we return to tourism and show how these various cultural changes and the development of the service and middle classes profoundly affect tourism.

Mediated Tourism

Indeed it is only through the analysis of wider cultural changes that specific tourist developments can be understood. We begin with some comments on the tastes of the service class and their impact upon seaside resorts.

Such tastes involve the prioritisation of 'culture' over a particular construction of 'nature' or 'natural desires'. Bourdieu expresses this well: 'The nature against which culture is here constructed is nothing other than what is "popular", "low", "vulgar", "common" ... a "social promotion" experienced as an ontological promotion, a process of "civilization" ... a leap from nature to culture, from the animal to the human' (1984: 251).

The British seaside resort embodied a particular construction of nature – as uncivilised, tasteless, animalistic, to be counterposed to the civilisation of culture. Such an attitude can be seen even among socialist critics. George Orwell imagined a modern design for Coleridge's 'Kubla Khan' as consisting of a holiday camp where air-conditioned caverns were transformed into a series of tea-grottoes in Moorish, Caucasian and Hawaiian styles. The sacred river would be turned into an artificially warmed bathing pool and muzak would be playing in the background 'to prevent the onset of that dreaded thing – thought' (quoted in Hebdige, 1988: 51). Likewise, Richard Hoggart set one of his parodies of cheap romantic fiction in what he called the Kosy Holiday Camp where there was a 'shiny barbarism', a 'spiritual dry-rot' and a 'Candy Floss World' (Hebdige, 1988: 52). Having good taste involves looking down on such places and only passing through, to view them as a voyeur would (as an Orwell or a Hoggart), but never to stay. The uncivilised resorts are not to be taken seriously, but can perhaps be played at or with.

At the same time an alternative construction of nature is also part of the service class habitus. There is a pronounced cultural emphasis on certain aspects of the natural. When discussing Bourdieu, it was argued that intellectuals subvert the bourgeois order through mini-mal luxury, functionalism and an ascetic aesthetics (1984: 287). This pattern is further reflected in an extraordinary range of contempo-rary cultural symbols and practices: health foods, real ale, real bread, vegetarianism, nouvelle cuisine, traditional, non-western science and medicine, natural childbirth, wool, lace and cotton rather 'man-made' fibres, antiques rather than 'man-made' reproductions, restored houses/warehouses, jogging, yoga, cycling, mountaineering, and fell-walking rather than organised, 'contrived' leisure. The middle-class ambiva-lence to the 'natural' is well captured in Campbell's account of how fishing has been affected by the naturalistic myth of the 'sportsman' (1989; Macnaghten and Urry, 2000b).

One reflection of the real or natural in tourism has been the 'Campaign for Real Holidays' conducted in the late 1980s in a key newspaper of the British service class, the *Independent*. This cam-paign resulted in the novel travel guide *The Independent Guide to Real Holidays Abroad* (Barrett, 1989a). The author states that it is increasingly difficult to have a 'real holiday' because the 'rise and rise of the package holiday has imposed on travel the same problems that mass production has inflicted on beer, bread, ice cream and many other things' (Barrett, 1989a: 1). A supposedly real holiday has two main characteristics. First, it involves visiting somewhere well away from where the mass of the population will be visiting. Real holidays thus involve the romantic tourist gaze, which has the effect of incorporating almost everywhere in the world as part of the 'pleasure periphery'. Second, the real holidaymaker will use small specialist agents/operators to get to their destination. The *Guide* bemoaned the fact that three-quarters of all foreign holidays taken by Britons are sold by five major companies. The *Guide* favours instead the development of smaller companies specialising in particular segments of the 'traveller market'. It talks of the development of the 'delicatessen' travel agent – these are specialist agencies that promote particular operators to 'a discriminating, independent-minded clientele' (Barrett, 1989a: 4, 1989b).

The existing companies have not been slow in recognising this trend to 'real' holidays, involving the culture of 'travel' rather than 'tourism', the romantic rather than the collective gaze and small niche suppliers rather than mass production/consumption operators. Thomas Cook tells us that this 'is not a trip for the tourist but a voyage of discovery for the traveller ... there is no packaging. ... Thomas Cook treats you not just as an individual but as a VIP. ... Thomas Cook provides a service that is both personal and global. This is truly travel à la carte' (*Thomas Cook Escorted Journeys*, Jan. 1989–Dec. 1989). Accompanying the description of each holiday or travel experience is a reading list of useful books on the particular country. There are various emphases to be noted here: travel rather than tourism, individual choice, avoiding the package holidaymaker, the need to be an educated traveller, and a global operation that permits individual care and attention.

The service-class preference for the 'real' or the 'natural' can also be seen in the increasing attraction of both visiting the countryside and protecting it. This is not new (Williams, 1973; Macnaghten and Urry, 1998). This image of the English countryside, 'a bucolic vision of an ordered, comforting, peaceful and, above all, deferential past', is a fundamentally constructed one, comprising elements that never existed together (Thrift, 1989: 26). The countryside today is even less like 'ye Olde English village', even less like Gray's description of Grasmere in the Lake District: 'This little unsuspected paradise, where all is peace, rusticity and happy poverty' (especially given the countryside's regular harbouring of diseased and factory-farmed animals).

But at the moment when rural life is being transformed because of changes in modern agriculture, so the countryside is an attractive object of the tourist gaze. One reflection of this is the rise in membership of many organisations concerned with simultaneously protecting the countryside and facilitating access to it. The current membership of the National Trust of England and Wales is 3.5 million and the RSPB 1 million. Connected with this has been the proliferation of 'new traditionalist' magazines that help to construct ever more redolent signs of the fast-disappearing countryside. These include *Country Homes and Interiors*, *Country Living*, *Country Homes* (Thrift, 1989: 28). Thrift argues that it is the service class which 'seems to be the social group that has taken the countryside and heritage traditions most to heart' (1989: 31). This class has been leading the push to move into the countryside and, indeed, historically led the campaigns to open up the countryside against the landlord class (see Urry, 1995b, on this class struggle). Thrift talks of the 'service-class character of places replete with manicured countryside' (1989: 34; Cloke et al., 1995; Urry, 1995b). This led to the gentrification of run-down rural property, and especially ruined farm buildings, as well as the building of new estates in vernacular or rustic style, such estates being usually described as 'villages' (Cloke, Phillips and Thrift, 1995).

In the Scandinavian countries this desire for the countryside has revitalised the 'coolness' of summer cottages (Bærenholdt et al., 2004). This will expand as many other people, following the example of the service class, seek to realise the 'village in their mind', to develop rural place-based consumption. Furthermore, those with professional-managerial jobs are twice as likely as those with manual jobs to visit, and they are more likely to be frequent visitors (Urry, 1995b: 211–12). However, differences can be identified between those more likely to work in the public sector who engage in 'natural' pursuits in the countryside, such as walking, climbing, camping and so on, and those private-sector managers who engage in country pursuits such as shooting, fishing, sailing, or golf (Urry, 1995b: 212–13; Savage et al., 1992). Moreover, there is a relationship here between postmodernism and this current obsession with the countryside. The attractions of the countryside derive in part from the disillusionment with the modern, particularly with the attempt to effect wholesale reconstruction of towns and cities in the post-war period. The countryside is *thought* to embody some or all of the following: a lack of planning and regimentation, a vernacular quaint architecture, winding lanes and a generally labyrinthine road system, and the virtues of tradition and the lack of social intervention. It hardly needs to be said that rural areas in most countries have in fact been subject to a wide range of modernising processes, especially large-scale agriculture, considerable attempts at land-use planning and extensive private-sector rural development. Moreover, only certain sorts of countryside are attractive to the prospective visitor, particularly those consistent with the idea of 'landscape'. Cosgrove summarises how

> the landscape idea was active within a process of undermining collective appropriation of nature for use. It was locked into an individualist way of seeing ... it is a way of seeing which separates subject and object, giving lordship to the eye of a single observer. In this the landscape idea either denies collective experience ... or mystifies it in an appeal to transcendental qualities of a particular area. (1984: 262; Schama, 1995)

Thus, 'landscape' is a *human* way of visually forming, through cultivated eyes, skilful techniques and technologies of representing, a physical environment. Hence, 'a landscape is a cultural image, a pictorial way of representing, structuring or symbolising surroundings' (Cosgrove, 1984: 1). 'Landscape' is about how humans take control and possession of, and derive pleasures from, 'nature'. It is a specific way of relating to 'nature' that fuses 'reality' with images and representations. It is about appearances and the look of places; it de-materialises place.

Landscape implies separation and individual observation (Williams, 1973: 120). Landscape 'is what the viewer has selected from the land, edited and modified in accordance with certain conventional ideas about what constitutes a 'good view'. It is land organised and reduced to the point 'where the human eye can comprehend its breadth and depth within one frame or short scan' (Andrews, 1989: 4). In other words, 'landscape' is a skilled, learned performance that visually and imaginatively works upon nature that, in turn, is rendered passive and submissive. This landscape vision depends on various objects and mundane technologies, and it undercut 'simple dichotomies of what is natural and unnatural, what is countryside and what is urban, and what are subjects and what are supposedly objects' (Macnaghten and Urry, 2000c: 2). While culturally constituted, 'landscape' is not without a material reality: it circulates in mobile cultural objects; it is built into the environment; and embodied landscape performances takes place in and have effects upon it. The social construction of landscape 'entails, at a minimum, the circulation of paper and bodies and manifold other materials' (Michael, 2000: 50). Landscape representations are travelling objects, at once informational and material: 'in this sense, landscape representations become dynamic vehicles for the circulation of place through space and time. ... Like Latour's scientific circulating references, landscape-objects allow us to "pack the world in a box" and move about it, contributing to the shaping of the knowledge of the world itself' (della Dora, 2007: 293, 2009).

Such a 'rural landscape' normally has erased from it farm machinery, labourers, tractors, telegraph wires, concrete farm buildings, motorways, derelict land, polluted water, nuclear power stations and dead and diseased animals. What people see is selective, and it is this focused gaze that is central to people's appropriation. The countryside is there to be gazed upon, and ideally one should not be gazing upon other people, whether workers or other tourists. Raymond Williams says that 'a working country is hardly ever a landscape. The very idea of landscape implies separation and observation' (1973: 120). The service class and the 'romantic gaze' are leading the way in sustaining this picture of the countryside as 'landscape'. But it is a gaze which has become more complex and playful, as rural images are central to mainstream popular culture, particularly advertising:

> From such a post-modern perspective landscape seems less like a palimpsest whose 'real' or 'authentic' meanings can somehow be recovered with the correct techniques, theories or ideologies, than a flickering text ... whose meaning can be created, extended, altered, elaborated and finally obliterated by the touch of a button. (Daniels and Cosgrove, 1988: 8; Macnaghten and Urry, 1998: ch. 6)

There is an alternative approach to that of 'landscape', of 'land' that is a physical, tangible resource that is ploughed, sown, grazed and built upon by human hands. It involves bodily proximity and physical engagement with, or 'dwelling within', the environment (Milton, 1993; Ingold and Kurttila, 2000; this is discussed in Chapter 8). The inter-war period in Britain saw attempts, especially by the northern urban working class, to gain access to wild upland countryside for walking, rambling and cycling, for leisure through land. Central to these campaigns was an element of class struggle, against the landowners who historically restricted access. The most famous access campaign took place at Kinder Scout in the Peak District in 1932. The aim of the organisers, such as Tom Stephenson, 'were not to *see* landscape, so much as to experience it physically – to walk it, climb it or cycle through it' (Cosgrove, 1984: 268). They stepped into the 'landscape picture' and engaged bodily, sensuously and expressively with their material affordances, much like contemporary adventure tourism where nature's materiality is experienced through the active, moving, hybridised body. 'Nature, for many tourist consumers, has evolved from something to look at, to something to leap into, jet boat through, or turn completely upside down: the inverted sublime!' (Bell and Lyall, 2002: 27)

Samuel argues that for the young ramblers of the north in the 1930s: 'the countryside was seen as an energizer: their intention was not so much to see the landscape as to experience it, to touch it with all the senses' (1998: 146). These new multi-sensuous practices ignored the existing farming activities of the countryside. Rather than being regarded as visual enticements, villages in the inter-war period were 'rural slums, with rising damp, leaky roofs, tiny windows, and squalid interiors' (Samuel, 1998: 146). Those rambling, climbing, cycling, camping and so on mostly ignored the lives and habitats of the people living and working in that countryside.

To the extent to which contemporary appropriations of the countryside involve treating it as a spectacle, even a 'theme', this is a postmodern attitude to be contrasted with an approach emphasising its 'use' or dwelling (Macnaghten and Urry, 1998). In response to the former, many living in rural areas develop packaged, themed environments whereby relatively sanitised representations of rural life are designed, constructed and presented to visitors:

> We seem to find it far easier to schedule areas for preservation as outstanding landscape for those who would passively view their scenery than to delegate authority for their shaping to those who live, work and actively recreate in them. ... Such preserved landscapes have in fact become a national commodity, advertised and sold abroad by the travel industry. (Cosgrove, 1984: 269)

The category of tourist is a relatively privileged one in rural areas. To be able to claim such a status it is normally necessary to be white and wealthy enough to own a car, and be able to organise and purchase certain kinds of accommodation (hotel bed, caravan or recognised camp site). It is also necessary, if people are visiting as a group, to use certain kinds of transport, such as coach or train, and not others, such as a convoy of cars or motorbikes, or a hippie convoy of travellers (see Hetherington, 2000b, on new age travellers). It is also necessary to engage in certain kinds of behaviour deemed appropriate and not others (known in Britain as the 'country code').

In particular, there has been some development of eco-tourism which stems from a selective repudiation of modern forms of transport, energy and industrial and agricultural production. Particular hostility has been shown to the 'modernised' planting of extensive forests of conifers, especially by the Forestry Commission but also by private landlords. Such forests are thought to have deleterious environmental and social consequences: the loss of a distinctive wildlife, including indigenous birds of prey; reduced levels of employment compared with those that would be supported by tourism; and the elimination of the wild, open and 'romantic' moors that are of such appeal. Indeed, a greater influence exercised by tourists would probably preserve the open moorlands against modernised planting of more and more rows of conifers (see Shoard, 1987: 223–5; see Macnaghten and Urry, 2000a, on woodland walking). Thus some important features of rural tourism stem from the broader development of environmental politics in the past two to three decades and the resistance to widespread attempts to 'modernise' particular areas or localities.

One element briefly mentioned above is that of playfulness. Feifer develops this idea through her notion of 'post-tourism' (1985). She highlights three features. The first is that the post-tourist does not have to leave his or her house in order to *see* many of the typical objects of the tourist gaze, with TV, video and the internet, all sorts of places can be gazed upon, compared, contextualised and gazed upon again. It is possible to imagine oneself 'really' there, seeing the sunset, the mountain range or the turquoise-coloured sea. The typical tourist experience is anyway to see *named* scenes through a *frame*, such as the hotel window, the car windscreen or the window of the coach. But this can now be experienced in one's own living room, at the flick of a switch, and it can be repeated time and time again. There is much less of the sense of the authentic, the once-in-a-lifetime gaze, and much more of the endless availability of gazes through a frame at the flick of a switch or a click. The distinctiveness of the 'tourist gaze' is lost as such gazes are part of a postmodern popular culture. Consequently, we can speak of the 'end of tourism' 'since people are tourists most of the time, whether they are literally mobile or only experience simulated mobility through the incredible fluidity of multiple signs and electronic images' (Lash and Urry, 1994: 259). In Chapter 9 we reconsider this in relationship to the risks of climate change and the capacity to travel and consume other places 'virtually'.

Second, the post-tourist is aware of change and delights in the multitude of choice: 'Now he [sic] wants to behold something sacred; now something informative, to broaden him, now something beautiful, to lift him and make him finer; and now something just different, because he's bored' (Feifer, 1985: 269). The post-tourist is freed from the constraints of 'high culture', on the one hand, and the untrammelled pursuit of the 'pleasure principle' on the other. He or she can move easily from one to the other and indeed can gain pleasure from the contrasts between the two. The world is a stage and the post-tourist can delight in the multitude of games to be played. When the miniature replica of the Eiffel Tower is purchased, it can be simultaneously enjoyed as a piece of kitsch, an exercise in geometric formalism and as a socially revealing artefact (see Feifer, 1985: 270). There is no need to make a fetish out of the correct interpretation since the post-tourist can enjoy playing at it being all three.

Third, and most important, the post-tourist knows they are a tourist and tourism is a series of games with multiple texts and no single, authentic tourist experience. The post-tourist thus knows that he or she will have to queue time and time again, that the glossy brochure is a piece of pop culture, that the apparently authentic local entertainment is as socially contrived as the ethnic bar, and that the supposedly quaint and traditional fishing village could not survive without the income from tourism. The post-tourist knows that he [*sic*] is: 'not a time-traveller when he goes somewhere historic; not an instant noble savage when he stays on a tropical beach; not an invisible observer when he visits a native compound. Resolutely "realistic", he cannot evade his condition of outsider' (Feifer, 1985: 271).

One game played by tourists is being a 'child'. This is especially clear in guided coach tours. One is told where to go, how long to go for, when one can eat, how long one has to visit the toilet and so on. The group (or class) are also asked inane questions and much of the discourse consists of setting up imaginary hostilities between people visiting from different places. And yet such tours seem much appreciated even by those who understand that they are 'playing at being a tourist', and one of the games to be embraced is 'being a child'.

If post-tourism is important it will affect existing tourist practices. The pleasures of tourism stem from complex processes of both production and consumption. We emphasised the socially constructed character of the tourist gaze, that both production and consumption are socially organised, and that the gaze must be directed to certain objects or features which are extraordinary, which distinguish that site/sight of the gaze from others. Normally there is something about its physical properties which makes it distinct, although these are often both manufactured and have to be learnt. But sometimes it is merely a place's historical or literary associations which make it extraordinary, such as the tunnel in Paris where Princess Diana died, or the vicarage in Haworth, Yorkshire where the Brontës lived.

The development of post-tourism transforms these processes by which the tourist gaze is produced and consumed. Mercer, for instance, notes that popular pleasures 'require a wholehearted and unselfconscious involvement in a cultural event, form or text' (1983: 84). Particularly important in tourist pleasures are those that involve the energetic breaking of the mild taboos that operate on various forms of consumption, such as eating or drinking to excess, spending money recklessly, wearing outrageous clothes, keeping wildly different time patterns and so on. As Thompson says: 'People are encouraged to spend by this *disorganisation* of the normal, "acceptable" routines of consumption' (1983: 129). But the post-tourist emphasis on playfulness, variety and self-consciousness makes it harder to find simple pleasures in such mild and socially tolerated rule-breaking. The post-tourist is above all self-conscious, 'cool' and role-distanced. Pleasure hence comes to be anticipated and experienced in different ways from before. A number of changes are occurring here.

The universal availability of the predominantly visual media in advanced western societies has resulted in a massive upward shift in the level of what is 'ordinary' and hence what people view as 'extraordinary'. Moreover, to the extent to which it is true that the media have ushered in a 'three-minute' culture, so this is also likely to encourage people to switch forms and sites of pleasures. It is almost certain that people will gain relatively less satisfaction from continuing to do what they, or more particularly their family, have always done. Thus, holidays have become less to do with the reinforcing of collective memories and experiences, especially around family and neighborhood, and more to do with immediate pleasure. As a result, people keep demanding new out-of-the-ordinary experiences. It is an interesting question whether it is in fact possible to construct a postmodern tourist site around absolutely any object. Mercer, though, argues that to experience pleasure in this more distanced, playful way makes all pleasures less satisfying. And in particular it makes it much harder to enjoy 'simple' pleasures such as those once found in seaside resorts.

Yet 'post-tourism', this de-differentiation between the everyday and touristic gazing, does not always substitute desires for seeing places directly and bodily. Another feature is the mediation of experiences and places. Media cultures also create desires for tourism, novel destinations and for new forms of mediated gazing, what in Chapter 1 we called 'mediatised gazing'. There are complex intersections between these different modes of virtual, imaginative and corporeal travelling that are increasingly de-differentiated from one another.

The tourist gaze is increasingly media-mediated. In postmodernity, tourists are constantly folded into a world of texts and images – books, magazines, paintings, postcards, ads, soap operas, movies, video games, music videos and so on – when gazing in and upon places. With the tourist gaze's widespread globalisation most places are 'on the move' and 'connected' through a circuit of images; faraway places are relentlessly travelling in and through the everyday spaces of those living in the 'rich North' of the world (Urry, 2007; Haldrup and Larsen, 2010). It is virtually impossible to visit places which people have not travelled to 'imaginatively' at some time. We have all been to New York via *NYPD Blue*, *Spin City*, *Seinfeld*, *Friends* and *Sex in the City*, through the eyes of Woody Allen, Spike Lee and Wayne Wang, and not least through the 9/11 terror attacks. Walking the streets of New York trigger memories of countless media-circulated images (Larsen, 2005; Mazierska and Walton, 2006).

Through representational performances, most tourist places have over time been inscribed with specific 'imaginative geographies' materialised and mobilised in and through books, brochures, postcards and photo albums. Tourist places are not given or fixed; they can appear and disappear, change meaning and character, and move about according to how they are produced and reproduced in media cultures (Shields, 1990; Coleman and Crang, 2002b; Bærenholdt et al., 2004). As literary theorist Edward Said says: 'people, places, and experiences can always be described by a book, so much that the book acquires greater authority, and use, even than the actuality it describes' (1995: 93).

'Markers' of tourism seem to be everywhere these days, where the tourist gaze and media gaze highly overlap and reinforce each other, whether people travel corporeally or simply imaginatively through the incredible range of global images that make up everyday media cultures. Major films and soap operas often cause tourist flows where few roamed before the location was made visible upon the silver screen (Tooke and Baker, 1996; Riley et al., 1998; Beeton, 2005; Couldry, 2005; Tzanelli, 2008; Mordue, 2009). There has been an upsurge in 'media pilgrimage', according to media scholar Couldry, which 'is both a real journey across space, and an acting out in space of the constructed "distance" between "ordinary world" and "media world"' (2005: 72). Such media pilgrimages in search for the reality of a film or soap opera travel in a form of postmodern hyper-reality (Eco, 1986) where model and reality are confused in a world where access to unmediated reality is impossible. Here we have a situation where film landscapes identify with and represent actual land-scapes, so that tourism destinations in part become *fantasylands* or *mediaworlds*.

As Mordue argues in relation to the contemporary TV programme *Heartbeat*, which revolves around the life of a country policeman living in Goathland in 1960s Britain: 'The stage management of Goathland for *Heartbeat* tourism has meant that its identity as a "traditional" rural village and its media identity as Aidensfield are, visually, completely intertwined. ... At virtually every corner of the village center there is some reminder, through a sign or souvenir, that you are in the heart of Heartbeat Country' (2009: 336). The popularity of this series represents a nostalgia for rural life, and when the programme reached wide popularity annual visitor numbers to the area increased from 200,000 to 1.2 million (Mordue, 2009: 332).

At the same time film studios have become 'tourist destinations'. Indeed, tourism organizations around the world quickly realised the potential of popular 'film geographies' which enables them to invent new destinations or inscribe old destinations with new imaginative geographies or place myths. In 1996, the British Tourist Authority (BTA) launched a *Movie Map* and a *Movie Map Web Site* to promote Britain's cinematic geographies as tourist geographies. Their new slogan is 'vacation on location' (www.visitbritian.com/corporate/links/visitbritian/campaigns.htm; accessed 22.03.10). This movie map reflects 'that an increasing number of visitors to Britain come in search of the locations featured in their favourite films and TV shows'. One campaign utilised the tremendous global success of *Harry Potter* as the lens to discover the magic of Britain, its 'magical and mysterious attractions' (Edensor, 2002; Larsen, 2005). In their attempt to boost their national brand, Scottish tourist authorities deployed the Hollywood blockbuster movie of *Braveheart* (Edensor, 2002).

Given that one film reviewer commented that the film *Captain Corelli's Mandolin* is 'a fine holiday ad but a rather dull movie' (Channel 4), it is unsurprising that tour operators tried to sell Kefalonia through its cinematic representation. To cite Thompson: 'Castaway Kefalonia – the island of Captain Corelli fame' (quoted Crang and Travlou, 2009: 86).

And the novels *The Lord of the Rings* were written by the British novelist Tolkien, bearing no specific relation to New Zealand. However, the films are directed by the New Zealander Peter Jackson and shot in New Zealand. This led many tourism providers in New Zealand to capitalise upon its worldwide popularity. Indeed, even though most scenes are a mix of 'real' landscapes, film sets and postproduction digital modifications, the official New Zealand tourist organisation branded itself the 'Home of Middle Earth'. Various companies arranged shorter and longer tours to the major sights of the film although no 'remnants' now remain; one can travel with 'the Lords of the Rings location guidebook' through this fictional and virtual environment. In this LOTR industry, 'place' and 'culture' are not exclusively attached to physical loci but also to fictional and virtual environments. According to Tzanelli, 'virtual tourism' does not simply re-narrate 'place' and 'culture' but the fictional, cinematic, narrative itself becomes the destination for the 'archetypal tourist' of the LOTR sign industry (2008: ch. 3).

Conclusion

So in this chapter we explored some major shifts in contemporary culture which has been expressed in terms of the move from the modern to the postmodern. We examined especially various de-differentiations between multiple domains, the proliferating middle-class taste wars and many aspects of the mediatising of tourism. Much of this argument was demonstrated in relationship to the attractions and allure of the rural and of the natural. Overall, we saw how 'culture' is more significant to tourism as economies are more and more economies of signs. We ended with exploring the notion of the 'post-tourist' involving de-differentiation between the everyday and tourism. Generally, we examined how media cultures also create desires for tourist travel, novel destinations and new forms of 'mediatised gazing'.

The effects upon tourist experiences, though, have been left partly unspecified. So in the next chapter we examine the impacts of these cultural shifts upon places, buildings and design. How are various tourist gazes impacting upon the built form of place, of various old and new buildings and of their design and, indeed, redesign 'for the gaze'? Signs are not just signs, we might say, since they have many material effects.

6

Places, Buildings and Design

Places

In much tourism *writing*, the main focus is upon tourists and what they do and why they are motivated to go to certain kinds of place at particular periods of the year. There is a focus upon human subjects. But in this book we are also concerned with the places that are made and remade through the different forms of the gaze of such tourists. Indeed, we are interested in how places are intertwined with people through systems that generate and reproduce performances in and of place (and by comparison with other places). In *Performing Tourist Places*, we analysed tourist places through the metaphor of the 'sandcastle' (Baerenholdt et al., 2004; Coleman and Crang, 2002a; see Chapter 8). A particular physical environment does not in itself produce a tourist place. A pile of appropriately textured sand is nothing until it is turned into a sandcastle. It has to be designed into buildings, sociabilities, family life, friendship and memories. Places emerge as 'tourist places' when they are inscribed in circles of anticipation, performance and remembrance. They are economically, politically and culturally produced through networked mobilities of capital, persons, objects, signs and information. And it is out of these complex movements that certain places to play are assembled. Places are not fixed or given or simply bounded. They are 'in play' in relationship to multiple tourist gazes stretching in, through, and over apparently distinct places.

In this chapter we thus de-centre tourist studies away from 'tourists' and on to the networks and discourses that enable or perform various places. Places are thus (re)produced through tourist performances that are made possible through networked relationships with other organisations, machines, and especially buildings. Places are in the thick of such 'touring' processes and in part consist of anticipated, designed and remembered buildings. We thus consider in this chapter various connections between buildings, their design and the places that tourists may gaze upon.

In the next section we consider the design and architecture of such developments. Tourism is about finding certain sorts of place pleasant and interesting to gaze upon, and it necessarily comes up against the design of the buildings within such places. We begin with issues of design and the redesign of place, and then turn briefly to the designing and using of themes and malls. We then go on to consider questions of heritage and especially the look of heritage buildings. And finally, we examine the changing character of museums and especially the designing and using of postmodern museums.

Designing for the Gaze

Given how much tourist consumption involves the visual, and the significance of buildings as objects upon which the gaze is directed, it is essential to consider changing aesthetic design, patterns, forms and themes that those buildings might take. Here we turn to discussions of the experience economy and staging, Disneyization and especially postmodern buildings, the sphere which many would say best demonstrates such a cultural paradigm.

We argue, first, that there are a number of contemporary architectures. There are *after* the modern; *return* to the premodern; and *anti* the modern. We briefly describe the architectural style associated with each.

After the modern is 'consumerist postmodernism'. This takes its cue from Venturi's cry to 'learn from Las Vegas' (1972; Jencks, 1977; Frampton, 1988; Ibelings, 1998). Such consumerist postmodernism is the stylistic hallmark of post-Fordism and, more recently, the 'experience economy'. Luxor Las Vegas, Caesars Palace, Bellagio and The Venetian hotel in Las Vegas or Disneyland are its icons, celebrating commercialism and postmodern 'theming' (Harris and Lipman, 1986: 844–5; Klingmann, 2007: 194–205); see Figure 6.1. Art and life are fused or pastiched in the playful and shameless borrowing of ornamental style (see the Trafford Centre in Figure 6.2 on page 131, or the designs of John Jerde). Previous elements of high culture are mass-produced and no longer signify a single style. This is an architecture of surfaces and appearances, of playfulness and pastiche. It is mannerist – as if all the historical styles and conventions of architecture are there to be endlessly drawn on, juxtaposed and drawn on yet again. The past is an 'inexhaustible repertoire of forms, "styles" that everyone could re-cycle' (Ibelings, 1998: 21). The visual spectacle of Las Vegas shows how architecture can be liberated from the deadness of modern architecture's 'pure forms'.

Figure 6.1   *The Venetian experience, Las Vegas*

Las Vegas' heightened symbolism builds a fictional fantasy landscape. Its architecture of signs and styles appears almost a-spatial, with theming overshadowing function. It is an architecture of narrative content that liberates architecture from its visual silence by turning it into an 'imaginary world of appearance'. One lesson learnt from Las Vegas is that pleasure-zone architecture should have a narrative structure with the power to engulf people in an imaginary role (Venturi, 1972: 53). It is a kind of architecture that caters for collective and spectatorial gazes.

This architecture, as in John Jerde's designed malls, is now crucial to the 'experience economy'. Klingmann links the experience economy and architecture: '[F]or architecture, in the experience economy, the relative success of design lies in the sensation a consumer derives from it – in the enjoyment it offers and the resulting pleasures it evokes' (2007: 19). Whereas modern architecture was largely concerned with forms and function, Klingmann argues that design in the 'experience economy' focuses on experiences and engenders affective sensations. It is no longer the formal design of a building that determines its quality, but rather its powers of affecting and engaging users, emotionally, bodily and mentally. The key becomes what it does rather than what it is (Klingmann, 2007: 317). Its transitional and performative powers are central. And architects come to think of themselves as choreographers of dynamic themes and situations (Klingmann, 2007: 214).

By contrast, there is the style associated with the return to the premodern. Here, what is celebrated is the classical form, the architecture of an elite and the romantic gaze. Leon Krier summarises its attraction: 'People never protested against the tradition of classical architecture. … Architecture has reached its highest possible form in the classical principles and orders … [which] have the same inexhaustible capacities as the principles which govern nature and the universe itself' (1984: 87, 119).

This reconstructed classicism springs from those who believe they have distinct powers of insight, who will be able to return to the aura of the fine building. Architecture here is a self-determining practice, an autonomous discipline able to reproduce the three classical orders. This is linked to the belief that such classicism is really what people would want if only their choices were not distorted by 'modern architecture'.

To the extent to which such contemporary classical buildings mirror the English Georgian style, they will be popular objects of the tourist gaze. If there is a single style of house which tourists at least in Britain want to gaze upon, it is the classical Georgian country house (Hewison, 1987: ch. 3). Much Georgian building is preserved in many towns and cities in Britain. The most striking Georgian townscape is Bath where the housing stock is a positional good (see Chapter 9). One could describe many of the residents as living in a museum and simultaneously surrounded by museums. The city is almost definitive of good taste and a setting in which part of the cultural capital possessed by its residents is the knowledge of such housing and the skills necessary to improve it, while at the same time appearing to conserve it. The renaissance of Bath is just as important an icon of the postmodern (in the return to the premodern sense) as the latest jokey theme park or shopping mall.

The third variant is *against* the modern. This is found in Frampton's concept of 'critical regionalism' (1988) and Foster's notion of a 'critical postmodernism' (1985a, 1985b). The latter defines the critique of modernism as a Eurocentric and phallocentric set of discourses (see Hebdige, 1986–7: 8–9). It is argued that modernism (like premodern classicism) privileges the metropolitan centre over provincial towns and cities, the developed world over developing countries, the north Atlantic rim over the Pacific rim, western art forms over those from the 'east' and the 'south', men's art over women's art, the professional over the people and so on. This variant involves challenging these dominant discourses, seeing space as localised, specific, context-dependent, and particularistic, by contrast with modernist space which is absolute, generalised, and independent of context (Harvey, 1989).

Leon Krier talks of the need to create 'localities of human dignity' (1984: 87). The locality is central. And there are important resistances in contemporary societies which have made local vernacular architecture particularly popular, at least outside the metropolitan centres. There is the apparent desire of people living in particular places to conserve or to develop buildings, at least in their public spaces, which express the particular locality in which they live. Such old buildings appear to have a number of characteristics: solidity, since they have survived wars, erosions, developers and town planning; continuity, since they provide links between past generations and the present; authority, since they signify that age and tradition are worthy or preservation; and craft, since they were mostly built using otherwise underrated premodern techniques and materials (Lowenthal, 1985: 52–63). A significant London example of this is the Tate Modern gallery housed in a former power station on the south bank of the Thames which attracted five million visitors in its first year of operation.

And because of the globalisation of the tourist gaze, all sorts of places (indeed almost everywhere) have come to construct themselves as objects of the tourist gaze; in other words, not only as centres of production or symbols of power, but as sites of pleasure. Once people visit places outside capital cities and other major centres, what they find pleasurable are buildings which seem appropriate to that place and which mark it off from others. One strong objection to modern architecture was how it generated uniformity or placelessness, and was therefore unlikely to generate many distinct buildings attractive to potential tourists. The main exceptions to this are in major cities, such as Richard Rogers and Renzo Piano's high-tech Pompidou Centre in Paris, which now attracts more visitors than the Louvre, or Frank Gehry's Guggenheim Museum in Bilbao, perhaps the single best-known new building across the globe. Outside the major cities the tourist gaze has made most other places enhance difference often through the rediscovery of local vernacular styles that convey particular histories. As Lynch asks, 'what time is this place?' (1973). In other words, places indicate particular times or histories and in that process vernacular postmodernism is important. Wright talks of the 'abstract and artificial aestheticisation of the ordinary and the old', although different places signify very different 'old' times (1985: 230).

Moreover, each such place will be viewed from various perspectives. There will be differences between what visitors and locals 'see' in a place, and between the viewpoints of old and new residents. Wright maintains: 'People live in different worlds even though they share the same locality: *there is no single community or quarter*. What is pleasantly old for one person is decayed and broken for another' (1985: 237, italics in original).

So far we have talked about various kinds of architecture and how these do or do not coincide with the likely gazes of both local residents and visitors. We briefly consider the respective influences of architects and developers in developing different tourist sites. In the USA, there has been expanding employment of architects in small- and medium-sized towns where a middle class has given rise to localities with high incomes, environmental sensitivity and a consciousness of design (see Knox, 1987; Blau, 1988). Partly influenced by some of these locally based architects, a more participatory and activist-influenced planning developed in some places, 'aimed not only at halting renewal schemes but also at preserving and enhancing the neighborhood lifeworld' (Knox, 1988: 5). The effectiveness has varied and often schemes for the desired conservation of an area turn out to have unexpected consequences. The renewal of Covent

Garden in London as a result of a planning decision influenced by activists concerned to conserve the buildings after the ending of its market function generated an immensely successful tourist site (with resulting congestion, inflated prices and piles of uncollected rubbish).

Themed Spaces

We now turn to two specific aspects of contemporary architecture: theming and malls. Theming 'involves the use of an overarching theme, such as western, to create a holistic and integrated spatial organization' (Lukas, 2008: 67). It is a process of signification where certain geographical representations and meanings are selectively invented, reworked or borrowed in the material and symbolic design of self-enclosed leisure or tourism spaces (Hollinshead, 2009). We consider aspects of recent theme parks before turning to the themed character of contemporary shopping malls and resort hotels. In this section we further explore similarities between consumerist architecture and Disneyization. We show that much theming revolves around the tourist gaze. Themed environments stimulate primarily the visual sense through spectacular but also predictable and well-known signs. They rest upon hyper-sensuous experiences in which vision are reduced to a limited array of features, are then exaggerated, and finally come to dominate other senses. Offensive smells are eliminated and reduced to a light deodorized breeze. Touristic theming often happens through importing signs of iconic tourist places elsewhere and in other times.

Theming is about importing places and stimulating imaginative travel elsewhere. Themed spaces represent a paradoxical mix of presence and absence, here and there. They are also typified by high capital investment, private ownership, international 'brands' and surveillance. They indicate that public space is increasingly privatised, commodified and regulated.

The first kind of theme is the dividing up of countries in terms of new spatial divisions with new place names. In the north of England there is 'Last of the Summer Wine Country', 'Emmerdale Farm Country', 'James Herriot Country', 'Robin Hood Country', 'Catherine Cookson Country', 'Brontë Country' and so on. Space is divided up in terms of signs that signify particular themes – but not themes that necessarily relate to actual historical or geographical processes. In Canada the theme of 'Maritimicity' developed since the 1920s as a result of the provincial state and private capital seeking to mobilise modern tourism in Nova Scotia. McKay describes it as 'a peculiar petit-bourgeois rhetoric of lobster pots, grizzled fishermen, wharves and schooners ... a Golden Age mythology in a region that has become economically dependent on tourism' (1988: 30). Peggy's Cove has over the years become a purer and purer simulacrum, a copy of a prosperous and tranquil fishing village that never really existed.

Themed attractions in Britain include the Jorvik Centre in York, the Camelot theme park in Lancashire, the American Adventure in the Peak District, the Oxford Story, the Crusades experience in Winchester ('history brought to life') and the Pilgrim's Way in Canterbury. The last is described in the advertising material as 'a pilgrimage to the past'. However, the sense of history is bizarre since 'a man on children's television is the model for a dummy who is the adjunct to a non-existent scene in a mediaeval religious poem, none of whose words you hear' (Faulks, 1988). Another example is in Llandrindod Wells in Wales. Once a year most of the population dresses up in Edwardian costume. But it was suggested that the population could be dressed that way *for the entire year*. Thus the whole town and its population would be turned into a permanent Edwardian themed town. Already Visby in Sweden, an island in the Baltic, experiences a 'medieval week' when everyone dresses up in medieval costume, bringing the medieval 'theme' to life. Nowhere is theming more prevalent than in the USA, with some 700 themed attractions across the country even by the mid-1980s (see US examples in Hollinshead, 2009, and below).

Themes are, in Debord's terms, elements of the 'society of the spectacle' (1983). Those developing Jorvik or the Oxford Story attempt to make the experience authentic. In such themed areas the objects observed seem real and absolute through the use of smell as well as visual and aural simulation. The scenes are more real than the original or hyper-real. Or at least the surfaces, as grasped through the immediate senses, are more real. Lowenthal notes that 'habituation to replicas tends to persuade us that antiquities should look complete and "new"' (1985: 293). The representations thus approximate more closely to our expectations of reality, of the signs that we carry around waiting to be realised: 'Disneyland tells us that faked nature corresponds much more to our daydream demands ... Disneyland tells us that technology can give us more reality than nature can' (Eco, 1986: 44; Lukas, 2007, 2008).

This technological ability to create new themes which appear more real than the original has spread far and wide. The symbolic architecture of recent mega-hotels in Las Vegas involves an astonishing level of theming through drawing upon iconic tourist places from elsewhere. Luxor Las Vegas is themed as a postmodern Orientalist simulacra of timeless 'tourist Egypt', of iconic monuments, ruins, camels and pyramids. This theming, according to Cass, represents 'Egypt on steroids' (2004). 'Italy' is also present in Las Vegas. The luxury mega-hotels of Caesars Palace, Bellagio and The Venetian are all themed upon a simulated landscape of typical 'Italian' architecture, art and sights (Raento and Flusty, 2006) (see Figure 6.1 on page 121).

Many more or less all-inclusive mega-hotels catering for western tourists in non-western countries such as India, Turkey and Kenya also employ the architectural and performative 'theming' of exotic otherness, but within a controlled environment and without the dangers and messy sensuous geographies lurking outside. There is a colonial element to such enclavic spaces in the developing countries that often happen to be former colonies, such as India. Edensor speaks of such luxury 'camps' as enclavic places where tourists are cut off from surrounding places. He argues that 'above all the tourist enclave is designed for gazing', with exotic interior, evening shows and performing waiters. They are 'environmental bubbles' where tourists are shielded from offensive smells, tastes and sites (Edensor, 1998: 51; Edensor and Kothari, 2004). They are familial places where tourists feel at-home-away-from-home. Tourists are surrounded by like-minded tourists, international interior and amenities, western-style food, English-speaking staff and so on.

The theming of enclavic spaces of Mediterranean mass tourism ties into what Billig terms 'banal nationalism' (1997). Nationally themed bars and restaurants often outnumber those presenting themselves as locally authentic; thus, tourists can eat and drink foodstuffs from their native country surrounded by tourists of the same nationality as well as by flags and other symbols of their homeland (Jacobsen, 2003; Haldrup and Larsen, 2010). A recent ethnography of Britishness in charter-based tourism in Mallorca shows:

> For example, place names are resonant of those found in the UK, with café-bars called *The Britannia*, *The Willows*, *The Red Lion*, and others that make reference to British popular culture – Benny Hill and Eastenders, for instance. Added to this, English is the main language spoken and British sporting fixtures, news and other TV programmes are beamed in by satellite or played from video recordings. Food has a distinctly British flavour, with British bread, milk, bacon and sausages being a few of the items imported and advertised for sale. (Andrews, 2005: 252; see also West, 2006)

Many shopping malls have now become major tourist attractions in their own right and represent exceptional de-differentiation through theming. Consider the West Edmonton Mall:

> Imagine visiting Disneyland, Malibu Beach, Bourbon Street, the San Diego Zoo, Rodeo Drive in Beverly Hills and Australia's Great Barrier Reef ... in one weekend – and under one roof. ... Billed as the world's largest shopping complex of its kind, the Mall covers 110 acres and features 828 stores, 110 restaurants, 19 theatres ... a five-acre water park with a glass dome that is over 19 storeys high ... Contemplate the Mall's indoor lake complete with four submarines from which you can view sharks, octopi, tropical marine life, and a replica of the Great Barrier Reef. ... Fantasyland Hotel has given its rooms a variety of themes: one floor holds Classical Roman rooms, another *1001 Nights* Arabian rooms, another, Polynesian rooms ... (Travel Alberta, undated)

This mall has been very successful, attracting over nine million visitors a year as early as 1987. It represents a symbolic rejection of the normally understood world geography in which there are cultural centres with Edmonton located upon the world's periphery. What is asserted is a new collective sense of place based on transcending the barriers of distance and of place. The real-space relations of the globe are thus replaced by imaginary-space relations (Shields, 1989: 153).

This has only been possible because of the pervasiveness of tourist signs, of the rapid circulation of photographic and moving images. It is this exchange of signs which makes possible the construction of a pastiche of themes, each of which seems more real than the original, particularly because of the way that shopping malls in general emphasise newness and cleanliness: '[I]t is a world where Spanish galleons sail up Main Street past Marks and Spencer to put in at "New Orleans", where everything is tame and happy shoppers mingle with smiling dolphins' (Shields, 1989: 154).

The Metrocentre in the north-east of England is located in Gateshead, a place that has also been considered peripheral to British and European life. Its themes are 'Antique Village'; a 'Roman Forum', with areas on which to recline Roman-style; and a 'Mediterranean Village', with Italian, Greek and Lebanese restaurants lining a windingly quaint Mediterranean street. Shopping here is only part of its appeal, which also concerns leisure and tourism. There is a de-differentiation of the gaze of the shopper and tourist. Within a few minutes' walk people consume many tourist themes and services, they can stroll, and they can gaze and be gazed upon as though 'on holiday'.

The Trafford Centre near Manchester looks like a mix of a Classical Roman building and the Taj Mahal. The main entrance is a colonnaded granite and stone open space with sculptures, fountains and decorated benches. Once one is inside the 'port', palm trees and an ocean liner invite visitors to go on a 'great tourist escape'. Of all tourism icons, the palm tree is one of the most connotative, signifying paradise, liminality, 'Otherness', extravagant consumption and bodily pleasure (Osborne, 2000: 107). The Trafford ocean liner is no pale imitation of a 'real' ocean liner, possessing lifeboats, lifebelts, port holes, a swimming pool and a white surface with reddish-brown spots showing many years at sea! The main deck is a 1600-seater food court where costumers are entertained by live-performances, 'Trafford-TV' or gazing at fellow cruisers. There is a spectacular sky-effect ceiling that takes visitors from day to night and back again via dusk and dawn by-the-hour.

Visitors can step smoothly into different worlds: China, Italy, New York and New Orleans. In the New Orleans French Quarter, one is welcomed by a statue of four smiling black trumpeters and restaurants with 'outside' tables. Laundry is hanging out of the windows and the balconies proliferate with flowers and ornamentation (see Figure 6.2). Once New Orleans is consumed (with no hurricanes in sight!), the journey continues into the shopping streets. Regent Crescent gives the feeling of Ancient Rome and Greece with its neo-classically inspired ornaments, while the Festival Village is themed as a traditional English market.

The Trafford Centre has learnt lessons from Las Vegas and Disney. First, the Centre is virtually nothing but surface effects, images, decorations and ornaments. It is a glossy visual feast: an ecstasy of looking. Second, it quotes vicariously from historical forms. However, classical greatness is here invoked with touches of both nostalgia and humour – as part of a narrative. This is not architecture as art, but as popular storytelling, a story about the world as nothing but the 'tourist's oyster' (Bauman, 1993: 241). What such spectacular malls offer are staged environments and themed experiences as much as consumer goods. In this sense, they have redesigned themselves and become some of the main movers of the experience economy. To cite Klingmann: 'Within a generation, shopping malls have gone from functional shopping machines to highly immersive environments where lighting, music, and a careful selection of materials not only displays the merchandise as such but provides the right ambience' (2007: 36). One featured postmodern design was that architecture after the modern 'international style' should be sensitive to

∧∧

context and identity. It should promote difference and heterogeneous landscapes (Ibelings, 1998: 18). Yet there are very few historical references, architectural styles or cultural icons which identify the Trafford Centre with Manchester or actually northwest England.

This highlights how much postmodern theming no longer respects local 'semiotics' and styles but has become 'global', what Castells calls 'an architecture of the space of the flows'. It expresses 'in almost direct terms, the new dominant ideology, the end of ideology: the end of history and suppression of places in spaces of flows. Because if we are at the end of history can we now mix up everything we knew before. Because we do not belong any longer to any place, to any culture, the extreme version of postmodernism imposes codified code-breaking anywhere something is built' (Castells, 1996: 419).

A further reading of the Trafford Centre is that it is designed to be warm and inclusive. As the public-relations manager says:

> We have gone out to create a building that is warm, where you feel protected, feel part of it. It is not somewhere that is contemporary or modern or clinical. The whole building has been built to be a huge stately home. The architectural details go back to neo-classical design that gives a sense of warm feeling … it has a nice ambience and a nice atmosphere.

This is the ambience that much postmodernist architecture strives to achieve. The public-relations manager reproduces the widespread contempt of modern architect as alienating and soulless. Postmodern architecture is populist compared with the elitism of modern architecture. The Trafford Centre is said to be an 'inclusive' architecture for 'real' people (Jencks, 1977: 8).

Theme parks, malls and resorts represent membership of a community of consumers. To be in attendance at the 'court of commodities' is to be recognised as a citizen in contemporary society, as a consumer. However, recent marketing philosophy has been to develop spectacles of 'diversity and market segmentation'. Developments of this sort also represent the changing nature of public space in contemporary societies. An increasingly central role is being played by privately owned and controlled consumption spaces, as in the Trafford Centre and the refurbished Gum shopping arcades next to Red Square in Moscow. These involve high levels of surveillance where certain types of behaviour, clothing and comportment are expected, such as not sitting on the floor. The entrance and pathways of malls are often 'policed' by private security firms (similarly to airports) and 'undesirables' such as the homeless are excluded.

Figure 6.2 'New Orleans' at the Trafford Centre, Manchester

Every movement of consumers is the target of the omnipresent, all-recording gaze of the CCTV cameras. Gazers are constantly being gazed upon by hidden cameras. Shopping malls often boast that they are the safest places in Britain to shop while resort hotels protect tourists from supposedly dangerous, filthy and noisy outside worlds. There are some analogies between Bentham's panopticon prison and the visual and electronic surveillance found in these themed spaces. A Foucaultian take on themed spaces would stress that we are 'neither in the amphitheatre, nor on the stage, but in the panopticon machine (Foucault, 1979: 217; Hollinshead, 1999). As the public-relations manager of the Trafford Centre says: 'You can't escape the surveillance' (Larsen, 2000: 54). Themed spaces are also conspicuous for cleanliness and newness, with no space for untidy litter, the old, the shabby or the worn (Fiske, 1989: 39–42; Larsen, 2000).

A further setting for themed environments is that of world fairs. These are enormous international tourist attractions. For example, over 500,000 visitors a day attended the 1992 Expo in Seville (Harvey, 1996: 155). More than one hundred countries participated in Expo 2008 in Zaragoza. Some 70–100 million – mainly Chinese – people were expected to visit the 2010 Expo in Shanghai, China over a six-month period. The development and popularity of world fairs are a further example of the de-differentiation of leisure, tourism, shopping, culture, education, eating and so on.

Expos are organised around different national displays (Harvey, 1996: ch. 3). There are many themed environments based on national stereotypes, such as the British pub, American achievement in sport, the German beer garden and South Sea exotic dancing. Such themes are designed to demonstrate national pride in the cultural activities presumed specific to that country. Generally, this pride is revealed either in repackaging aspects of each country's traditions and heritage or in demonstrating the modern technology that each country has achieved.

Involved in such national displays are the mobilities of people, objects, signs and even rooted attractions. The iconic attraction of the tourist gaze in Copenhagen, the Little Mermaid, was plucked from her rock in Copenhagen harbour and than sat in an artificial pond at the centre of the Danish pavilion at the Shanghai Expo. This is not a postmodern copy but the original, travelling to a nation where she is an iconic figure popularised through the novelist Hans Christian Andersen. As the architect of the Danish Pavilion, Bjarke Ingles, said: 'When the Danish politicians learnt that all of the

Chinese actually grew up with the mermaid as part of their education, everybody thought it would be a beautiful gesture to send their mermaid to China for six months.' On the night of its unveiling, Shanghai's vice-mayor predicted it would become 'one of the shining stars of the whole Expo Park' (http://news.bbc.co.uk/2/hi/asia-pacific/8644013.stm; accessed 18.11.10). There is hardly a more spectacular way of branding Denmark to China, a country that soon will generate the most outbound tourists worldwide (see Figure 6.3 and Chapter 9 below).

No single hegemonic set of messages is conveyed by Expos and world fairs. They are a kind of micro-version of international tourism. Rather than tourists having to travel worldwide to experience and gaze upon different signs, they are conveniently brought together in one location. Harvey says more generally: 'it is now possible to experience the world's geography vicariously, as a simulacrum' (1989: 300). This can be seen from the entertainment provided at such world fairs. At the Vancouver Expo in 1986 there were 43,000 free on-site performances given by 80,000 performers (Ley and Olds, 1988: 203). Although there was high culture, including a presentation from *La Scala* to an audience of 40,000, most entertainment consisted of folk or popular forms, a postmodern cultural pastiche, rather like the availability of cuisines from across the world now available in cities round the world (Pillsbury, 1990). Most performances were recognisably from a specific country and consisted of the sort of ethnic entertainment that is provided for tourists in each country that they visit. The difference here was that the visitors only had to walk from one tent or display to the next in order to gaze upon another cultural event, signifying yet another nation.

Such exhibitions operate as a technology of nationhood, providing narrative possibilities for the imagining of national cultures and, indeed, the national 'brand' (Harvey, 1996: ch. 3). Through powerful images, symbols and icons, nation-states are represented as repositories of stability, continuity, uniqueness and harmony. However, the Expo of Seville was also a place of international capital, funding various national displays, the Expo as a whole and their own exhibition spaces, especially with communicational and informational advances that transcend national borders. In these displays the emphasis is placed upon consumer desire, individual choice, cosmopolitanism and the freedom of the market to cross national borders (the tourist crossing of borders is also to be found in collecting stamps in the Exhibition Passport). Universal exhibitions are thus places to celebrate global scapes and flows and of the companies that mobilise

Figure 6.3   *The Little Mermaid in Shanghai Expo 2010*

such mobilities. Nations are principally there as spectacle and sign in the branding processes that Expos construct and celebrate (see McCrone et al., 1995, on Scotland the brand).

Many displays in Expos purport to be educational, and indeed groups of school-age children constitute a major category of visitors. And this is a further feature of the de-differentiation of the cultural spheres. Education and entertainment are becoming merged, a process much assisted by the increasingly central role of the visual and electronic media in both. Indeed, themed spaces are involved in providing 'edu-tainment'. Holidays are thus not so straightforwardly contrasted with education and learning as in the past. In many ways much tourism is more closely interwoven with learning, returning, in a way, to the Grand Tour. We consider below the increasing popularity of museums, the fascination with the lives of industrial workers in particular and the popularity of hyper-real historical re-creations. We turn to assess the significance of the heritage industry and subsequently of museums to contemporary tourism.

Heritage

There has been much debate as to the causes of the contemporary fascination with gazing upon the historical or what is often seen as heritage. Places like the refurbished 'colonial' Havana in Cuba (see Figure 6.4; Lasanky, 2004), the Wigan Pier Heritage Centre (closed in 2007) in Lancashire or the restored mills in Lowell, Massachusetts, the first industrial town in the USA, are all examples of heritage. Some indicators of this phenomenon in Britain include 500,000 listed buildings, 17,000 protected monuments and 5,500 conservation areas. A new museum was said to open every fortnight in the UK, there are 78 museums devoted to railways and 180 watermills and windmills are open to the public (Samuel, 1994: Part II). Of the 1,750 museums in 1987, half were started since 1971. There are many heritage centres in the UK, including Ironbridge Gorge near Telford, the Wigan Pier Heritage Centre, Black Country World near Dudley, the Beamish Open Air Museum near Newcastle and the Jorvik Viking Centre in York. In the Rhondda valley a museum and heritage park were established in the former Lewis Merthyr coalmine (Dicks, 2000). Almost everywhere and everything from the past may be conserved. In Lancashire environmentalists have sought to preserve the largest slag heap in Britain, which the former British Coal had wanted to remove. A former director of the Science Museum has said of this growth in heritage that: 'You can't project that sort of rate

Figure 6.4   *The restoration of 'colonial' Havana*

of growth much further before the whole country becomes one big open air museum, and you just join it as you get off at Heathrow' (quoted in Hewison, 1987: 24). The seventeenth-century disease of nostalgia seems to have become a contemporary epidemic.

Similarly, Lowenthal says of the USA that 'the trappings of history now festoon the whole country' (1985: xv). The number of properties listed in the US National Register of Historic Places rose from 1,200 in 1968 to 37,000 in 1985 (Frieden and Sagalyn, 1989: 201). Likewise most other countries developing their tourism have also sought to recreate the 'heritage' of the built environment even if this is of an epoch now denigrated, as strikingly so in Cuba and its 'colonial architecture'.

Other heritage destinations, now components of global tourism, include various 'dark tourist' heritage sites. These include Auschwitz-Birkenau, Nazi-occupation sites in the Channel Islands, Dachau, Robben Island in South Africa, Alcatraz, Sarajevo's 'massacre trail', Ground Zero and the United States Holocaust Memorial Museum in Washington (see Figure 6.5). Such dark tourist sites are heritage sites of death, disaster and depravity (Lennon and Foley, 2000; Strange and Kempla, 2003; Lisle, 2004). And with the collapse of the communist regimes in eastern Europe in 1989, many westerners travel to 'gaze on communism', to experience this 'other' political, economic and social system and 'architecture' that was the antithesis of western capitalism (Hoffman and Musil, 1999; Light, 2001). Such 'communist heritage tourists' in search of material signs of a communist past are causing dilemmas. While they are an important source of revenue, tourists longing for a communist past are at odds with the former communist countries' quest for constructing new post-communist identities (Light, 2001).

Many of these recent developments result from the increased privatisation of the heritage/museum industry, with 56 per cent of UK museums opening in the 1980s being in the private sector (Hewison, 1987: 1, ch. 4). Many private initiatives have involved new ways of representing history, through commodifying the past in novel forms often in combination with local activists and enthusiasts. Very large numbers of people visit museums and heritage sites. The proportion of the service class visiting museum and heritage centres is about three times the proportion of manual workers. Visits to such sites vary ethnically, with 'white' people more likely to visit historic buildings or museums than either 'black' or 'Asian' people, who wish to learn about various heritage experience and not just that of 'England'. However, there is very widespread support for sustaining English heritage sites, with three-quarters of the population believing that their lives are

Figure 6.5   *United States Holocaust Memorial Museum, Washington, DC*

richer for having the opportunity to visit sites of heritage. Nine out of ten people support the use of public funds to preserve heritage.

Raban talks of a willingness of people to present a particular impression of the heritage of village England: 'nowhere outside Africa ... were the tribespeople so willing to dress up in "traditional" costumes and cater for the entertainment of their visitors. ... The thing had become a national industry. Year by year, England was being made more picturesquely merrie' (1986: 194–5). Some of these events are now organised as 'costume dramas' by English Heritage, the main body in England concerned with protecting heritage sites. The tendency to visit grand country houses also remains immensely popular, with 12 million people a year visiting National Trust properties. There are over 800 museums containing rural exhibits, some of which have been described as 'pretend farms', with wheelwrights, blacksmiths, horse breeders, farriers and so on.

Indeed, there has been a remarkable increase in encountering the real lives of industrial/mining workers. MacCannell points out the irony of these changes: 'Modern Man [*sic*] is losing his attachments to the work bench, the neighbourhood, the town, the family, which he once called "his own" but, at the same time, he is developing an interest in the "real lives" of others' (1999: 91). This is particularly marked in the north of Britain, where much heavy industry had been located. It is such industries which are of most interest to visitors, particularly because of the apparently heroic quality of the work, as with a coal mine or steel works. This fascination with other people's work is bound up with the postmodern breaking down of boundaries, particularly between the front and backstage of people's lives. Such a development is also part of a postmodern museum culture in which almost anything can become an object of curiosity for visitors (and see next section).

The remarkably rapid de-industrialisation of Britain during the 1980s and 1990s created a profound sense of loss, both of certain kinds of technology (steam engines, blast furnaces, pit workings) and of the social life that had developed around those technologies. The rapidity of such change was especially concentrated in the north of England, South Wales and central Scotland. Moreover, much of this industry had historically been based in inner-city Victorian premises, many of which became available for alternative uses. Such buildings were either attractive in their own right (such as the Albert Dock in Liverpool), or could be refurbished in a suitable heritage style for housing, offices, museums or restaurants. Such a style is normally picturesque, complete with sandblasted walls, replaced 'authentic-looking' windows and attractive street furniture. This process of de-industrialisation occurred in Britain at a time when many local authorities were developing more of a strategic role with regard to economic development and saw in tourism a way of generating jobs directly and through more general publicity about their place.

And with globalisation different countries have come to specialise in different sectors of the holiday market. Britain has in part come to specialise in holidays for overseas visitors that emphasise the historical and the quaint (North Americans often refer to Britain as that 'quaint country' or that 'old country'). This location within the global division of tourism has further reinforced the particular strength of heritage in Britain. So heritage is particularly important within British tourism and is more central to the gaze in Britain than in many other places.

But what is meant by heritage, particularly in relationship to notions of history and authenticity (Uzzell, 1989)? A lively debate has been raging concerned with interpreting the causes and consequences of heritage stimulated by Hewison's book subtitled *Britain in a Climate of Decline* (1987). He begins with the comment that, instead of manufacturing goods, Britain is increasingly manufacturing heritage. This has come about because of the perception that Britain is in some kind of terminal decline. And the development of heritage not only involves the reassertion of values which are anti-democratic, but the heightening of decline through a stifling of the culture of the present. A critical culture based on the understanding of history is what is needed, not, Hewison says, a set of heritage fantasies.

Hewison is concerned with analysing the conditions in which nostalgia is generated. He argues that it is felt most strongly at a time of discontent, anxiety or disappointment. And yet the times for which we feel most nostalgia were themselves periods of considerable disturbance. Furthermore, nostalgic memory is quite different from total recall; it is a socially organised construction.

Hewison notes how much contemporary nostalgia is for the *industrial* past. The Association for Industrial Archaeology was founded in 1973 and by the 1980s industrial museums were developing almost everywhere in the northern half of Britain. Hewison makes much of the contrasts between the development of the industrial museum at Beamish and the devastation brought about by the more or less simultaneous closure of the steel works at Consett, just ten miles away. The protection of the past conceals the destruction of the present. There is a distinction between authentic history (continuing and therefore dangerous) and heritage (past, dead and safe). The latter, in short, conceals social and spatial inequalities, masks a shallow commercialism and consumerism, and may in part at least destroy elements of the buildings or artefacts supposedly being conserved. Hewison argues that: 'If we really are interested in our history, then we may have to preserve it from the conservationists' (1987: 98). The novelist Tom Wolfe proposed that the British population service a national Disneyland for foreign tourists. And a fantasy of this sort can be seen in Julian Barnes' novel *England, England*, with a proposed theme park covering the whole of the Isle of Wight. This would be known as *Englandland* and contain scaled-down replicas of almost all the well-known historic buildings in England (Barnes, 1999).

However, these various criticisms of the heritage industry bear much similarity with the critique of the so-called mass society. Indeed, social scientists may well be prone to a kind of nostalgia, that is, for a Golden Age when the mass of the population was not taken in by new and distorting cultural forms (Stauth and Turner, 1988). There has, of course, never been such a period. Moreover, Hewison ignores the enormously important popular bases of conservation. For example, he sees the [English] National Trust as a gigantic system of outdoor relief for the old upper classes to maintain their stately homes. But this ignores the widespread support for such conservation. The National Trust with 3.5 million members is the largest mass organisation in England (see McCrone et al., 1995, on the Scottish equivalent). Moreover, much of the early conservation movement was plebeian in character – for example, railway preservation, industrial archaeology, steam traction rallies and the like in the 1960s – well before more obvious indicators of economic decline materialised in Britain. As noted, Covent Garden in central London, which might be critiqued as a 'heritage playground', only became transformed into a tourist site because of a conservation campaign conducted by local residents (Januszczak, 1987; Samuel, 1994). Likewise the preservation of some derelict coal mines in Wales resulted from pressure by local groups of miners and their families who sought to hold on to aspects of 'their' history; indeed, visitors to Big Pit in South Wales, for example, are said to be pleased that it has not been made 'pretty' for visitors (Urry, 1996).

Generally, the critics of the heritage industry also fail to link the pressure for conservation with the much broader development of environmental and cultural politics. Thus research on the membership of the National Trust for Scotland shows that Scottish heritage is a significant element in the development of cultural nationalism (McCrone et al., 1995). Heritage is seen as involving a strong sense of lineage and inheritance. It has an identity-conferring status. For most of the respondents, conserving Scottish heritage is a centrally important enthusiasm. McCrone, Morris and Kiely thus write of the membership of the National Trust of Scotland:

> There is a rich network of local activity groups, travel outings, and active participation in heritage conservation through voluntary labour. What is available to life members is a coordinated lifestyle achieved through association ... 'a timeless organisation upholding traditional values'. (1995: 155)

Hewison, moreover, presumes a rather simple model by which certain meanings, such as nostalgia for times past, are unambiguously transferred to visitors by these heritage sites (1987). There is little sense of the complexity by which different visitors can gaze upon the same set of objects and read and perform them in a different ways (see Urry, 1996; Franklin, 2003). Indeed, sites are not uniformly understood and passively accepted by visitors. Macdonald shows in an exhibition at the Science Museum how visitors frame and interpret the visit in ways not expected or planned for by its designers (1995: 21). Such visitors connect together exhibits that were not meant to be linked, they read the exhibits as prescriptive when they are not intended to be, and mostly they do not describe the exhibition in ways that the designers had intended it should be so described (and see Shaw et al., 2000: 276).

Research at the Albert Dock in Liverpool further shows that people actively use sites as bases for reminiscence, 'as the point of departure for their own memories of a way of life in which economic hardship and exploited labour were offset by a sense of community, neighbourliness and mutuality' (Mellor, 1991: 100). 'Reminiscence' may indeed be a major 'practice' at such sites. And reminiscing involves performance – both by those 'real' performers who are there to stimulate memories, and by visitors who often have to work cooperatively with others in order to produce their memories. Reminiscencing is not an apparently passive process of individual visual consumption. In some ways, it is similar to various other spatial practices taking place at tourist sites, such as walking, talking, sitting, photographing and so on, generally carried out with others and especially family and friends (see Edensor, 1998; see Chapter 8 on performances).

There is something condescending about Hewison's view that such a presentation of heritage cannot be interpreted and performed in different ways, or that the fact that the experience may be enjoyable means that it cannot also be educational. This can be seen in the case of New Salem where Abraham Lincoln lived during the 1830s. The meaning of this site is not given and fixed (Bruner,

1994: 410–11). Tourists play with time frames and experiment with alternative realities. They reconstruct their sense of the past even as such sites possess a strong entertainment and playful character. Bruner concludes that: 'many tourists make associations between what they see at the site and their personal lives' (1994: 410; and see Chapters 1 and 8 on performance).

Hewison concentrates upon the Wigan Pier Centre (closed in 2007) in north-west England as emblematic of this turning of history into heritage. However, this criticism is partly unfair since the Centre is scholarly and educational; it presents a history of intense popular struggle; it identifies the bosses as partly to blame for mining disasters; it celebrates a non-elite popular culture; and was in part organised by a local council with the objective of remembering past 'heroic labour'. Compared with most people's understanding of history it conveys something of the social processes involved in that history, even if it is hard to see how to build on that history in the future. Indeed, it is not at all clear just what understanding of 'history' most people have anyway. In the absence of the heritage industry, just how is the past normally understood by people (see Lowenthal, 1985: 411)? For many people history will be acquired at best through reading biographies and historical novels and seeing historical dramas on TV. It is not obvious that the heritage industry's account is more misleading. However, what is important is that heritage history is problematic because it is visual. Visitors *see* an array of artefacts, including buildings (either 'real' or 'manufactured'), and they then have to imagine the patterns of life that would have emerged around those seen objects (see Bruner, 1994). This is an 'artefactual' history, in which various kinds of *social* experiences are in effect ignored or trivialised, such as the relations of war, exploitation, hunger, disease, the law and so on, which cannot be seen as such.

Previously we noted that there is often considerable local support for conserving buildings as markers of place. However, conservation groups vary considerably between places. For example, in 1980, while there were 5.1 members of 'amenity societies' per 1,000 people in the UK as a whole, the ratio was over 20 per 1,000 in Hampshire and over 10 per 1,000 in most of the counties around London, in Devon, North Yorkshire and Cumbria (Lowe and Goyder, 1983: 28–30). Clearly, part of the rationale of such groups is to prevent new developments that will harm the supposed 'character' of the locality. The role of the service and middle classes in such groups is crucial – and is a major means by which those possessing positional goods, such as a nice house in a nice village, seek to preserve their advantages. However, conservation movements can often have broader objectives: not merely to prevent development, but to bring about the refurbishment of existing public buildings and more generally to conserve and develop key features of the villagescape or townscape. Moreover, even if the objectives of the movement have nothing to do with tourism, the effect will increase the attractiveness of the locality to the tourist gaze.

One factor that strengthened conservation movements in the UK has been the lower rate of geographical mobility of at least the male members of the service class (see Savage, 1988). As a result, such people are likely to develop more of an attachment to place. One can talk therefore of the 'localisation of the service class' and this will have its impact, through the forming of amenity groups, on the level of conservation (Bagguley et al., 1989: 151–2). To the extent that such groups are successful, this will make the place more visually attractive to potential visitors. Thus the preservation of the quaint villagescape or townscape through middle-class collective action is almost certain to increase the number of tourists and the resulting congestion then experienced by residents.

Earlier we noted how competitive the tourist market has become, in part as all sorts of places are competing to attract the increasingly selective and discriminating post-tourist. As with many other commodities, the market is much more differentiated and particular places have been forced to develop tourism strategies based upon 'tourism reflexivity'. Such reflexivity has involved auditing local facilities, developing a plan of action and targeting appropriate marketing for the identified market niche. In some cases this has involved the local state almost initiating a tourist industry from scratch – as with Bradford (Williams, 1998). Local authorities also play an important role because of the structure of ownership in tourist towns. This is often fragmented and it is difficult to get local capital to implement appropriate actions from the viewpoint of the locality as a whole. The council can be often the only agent with the capacity to invest in new infrastructure (such as sea defences, conference centres, harbours), or to provide the sort of facilities which must be found in any such centre (entertainments, museums, swimming pools). Local councils have been willing to engage in promoting tourism because in a period of central government constraint this has been one area where there are sources of funding to initiate projects which may also benefit local residents (especially in the later 1990s through UK lottery funding). Furthermore, such facilities are important since they may also attract prospective employees and employers and then keep them satisfied.

Some of these points about gazing on history can be seen at Quarry Bank Mill at Styal in Cheshire (built by Samuel Greg in

1784). Surrounding the mill are the buildings of an entire factory community, two chapels, a school, shop, houses for mill workers and an apprentice house, all of which have remained physically well preserved. The museum was founded in 1976, described as 'a museum of the factory system', aiming to bring to life the role of the workforce, the Greg family and the circumstances which began the industrial revolution in the textile industry. The museum houses a number of displays on textile finishing and water power. Demonstrators, some dressed in appropriate clothing, show visitors how to spin cotton on a spinning jenny, how to hand-weave, how a carding machine operated, the workings of a weaving mule, and the domestic routines involved in cooking, cleaning and washing for the child workforce. Considerable research by professional historians was undertaken to produce both the displays and the large number of supporting documents, given to or sold to visitors (Rose, 1978). Engineers have also been centrally involved in the development of the museum, in order to get the often-derelict machinery reworking.

The mill has produced a range of supporting material for such visitors, including a 'Resource and Document Pack'. Up to 100 guides are employed in explaining aspects of the mill's workings to such visitors. There are also a number of other educational activities undertaken by the museum. Courses run by the mill include weaving, spinning, patchwork and quilting, embroidery and lace, experimental textiles, fashion and clothing, design for textiles, dyeing and printing and knitting. The mill has made energetic efforts to attract the 'non-museum visiting public' by specifically increasing the entertainment elements of display. This is partly achieved by the use of people to demonstrate many processes and to interact in a role-playing way with the visitors. It is also assisted by organising a variety of special events: Mothering Sunday lunches, a tent-making project, St George's Day celebrations, Spooky tours, Apprentices' Christmas and so on.

The mill had to grapple with the issue of authenticity. Although the building is 'genuine' and has not been particularly cleaned up, the machinery it houses does not stem from the eighteenth century. Some items had been in the mill since the nineteenth or early twentieth centuries, while quite a lot of it, including the immense waterwheel, was imported from other, often derelict, industrial sites. The work on the machinery has involved using 'traditional' techniques that had to be specially learnt. The mill tries to make explicit what is authentic, although this is not a straightforward exercise since what is thought to be authentic depends upon which particular period is being considered. Also, of course, existing 'authentic' factories contain machines from various periods. What Quarry Bank Mill ultimately shows is that there is no simple 'authentic' reconstruction of history but that all involve accommodation and reinterpretation.

Finally, the mill does not present an overly romanticised view of working-class life. There is evidence of the ill-health and squalor of industrial work. However, the mill literature also draws considerable attention to the views of contemporaries which suggested that conditions in rural factory communities such as Styal were better than those in the huge industrial cities such as neighbouring Manchester and Salford. Thus there seem to have been lower levels of industrial unrest, although this could also be related to forms of surveillance and control available locally. It was also suggested by the curator that visitors would not return for further visits if an overly depressing account of factory life were presented to visitors. However, Quarry Bank Mill is not a shrine to industrial technology – if anything the textile machinery is likely to be regarded by visitors as noisy, dangerous and dirty.

We now turn to discuss how *nations* promote heritage tourism and more broadly how heritage tourism and travel to national shrines and buildings are central to cultures, regions and nations. Being part of any culture almost always involves travel. Culture-developing-and-sustaining-travel can take a number of different forms: travel to the culture's sacred sites; to the location of central written or visual texts; to places where key events took place; to see particularly noteworthy individuals or their documentary record; and to view other cultures so as to reinforce one's own cultural attachments. This can be seen with Ground Zero. Shortly after the 'spectacular' 9/11 terror attacks millions of Americans and people from around the world ventured to New York in *record* numbers to gaze upon 'Ground Zero', to show national and cosmopolitan solidarity with the dead and to confirm the 'reality' of the collapse of those Twin Towers that everyone had seen on television. Ground Zero has turned into another tourist attraction full of photographing tourists and of souvenirs (Lisle, 2004).

Indeed, one way that nations present themselves to themselves and to others is through national and international tourism. As Edensor says:

> As tourism becomes the world's largest industry, national tourism strategies seek to compete in this global market by advertising their distinct charms: trying to carve out a unique niche that might attract the 'golden hordes'. This depends on both advertising generic landscapes and attractions, and promoting particular symbolic sites and events. Part of this imperative to entice tourists and to reward their choice of

destination with memorable experiences involves the staging of the nation. (2002: 85)

Central is the nation's narrative of itself. National histories tell a story, of a people passing through history, a story often beginning in the mists of time (Bhabha, 1990). Much of this history of its traditions and icons has been 'invented'. Late nineteenth-century Europe was a period of remarkable invention of such national heritage. In France, Jeanne d'Arc was only elevated from obscurity by the Catholic Church in the 1870s (McCrone, 1998: 45–6). *La Marseillaise* became the national anthem in 1879, Bastille Day was invented in 1880, in which year July 14th was designated for the national feast. More generally, the idea of 'France' was extended 'by a process akin to colonisation through communication (roads, railways and above all by the newspapers) so that by the end of nineteenth century popular and elite culture had come together' as a result of diverse mobilities (McCrone, 1998: 46). Key in this was the mass production of public monuments of the nation, especially in rebuilt Paris, monuments that were travelled to, seen, talked about and shared through paintings, photographs, films and the European tourism industry.

This collective participation and the more general nation-inducing role of travel were initiated with the 1851 Great Exhibition at London's Crystal Palace, the first ever national tourist event. Although the British population was only 18 million, six million visits were made to the Exhibition, many using the new railways to visit the national capital for the first time. In the second half of the nineteenth century similar mega-events took place across Europe with attendances at some reaching 30 million or so (Roche, 2000). In Australia, a Centennial International Exhibition was held in Melbourne in 1888 and it is thought that two-thirds of the Australian population attended (Spillman, 1997: 51). Visitors from home and abroad confirmed Australia's achievements and characteristics.

More generally, since the mid-nineteenth century, travel to see the key sites, texts, exhibitions, buildings, landscapes, restaurants and achievements of a society has developed the cultural sense of nationality. Particularly important in this has been the founding of national museums, the development of a national heritage, artists, architects, musicians, playwrights, novelists, historians and archaeologists (McCrone, 1998: 53–5; Kirshenblatt-Giblett, 1998; and see Chapter 7). Recently a global public stage has emerged upon which almost all nations have to appear, to compete, to mobilise themselves as spectacle and to attract large numbers of visitors. This placement particularly operates through mega-events such as the Olympics, World Cups and Expos

(Harvey, 1996). China in the last decade (Beijing Olympics and Shanghai Expo) and Brazil (World Cup and Olympics) in the next are 'nations' deploying global tourism events to announce themselves as having truly arrived upon the world's stage. These international events, premised upon mass tourism and cosmopolitanism, mean that national heritage is increasingly conceived in terms of such a location within, and on, this stage. It is that staging which facilitates travel to mega-events of the global order, especially the 'Olympics and Expos in the Growth of Global Culture' (Roche, 2000).

But such icons are continuously disputed. The power of national elites was, for example, strongly contested in the intense debates over the 1988 Australian bicentennial (Spillman, 1997: ch. 4). There was forceful Aboriginal opposition to the celebrations of Australian heritage. They termed Australia Day, which was a huge tourist event, 'Invasion Day'.

And there has been the proliferation of diverse, often localised, indigenous sociations seeking to save 'their particular history and heritage'. In Britain, Samuel documented the new democratic, familial, workerist, femininist, consumerist and domestic heritages that various sociations have saved, laid out for display, and sought to bring visitors in to see, touch, hear and remember (1994; see Macdonald, 1997, on Aros Gaelic heritage centre on the Isle of Skye). And as we have seen, former Welsh coal-mining communities show the importance of 'experience' sites of vernacular heritage. There are various 'alternative heritage' tours – such as the Black Atlantic tour that visits sites connected to the transatlantic slave trade. Thus, the role of heritage and history has become a major issue. Questions of heritage makes 'history' central to the nature of given cultures and demonstrates how heritage cannot be divorced from the various 'techniques of remembering', many involving tourist sites, festivals, events and so on (see Arellano, 2004).

The previously run-down area of El Raval in Barcelona has been transformed but in ways perceived to be partly detrimental to the people who have lived there for long periods. There are profoundly contested sensecapes, significant taste and place wars (Degen, 2008). Degen describes shifts in this area of bohemianism and permissiveness that operated in opposition to bourgeois Barcelona. She describes how if one had visited El Raval in the 1980s, one would avoid prolonged eye contact with most inhabitants who were on the margins of society, the poor, old, prostitutes and drug addicts. Breathing in the stale air, one would wander through a scattering of family-run grocery shops and workshops. El Raval evolved into a series of neighborhoods whose sensescapes reflected decay, it was a place of loss, a kind of third-world city which reflected more generally how Catalan Barcelona was neglected through the Franco period (Degen, 2008: 139). But with the democratisation of Spain in 1976, the reinstating of Barcelona as the Catalan capital in 1989, and its nomination in 1986 as host city for the 1992 Olympics this changed. Degen discusses the significance of the resulting 1992 Olympic Games in transforming and reimagining Barcelona:

> Although there were many heroic performances, it was unanimously agreed that a major winner of the Olympics was the city of Barcelona itself, the Game not only beamed its metamorphosed urban landscape (which often featured as a background to sporting events) into the world's gaze, but also re-asserted its Catalan pride and identity. The 1992 Olympic Games catapulted Barcelona onto a global stage and into the heart of the world's urban tourism networks. In less than 5 years the city had been transformed from a run-down industrial metropolis into one of Europe's most desired tourist venues. (2004: 131).

New 'Museums'

And in much of the heritage-isation of place there has been almost everywhere a spectacular growth in the number of museums. This is part of the process by which the past came to be more highly valued by comparison with the present and future. And the attraction of museums increases as people get older – so the 'greying' of the world's population adds to the number and range of museums.

Museums open to the public developed in the early nineteenth century, beginning with the Louvre in Paris, the Prado in Madrid and the Altes Museum in Berlin. Especially since the *Michelin Guides* first appeared, museums have been central to the tourist experience, especially for tourists with high 'cultural capital'. Horne describes the contemporary tourist as a modern pilgrim, carrying guidebooks as devotional texts (1984). What matters, he says, is what people are told they are seeing. The fame of the object becomes its meaning. There is thus a ceremonial agenda, in which it is established what should be seen and even the order in which the gazing should take place. Museums were based upon a special sense of aura. Horne summarises the typical tourist experience, in which the museum functions as a metaphor for the power of the state, the learning of the scholar and the genius of the artist:

> Tourists with little or no knowledge of painting are expected to pay their respects solely to the fame, costliness and authenticity of these

> sacred objects, remote in their frames. As 'works of art' from which tourists must keep their distance, the value of paintings can depend not on their nature, but on their authenticated scarcity. The gap between 'art' and the tourist's own environment is thereby maintained. (1984: 16)

Museums have thus been based upon the aura of authentic historical artefacts and particularly those that are scarce because of the supposed genius of their unique creator (Michelangelo) or their culture (the Greek).

However, we argue that how people gaze within museums has significantly changed. The sense of aura has been undermined through the 'postmodern museum', involving different modes of vision and use. First, there has been a marked broadening of the objects deemed worthy of being preserved. As seen in the previous section, there is a changed conception of history with a decline in the strength of a given, uncontested national history, which national museums exemplify. Instead, many alternative or vernacular histories have developed – social, economic, populist, feminist, ethnic, industrial and so on. There is a pluralisation and indeed a 'contemporary-isation' of history. The British Tourist Authority calculated that even in the 1980s there were up to 12,000 museum-type venues in Britain. Museums are concerned with 'representations' of history, and there has been a remarkable increase in the range of histories that are thought worthy of being represented. We have already noted some of these, especially rural and industrial museums. It is almost as though the worse the previous historical experience the more authentic and appealing the resulting attraction. No longer are visitors only interested in seeing great works of art or artefacts from very distant historical periods. People seem attracted by representations of the 'ordinary', of modest houses and mundane forms of work. Glass-blowing, engine driving, shop working, candle-making, cotton spinning, salt-making, cobbling, chemical manufacture, holiday-making, lace-making, domestic chores, coalmining and so on are all worthy of being represented and viewed in contemporary museums. There is a fascination with the 'mundane' and popular and a tendency to treat all kinds of object, whether the Mona Lisa or the old cake tin of a Lancashire cotton worker, as almost equally interesting. One can summarise this shift as being 'from aura to nostalgia', reflecting the anti-elitism of postmodernism (Edgar, 1987). Also all sorts of material are now preserved in museums, including moving images, radio, television, photographs, cinema, the environment and even the sets of TV soap operas (Lumley, 1988).

There has also been a marked change in the nature of museums themselves. No longer are visitors expected to stand in awe of the exhibits. More emphasis is being placed on visitors participating in the exhibits themselves. 'Living' museums replace 'dead' museums, open-air museums replace those under cover, sound replaces hushed silence, visitors are not separated from the exhibits by glass and there is a multi-mediatisation of the exhibit. Overall, the museum and various media are increasingly de-differentiated. The publicity for what was once called the Tyne & Wear museum expressed this trend towards participation: 'In our museum, the emphasis is on action, participation and fun. Out are the endless old-fashioned glass cases you pored over in hushed silence. In are professionally designed displays, working models to play with, complete period room settings to browse through and sound effects to complete the picture' (quoted in White, 1987: 10). Another example is The Farmers' Museum in Cooperstown in New York. This reconstructed heritage village stages the life of a simple farming community. Here 'rather than being expected to diligently absorb facts and figures, visitors are invited to engage in what would have a typical daily routine of the period. ... Each person becomes an actor in a staged drama and actively participates, with all of his or her senses involved, on a simulation of historical events' (Klingmann, 2007: 40).

A further example is the Viking Ship Museum in Roskilde, Denmark, which is a Michelin 3-star attraction (the highest possible). While the ships are displayed within an emblematic modern architectural space typified by simplicity, spatial order and lightness, an adjacent space affords spectacular sightseeing and joyful 'sightdoing'. Newly constructed replicas of fully equipped Viking ships invite tourists to step on board as fully clad Vikings. While intended for children and young families with the objects appearing as 'second-rate copies', many adults spend much time and take many pictures in this Viking experience. Almost everyone inspects the wood and the sails, sits in and walks around boats, hold objects in their hands and play with the various weapons. Many adults dress up in Viking costumes (Bærenholdt and Haldrup, 2004; Larsen, 2004b).

Museums are also becoming more aware of diverse publics and how to 'improve' the varied experiences of museum visiting. There is acknowledgement that visitors will come from different ethnic/national groups and museum staff must concern themselves with various ways in which visitors may interact with displays and different histories they present (Hooper-Greenhill, 1988: 228–30; Bærenholdt and Haldrup, 2004).

Museum displays are also less auratic. It is now common for it to be revealed how a particular exhibit was prepared for exhibition, and in some cases how it was made to appear 'authentic'. In various museums, actors play historical roles and interact with visitors, participating in historical sketches. At Beamish, people act out roles in the different shops, while at Wigan Pier visitors are encouraged to experience a simulated school lesson. Elsewhere ex-miners describe mining work to visitors, and people run machinery which does not actually produce anything but demonstrates the machinery, 'the working non-working industry' (White, 1987: 11). Lumley summarises these changes by arguing that they involve replacing the notion that the museum is a collection for scholarly use with the idea that it is a means of communication (1988: 15). There is the shift from 'legislator' to 'interpreter', as Bauman expresses it (1987). And this applies even to the visually impaired. The museum is still a place of visually seeing and collecting, and yet the visually impaired expect to find ways in which they can encounter museums non-visually, especially through using the tactile sense to touch the objects (Hetherington, 2000a).

In addition, there is a changed relationship between what is considered a museum and other social institutions. Some institutions have become more like museums. Shops, for example, can now look like museums with elaborate displays of high-quality goods where people will be attracted into the shop in order to wander and to gaze. One example is the Prada store Epicenter in New York designed by celebrity architect Rem Koolhaas (see Klingmann, 2007: 126–7). In places like the Albert Dock in Liverpool, which contains the Tate Gallery of the North, a maritime museum and many stylish shops, it is difficult to see quite what is distinctive about the shops as such since people seem to regard their contents as 'exhibits'. Stephen Bayley, from the London Design Museum, remarked:

> the old nineteenth century museum was somewhat like a shop ... a place where you go and look at values and ideas, and I think shopping really is becoming one of the great cultural experiences of the late twentieth century. ... The two things are merging. So you have museums becoming more commercial, shops becoming more intelligent and more cultural. (Quoted in Hewison, 1987: 139)

Museums have simultaneously become more like commercial businesses in which visitors treat their experiences as 'a matter for consumption – something akin to shopping and tourism' (Macdonald, 1995: 25). This has the consequence that 'the enterprise and flair of the High St is diffusing in the world of museums. ... Packaging means establishing a corporate identity. ... Shopping is not just making a purchase, it is about the whole experience, including the ambience of the shop, the style of the staff' (Pemberton, quoted in Lumley, 1988: 20). This poses difficulties for museum staff trying to fashion museums as different from commercial enterprise. The growth of theme parks, shopping malls and heritage centres have forced museums to compete and become more market-oriented, certainly to run a prominent museum 'shop' and café', but also to mount spectacular displays, as in the Canadian Museum of Civilization. Heritage centres, such as the Jorvik Viking Centre in York or the Pilgrim's Way in Canterbury, compete with existing museums and challenge given notions of authenticity. In such centres there is a curious mixing of the museum and theatre. Everything is meant to be authentic, even down to the smells, but nothing actually dates from the period, as Macdonald also describes in Aros, a Gaelic heritage centre on the Isle of Skye (1997).

Part of this evolving process involves the emergence of 'museum brands'. Several decades after the Solomon R. Guggenheim Museum (designed by Frank Lloyd Wright) was established in 1937 in New York, Guggenheim has become the leading global museum brand with spectacular franchised branches in Venice, New York, Berlin, Bilbao and Abu Dhabi (opening 2011; Ostling, 2007). The latter two are designed by celebrity architect Frank Gehry, who is himself a global brand. His extravagant Guggenheim Museum played a crucial role in re-imagining Bilbao (Ockman, 2004; Klingmann, 2007; Ostling, 2007). Architect and critic Giovannini highlights the significance of the Bilbao Guggenheim:

> The history of Bilbao, Spain, stretches back to medieval times, but it wasn't until Frank Gehry's Guggenheim Museum, with its façade of flowing titanium ribbons, that the Basque port on the Atlantic became internationally famous. The fame, however, was just not a serendipitous by-product of a startlingly original design, but the result of conscious move on the part of city fathers to reposition Bilbao on the world stage. The rust belt city, Spain's Pittsburgh, needed a postcard image comparable to the Eiffel Tower and the Sydney Opera House to symbolize its emergence as a player on the cheeseboard of a united Europe and a globalized economy. It needed a monument. One building and $110 million later, Bilbao is now a contender as a world-class city, and many of the world's second-and third-tier cities have called Mr Gehry's office, hoping for a comparable Cinderella transformation. (Quoted in Klingmann, 2007: 238)

The Guggenheim Museum in Bilbao was an instant success. Within its first year of opening, 1.3 million visitors had paid for its building costs and the city was energised by economic growth and a new social visibility (Ostling, 2007).

Thus the sovereignty of consumers and trends in popular taste are transforming the museum's social role. It is less the embodiment of a single high culture from which most of the population are excluded. Museums in the 1980s and 1990s became more accessible, especially to the service and middle classes (Merriman, 1989). In Britain, Liverpool is interesting in how it capitalised on its particular 'popular' cultural heritage and through its designation as one of the European Cities of Culture. Liverpool was home to the Beatles and advertises its 'brand' as 'Beatleland' (with its airport being the Liverpool John Lennon Airport). Strongly featured in its tourism profile is the daily 'Beatles Magical History Tour'. Museum visiting, with its previously high-cultural associations, now enables the acquisition of cultural capital made possible by people 'reading' and enjoying many different sorts of 'museums'.

Conclusion

Buildings, designed themes and diverse heritages are thus central to the tourist gaze. We have stressed that many tourist sights and resorts are designed as themed, with enclavic spaces stimulating primarily the visual sense. Such themed spaces can be contrasted analytically with what Edensor calls 'heterogeneous' tourism space, where tourists (especially backpackers) and locals share the same spaces, rub shoulders and the sensescape is more multi-sensuous and unpredictable (1998). And yet even in such heterogeneous tourist places 'theming' and 'banal nationalism' are often prevalent.

In this chapter we have de-centred tourist studies away from 'tourists' and onto the networks and discourses that enable or perform various places, especially as themed or as heritage. Places are thus (re)produced through performances made possible through networked relationships between organisations, machines and especially buildings. Places are in the thick of such 'touring' processes and in part consist of anticipated, designed and remembered buildings.

We explore places and buildings further in the next chapter through analysing the significance of photographing buildings which stand for place. Indeed, many such contemporary and refurbished heritage buildings are designed to be captured photographically and for those photographic gazes to be then globally circulated within mainstream media, new media and Web 2.0.

7

Vision and Photography

gazer + being gazed)

Introduction

We have argued that vision is central to tourism experience. However, there is nothing inevitable or natural about this organising power of vision. Indeed, there was a centuries-long struggle for visuality to break free from other senses with which it had been entangled. Here we begin by examining the history of visuality and what is meant by the idea of seeing and in turn being seen, and how vision became the dominating sense in modern societies. We pay particular attention to the profusion of new visual technologies and urban spaces.

Second, we link vision and the tourist gaze with the medium of photography, the most important technology for developing and extending the tourist gaze. Osborne describes: 'the ultimate inseparability of the medium [of photography] from tourism's general culture and economy and from the varieties of modern culture of which they are constitutive' (2000: 70). We show how the tourist gaze has been inseparably tied up with the development and popularisation of cameras and photographs. The gaze is constructed discursively and materially through images and performances of photography, and vice versa. We analyse significant *moments* within tourism photography and show how photographs enhance, frame and substitute for physical travel in complex and contingent ways, especially as photography is bodily central to the tourist encountering of the other. Tourists, as Sontag remarked, feel obliged to put the camera between themselves and whatever is remarkable in the encounter (1979).

Drawing on research, we show how photographs activate both 'imaginative mobility' and 'memory travel', and they frame tourists' gazes and the manipulation of their cameras. Photographs are more than just representations, and while photographic *images* are caught up with the moment, photographic *objects* have temporal and spatial duration. They are performative objects generating affective sensations. Photographs are 'blocks of space-time' that have effects beyond the people or place or events to which they refer.

We examine the performativity, or doings, of photographs, how they organise gazes, constructing and mobilising the places that tourists consume and remember. We need to think of photographs as corporeal, travelling, ageing and affective, rather than as bodiless, timeless, fixed and passive. And we stress that such photographs are not objective or innocent but produced within asymmetrical power relations and the need 'to situate tourism representation politically, examine what they include and exclude, and expose whose interests they serve' (Mellinger, 1994: 776). Both tourism organisations and tourists invest much energy in photographs. We show how the former use and deploy photographs so as to invoke anticipation and to construct the gaze of tourists. Also tourists take photographs so as to produce tangible memories to be cherished and consumed well after the journey. Through photographs, tourists strive to make fleeting gazes last longer.

Finally, we turn to how the digitisation of photography has transformed some at least of these relations. Many personal photographic images are now destined to live virtual, digital lives without material substance, in cameras, computers and on the internet. Emails, blogs and social networking sites dislocate photographic memories from the fixed physical home and object-ness, distributing them to desktops, folders, printers, photo paper, frames – or trash bins. Many such photographs possess complex biographies as they materialise, dematerialise and rematerialise, taking and retaking various forms and inhabiting different materialities as they travel at bewildering speed and become used as elements of multiple narratives and practices.

History of Visuality

The very idea of a tourist gaze stems from contestations within intellectual, governmental and religious thinking over the past few centuries. Febvre argues that in sixteenth-century Europe, 'Like their acute hearing and sharp sense of smell, the men of that time doubtless had keen sight. But that was just it. They had not yet set it apart from the other senses' (1982: 437; Cooper, 1997). As a result people were said to live within a fluid world where entities rapidly changed shape and size, boundaries quickly altered and where there was little systematic stabilisation of the social or physical worlds. 'Interaction' describes the fluid, changing forms of perception that characterised sixteenth-century life (Cooper, 1997).

Between then and 1800 there were many changes. Visual observation rather than the a priori knowledge of medieval cosmology came

SHIFT STUDY ⟶ see

to be viewed as the basis of scientific legitimacy. This subsequently developed into the very foundation of the scientific method of the west, based upon sense-data principally produced and guaranteed by sight. Foucault shows in *The Order of Things* how natural history involves the observable structure of the visible world and not functions and relationships invisible to the senses (1970). Various sciences of 'visible nature' developed and were organised around visual taxonomies, including especially that of Linnaeus (Gregory, 1994: 20). Such classifications were based upon the modern *episteme* of the individual subject, the seeing eye, and the observations, distinctions and classifications that the eye is able to make (Foucault, 1970).

Treatises on travel consequently shifted from a scholastic emphasis on touring as an opportunity for discourse via the ear, to travel as *eyewitness* observation. And with the development of scientific expeditions (the first recorded in 1735: Pratt, 1992: 1), travellers could no longer expect that their observations would become part of science itself. Travel came to be justified not through science but through the idea of connoisseurship – 'the well trained eye' (Adler, 1989: 22). A connoisseurship of buildings, works of art and of landscapes developed especially in the late eighteenth century with the growth of 'scenic tourism' in Britain and then across Europe. '[S]ightseeing became simultaneously a more effusive passionate activity and a more private one' (Adler, 1989: 22). Such connoisseurship came to involve new ways of seeing: a 'prolonged, contemplative [look] regarding the field of vision with a certain aloofness and disengagement, across a tranquil interval' (Bryson, 1983: 94; Taylor, 1994: 13).

During the eighteenth century a more specialised visual sense developed based upon the *camera obscura*, the Claude glass, the use of guidebooks, the widespread knowledge of routes, the art of sketching and the availability of sketchbooks, the balcony and so on (Ousby, 1990). This shift can be seen in the case of Sweden, between Linnaeus' scientific expeditions in the 1730s to collect flowers and minerals, to Linnerhielm's travels in the 1780s to collect views and moods. The latter expresses this shift in the nature of travel: 'I travel to see, not to study' (Löfgren, 1999: 17; also Pratt, 1992).

Claude glasses were significant in this shift. Named after the picturesque painter Claude Lorraine, these were lightweight, mobile convex mirrors that fitted into a (male) pocket and quickly became standard equipment among pre-photographic tourists in Europe (Andrews, 1989; Ousby, 1990: 155; Löfgren, 1999: 18). The gazer stood with his/her back to the scene and consumed it through the petite mirror in which the reflected landscape was neatly trimmed and recomposed in accordance to the eye's movement. One tourist explained: 'Where the objects are great and near, it removes them to a due distance, and shews them in the soft colours of nature, and the most regular perspective the eye can perceive, art teach, or science demonstrate' (quoted in Ousby, 1990: 155). Another stated: 'my convex mirror brought every scene within the compass of a picture' (quoted in Batchen, 1999: 73). Nature was tamed, put into perspective with, and by, the human eye, as a landscape picture, a single vision of order.

Special light effects à la Lorraine were also created through the use of filters. Such glasses perfected nature. Even before the invention and popularisation of cameras, seeing was mediated by hybridised and prosthetic technologies. To realise the desired picturesque – that is, 'picture-like' – scenery that the unassisted eye struggled to form and possess, these pre-photographic tourists employed the camera obscura and especially Claude glasses (Andrews, 1989; Ousby, 1990).

This visual sense enables people to take possession of objects and environments, often at a distance (as Simmel argues; Frisby and Featherstone, 1997: 116). It facilitates the world of the 'other' to be controlled from afar, combining detachment and mastery. It is by seeking distance that a proper 'view' is gained, abstracted from the hustle and bustle of everyday experience (see Pratt's account of 'imperial eyes': 1992). As Gregory shows, a powerful viewing-position of simultaneous immersion and standing apart enabled tourists to gaze upon Egypt as though they were inside *Arabian Nights*. One tourist wrote: 'viewed from a distance, this metropolis might really bear out … the enchanting pictures sketched out with true Eastern warmth in the *Arabian Nights* … [this] fancy may be captivated by a distant view of the city, a nearer acquaintance with it effects a sad reverse. Once entered, the spell is dissolved (quoted in Gregory, 2001: 9). The anticipated theatrical Egypt was produced by tourists searching out elevated positions and open vistas, especially by sailing down the Nile in a *dahabeeah* (a large luxury houseboat with cross-sails).

While areas of wild, barren nature, which were once sources of sublime terror and fear, were transformed into what Raymond Williams terms 'scenery, landscape, image, fresh air', places waiting at a distance for visual consumption by those visiting from towns and cities full of 'dark satanic mills' (1972: 160; Macnaghten and Urry, 1998: 114–15). Even before the end of the eighteenth century the Alps, which had been regarded as mountains of immense inhospitality, ugliness and terror, had become 'civilised'. Ring maintained that they 'are not simply the Alps. They are a unique visual, cultural, geological and natural phenomenon, indissolubly wed to European history' (2000: 9). Picturesque tourism was instrumental in transforming the Alps and 'mountainscapes' throughout the globe into visually atractive places. Löfgren writes how tourists in Norway spoke of 'Swiss views' and American mountain resorts competed to become 'the Switzerland of the USA' (1999: 34). Larsen describes how Bornholm became inscribed with associations with the Alps, as 'Denmark's Switzerland' (2006b). Also by the end of the eighteenth century 'tropical nature' had been romanticised by travellers who began to see scenery as though it were a 'painting' (Sheller, 2003).

Over the next century nature of all sorts came to be widely *NATURE.* regarded as scenery, views and perceptual sensation, partly because of the Romantics: 'Nature has largely to do with leisure and pleasure – tourism, spectacular entertainment, visual refreshment' (Green, 1990: 6, on mid-nineteenth-century France). By 1844 Wordsworth was noting that the development of the idea of landscape had recently developed; and he in effect promoted both the Alps and the Lake District as landscapes of attraction. He notes how previously barns and out-buildings had been placed in front of houses 'however beautiful the landscape which their windows might otherwise have commanded' (Wordsworth, 1984: 188). By the mid-nineteenth century houses were being built with regard to their 'prospects' as though they were a kind of 'camera' (Abercrombie and Longhurst, 1998: 79).

Larsen shows how hotels on Bornholm were also built 'as cameras' (2006b). They afforded a nicely framed view from the bedrooms and grand sweeping panoramas from the elevated porches and balconies; sitting safely and comfortably in the hotel armchair a painting of nature was put on to the stage for visitors. Working quarries were screened-off by fences so that they did not spoil the view. The Danish novelist Drachmann describes the *spectacle-isation* of fishing villages:

> In the midst of this Swiss fantasy one could still see the fishermen's cottages. ... The villas looked down on them. They needed to be down there or it wouldn't be a fishery village and the picture would miss its adornments. The villas wouldn't miss the huts, the boat with red sail, the pigsty, or the dozen half-naked children, but they would be less grand without them. The culture was successfully penetrated. But the original inhabitants must not disappear completely. They were needed as an assurance that one really lived by the sea. (1881: 62, our translation)

Benches and viewing stations, walking paths and promenades, affording respectively permanent views while-at-rest and many slow-moving views-in-leisurely-walking, were erected. Thus, what began as an imaginative geography of seeing, writing and fantasy eventually reconstructed, and became part of, the material make-up of many places (Larsen, 2006b). The language of views thus prescribed a particular visual structure to the experience of nature (Green, 1990: 88).

The building of piers, promenades and domesticated beaches enabled the visual consumption of the otherwise wild, untamed and 'natural' sea (Corbin, 1992). 'Sightseeing' is not passive looking or staring from everywhere. Landscapes and cities are seldom pleasing enough on their own; they have to be put into visual and spatial order as a framed and distanced picture.

But there is a further aspect of the nineteenth century. This concerns the emergence of relatively novel modes of visual perception which became part of the modern experience of visiting new urban centres, particularly the newly grand capital cities. This new visual experience has been characterised by Berman, who sees the rebuilding of Paris during the Second Empire in the mid-nineteenth century as constructing the conditions for the quintessentially modern experience (1983: section 3). It is one of the most celebrated of tourist gazes.

What is of central importance is the reconstruction of urban space which permits new ways of seeing and being seen. This was engendered by the massive rebuilding of Paris by Haussmann, who blasted a vast network of new boulevards through the heart of the old medieval city. The rebuilding of Paris displaced 350,000 people; by 1870 one-fifth of the streets of central Paris were Haussmann's creation; and at the height of the reconstruction one in five of all workers in the capital was employed in construction (Clark, 1984: 37).

The boulevards were central to this planned reconstruction – they were like arteries in a massive circulatory system, and were planned partly to facilitate rapid troop movements. However, they also restructured what could be seen or gazed upon. Haussmann's plan entailed the building of markets, bridges, parks, the Opera and other cultural palaces, with many located at the end of the various boulevards. Such boulevards came to structure the gaze, both of Parisians and later of visitors. For the first time in a major city people could see well into the distance and indeed where they were going and where they had come from. Great sweeping vistas were designed so that each walk led to a dramatic climax. As Berman says: 'All these qualities helped to make Paris a uniquely enticing spectacle, a visual and sensual feast … after centuries of life as a cluster of isolated cells, Paris was becoming a unified physical and human space' (1983: 151). Certain of these spectacular views have come to be signifiers of the entity 'Paris' (as opposed to the individual districts).

These boulevards brought enormous numbers of people together in ways that were relatively novel. The street level was lined with many small businesses, shops and especially cafés. These have come to be known all over the world as signs of *la vie Parisienne*, particularly as generations of painters, writers and photographers represented the patterns of life in and around them, beginning with the Impressionists in the 1860s (see Berman, 1983: 151; Clark, 1984). Lovers caught up in the extraordinary movement of modern Paris in the 1860s and 1870s could intensely experience their emotional affection. The traffic of people and horses transformed social experience in this modern urban setting. Urban life was rich and full of possibilities; and at the same time dangerous and frightening.

To be private in the midst of such danger and chaos created the perfect romantic setting of modern times, and millions of visitors have attempted to re-experience that particular quality among the boulevards and cafés of Paris. This romantic experience could be felt especially intensely in front of the endless parades of strangers moving up and down the boulevards – it was those strangers they gazed upon and who in turn gazed at them. Part then of the gaze in the new modern city of Paris was of the multitude of passers-by, who both enhanced the lovers' vision of themselves and in turn provided an endlessly fascinating source of curiosity.

Haussmann's reconstruction of Paris also meant that much of the working class was forced out of the centre of Paris, particularly because of the exceptionally high rents charged in the lavish apartment blocks that lined the new boulevards. Reconstruction therefore led to residential segregation and to the worst signs of deprivation being removed from the gaze of richer Parisians and especially from visitors.

Furthermore, Paris was said to be a city of vice, vulgarity and display – ostentation not luxury, frippery not fashion, consumption not trade (see Clark, 1984: 46–7). It was the city of the *flâneur* or stroller. The anonymity of the crowd provided an asylum for those on the margins of society who were able to move about unnoticed, observing and being observed, but not interacting with those encountered. The *flâneur* was the modern hero, able to travel, to arrive, to gaze, to move on, to be anonymous, to be in a liminal zone (see Benjamin, 1973; Wolff, 1985; Tester, 1994). The *flâneur* was invariably male and this rendered invisible the different ways in which women were both more restricted to the private sphere and at the same time were coming to colonise other emerging public spheres in the middle and late nineteenth century, especially the department store (see Wolff, 1985,

1993). The strolling *flâneur* was a forerunner of the twentieth-century tourist and the taking of photographs – of being seen and recorded, and of seeing others and recording them. Susan Sontag explicitly makes this link between the *flâneur* and photography. The latter:

> first comes into its own as an extension of the eye of the middle-class *flâneur*. … The photographer is an armed version of the solitary walker reconnoitering, stalking, cruising the urban inferno, the voyeuristic stroller who discovers the city as a landscape of voluptuous extremes. Adept of the joys of watching, connoisseur of empathy, the *flâneur* finds the world 'picturesque'. (1979: 55)

While the middle-class *flâneur* was attracted to the city's dark seamy corners, the twentieth-century photographer is attracted every-where, to every possible object, event and person. And at the same time the photographer is also observed and photographed. One is both see-er and seen.

The visual sense of possession developed across nineteenth-century western Europe and later into American urban spaces. The development of the skyscraper in Chicago in the 1880s led to fur-ther separation of the senses; its panoramic window afforded those inside to gaze down and across the crowd, while being insulated from its odours and potential touch. There was a growing separation of the senses, especially of vision from touch, smell and hearing. New technologies of the gaze began to be produced and circulated, includ-ing postcards, guidebooks, photographs, commodities, arcades, cafés, dioramas, mirrors, plate-glass windows, as well as places of incar-ceration based upon the 'unimpeded empire of the gaze' (Foucault, 1976: 39; Urry, 1992).

While the *flâneur* is a central figure of modernity, so too are the train passenger, car driver and jet-plane passenger. Their arrival changes the nature of vision. The 'static' forms of the tourist gaze, such as from a balcony, focuses upon the two-dimensional shape, colours and details of the view laid out before one and which can be moved around with one's eyes (Pratt, 1992: 222). Such a static gaze is paradigmatically captured through the still camera. By contrast, with what Schivelbusch terms a 'mobility of vision', there are swiftly passing panorama, a sense of multidimensional rush and the fluid interconnections of places, peoples and possibilities (1986: 66; simi-lar to the onrushing images encountered on TV and film). There are various *tourist glances*, the capturing of sights in passing from a rail-way carriage, through the car windscreen, the steamship porthole or the camcorder viewfinder (Larsen, 2001). As Schivelbusch argues:

'the traveller sees ... through the apparatus which moves him through the world. The machine and the motion it creates become integrated into his visual perception; thus he can only see things in motion (quoted in Osborne, 2000: 168).

The nineteenth-century development of the railway was momentous in developing this more mobilised gaze. From the railway carriage the landscape came to be viewed as a swiftly passing series of framed panorama, a 'panoramic perception', rather than something to be lingered over, sketched or painted or in any way captured (Schivelbusch, 1986). Nietzsche noted how 'everyone is like the traveller who gets to know a land and its people from a railway carriage' (quoted in Thrift, 1996: 286). The railroad had particular consequences on the very early development of tourism within the American frontier. Travellers noted how the railroad annihilated space through its exceptional speed that was not fully appreciated because of the comfort of the railway carriage. The railway journey produced an enormous sense of vastness, of scale, size and domination of the landscape that the train swept through (Retzinger, 1998: 221–4). A contemporary declared in 1888 that the railroad ride was like 'an airline through the woods to the ocean' (Löfgren, 1999: 3).

Similarly, the view through the car windscreen had significant consequences for the nature of the visual 'glance', enabling the *materiality* of the city or the landscape to be appreciated in passing (Larsen, 2001). Elsewhere Urry elaborates some moments in the history of automobility, including how in Europe inter-war motoring involved a kind of 'voyage through the life and history of a land' (2000: ch. 3). The increasingly domesticated middle classes, comfortably and safely located in their Morris Minors, 'began to tour England and take photographs in greater numbers than ever before' (Taylor, 1994: 122). While in post-war USA certain landscapes were substantially altered so as to produce a landscape of leisure '*pleasing* to the motorist ... using the land in a way that would "make an attractive *picture* from the Parkway"' (Wilson, 1992: 35, our italics). The state turned nature into something 'to be appreciated by the eyes alone' (Wilson, 1992: 37). The view through the car windscreen means that 'the faster we drive, the flatter the earth looks' (1992: 33). More generally, Baudrillard suggests that deserts in the USA constitute a metaphor of endless futurity, the obliteration of the past and the triumph of instantaneous time (1988: 6). Driving across the desert involves leaving one's past behind, driving on and on and seeing the ever-disappearing emptiness framed through the shape of the windscreen (Kaplan, 1996: 68–85).

We now turn to photography *per se*, beginning with the pre-history of photography that is intimately linked with the picturesque gazing discussed above (see Larsen, 2004a, for detail on the following).

Desires and the Origins of Photography

KODAKIZATION

We have seen how photography was invented around 1840 with Fox Talbot's and Daguerre's almost simultaneous announcement of the negative/positive process and the Daguerreotype. Yet the scientific basis of chemistry and physics to *project* and *fix* images had long been established. The optical principle of the camera was known for at least two thousand years and the knowledge that certain chemicals are light-sensitive was established as early as 1727 (Batchen, 1999). Gernsheim states that 'the circumstance that photography was not invented earlier remains the greatest mystery in its history' (1982: 6).

But this is less of a mystery if social desires rather than knowledge are understood as generative of technological innovation. By adopting Foucault's method of 'archaeology', Batchen shows that it was first in the late eighteenth century and early nineteenth century that the desire for what we can, retrospectively, call 'photography' emerged and manifested itself as 'a widespread, social imperative' among scientists, writers, painters and tourists (1999: 36). Pre-photographic tourists passionately desired 'something' that could fix the fleeting and elusive images of the camera obscura and Claude glasses. As Gilpin said in 1782:

> A succession of high-coloured pictures is continually gliding before the eye. They are like the visions of the imagination; or the brilliant landscapes of a dream. Forms, and colours in brightest array, fleet before us; and if the transient glance of a good composition happens to unite with them, we should *give any price to fix and appropriate the scene*. (Quoted in Batchen, 1999: 93–4, our italics)

Half a century later, while touring Italy, Fox Talbot's difficulties with the camera obscura generated a desire for a machine that would effortlessly fix nature's beauty upon paper. Pelizzari argues that 'photography was born, from Talbot's sense of inadequacy as an artist when faced with an attractive, foreign scene' (2003: 55). In the *Pencil of Nature* Talbot writes:

> One of the first days of the month of October 1833, I was amusing myself on the lovely shores of the Lake of Como, in Italy, taking sketches with Wollaston's Camera Lucida, or rather I should say,

attempting to take them: but with the smallest amount of success. ...
It was during these thoughts that the idea occurred to me ... how
charming it would be if it were possible to cause these natural images
to imprint themselves durably and remained fixed on paper. (1844–46,
unpaginated)

These desires animated the invention of what we now know as photography. As Talbot wrote in *Some Account of the Art of Photographic
Drawing*, 'to the traveller in distant lands, who is ignorant, as too
many unfortunately are, of the art of drawing, this little invention
may prove real service' (1839: 11). Travellers eagerly awaited its
invention. A French magazine reported that 'above all travellers –
and we know of more than one who has delayed his voyage to distant countries – await impatiently the demonstration of the
Daquerretype' (quoted in Schwartz, 1996: 18). Talbot described his
photographic invention as follows:

The most transitory of things, a shadow, the proverbial emblem of all
that is fleeting and momentary, may be fettered by the spells of our
'natural magic', and may be fixed forever in the position which it
seemed only destined for a single instant to occupy. ... Such is the fact,
that we may receive on paper the fleeting shadow, arrest it there and in
the space of a single minute fix it there so firmly as to be no more
capable of change. (1839: 12)

That 'natural magic' was realised in 1840. As seen in Chapter 1,
1840 is one of those remarkable moments when the world seems to
shift and new patterns of relationships are established. There is the
peculiar combining together of the means of collective travel, the
desire for travel and the techniques of photographic reproduction.
From 1840 onwards tourism and photography were assembled
together and they remake each other in an irreversible and momentous double helix. From then, we can say a 'tourist gaze' enters and
makes the mobile, modern world (Macnaghten and Urry, 1998:
180–5; Löfgren, 1999).

From 1840 onwards travelling photographers and mobile photographs mobilised and exhibited distant places; they created
spectacular displays that taught the art of gazing at the world
with touristic curiosity. They provided simulated mobility experiences that brought the countryside, ancient times and exoticism
to modern metropolises, resulting in a profound 'multiplication
of images' and an unprecedented 'geographical extension of the
field of the visible':

> The second half of the nineteenth century lives in a sort of frenzy of the visible. It is, of course, the effect of the social multiplication of images: ever-wider distribution of illustrated papers, waves of print, caricatures, etc. The effect also, however, of something of a geographical extension of the field of the visible and the representable: by journeys, explorations, colonizations, the world becomes visible at the same time that it becomes appropriatable. (Comolli, 1980: 122–3)

As Mitchell argues, the later nineteenth century conceived and arranged the world 'as an exhibition'. This era 'set the world up as a picture ... [and arranged] it before an audience as an object of display – to be viewed, investigated and experienced' (Mitchell, 1989: 220). The so-called 'real' world became thought of as one spectacular exhibition. Mitchell draws here upon Heidegger, who argued that modernity is 'the age of the world picture' (1993). The modern world-as-exhibition/picture means not only that the world became exhibited, but that it was conceived and grasped as if it were a picture. The rapid and sophisticated technologisation of the visual sense made the world-as-exhibition possible and thus seeing emerged as the master sense (Jay, 1993: 65–6).

The ability of photography to objectify the world as an exhibition, to arrange the entire globe for the tourist gaze, is stressed by Sontag: '[Photography's] main effect is to convert the world into a department store or a museum-without-walls in which every subject is depreciated into an article of consumption, promoted into an item for aesthetic appreciation' (1979: 110). As early as 1859, Oliver Wendall lamented how photography reduced the world to 'cheap and transportable' surfaces:

> There is only Coliseum or Pantheon; but how many millions of potential negatives have they shed – representatives of billions of pictures – since they were erected! Matter in large masses must always be fixed and dear; form is cheap and transportable. We have got the fruit of creation now and need not trouble ourselves with the core. Every conceivable object of Nature and Art will soon scale of its surfaces for us. We will hunt all curious, beautiful grand objects, as they hunt the cattle in South America, for their *skins*, and leave their carcasses as of little worth. (Quoted in Wells, 2001: 20)

Prior to photography, places did not travel well. While painters have always lifted particular places out of their 'dwelling' and transported them elsewhere, paintings were time-consuming to produce, relatively difficult to transport and one-of-a-kind. The multiplication of photographs especially took place with the introduction of the half-tone plate in the 1880s that made possible the mechanical reproduction of photographs in newspapers, periodicals, books and advertisements. Photography became coupled to consumer capitalism and the globe was now offered 'in limitless quantities, figures, landscapes, events which had not previously been utilised either at all, or only as pictures for one customer' (Benjamin, 1973: 163; Osborne, 2000: 11). With capitalism's arrangement of the world as a 'department store', 'the proliferation and circulation of representations ... achieved a spectacular and virtually inescapable global magnitude' (Grenblatt, 1991: 6). Gradually photographs became cheap mass-produced objects that made the world visible, aesthetic and desirable. Experiences were 'democratised' by translating them into cheap images (Sontag, 1977: 7; Tagg, 1988: 55–6). Light, small and mass-produced photographs became dynamic vehicles for the spatiotemporal circulation of places (della Dora, 2007: 293). Due to rapidly travelling images, places are, in effect, on the move, connected to other places and consume-able at a distance.

These mobilities of photographs do not destroy places, but rather constitute gazes and places within an economy of relations (Crang, 2006: 54–5). Instead of seeing photographs as reflections or distortions of a pre-existing world, they can be understood as a technology of world making. 'Images are not something that appear over or against reality, but parts of practices through which people work to establish realities. Rather than look to mirroring as a root metaphor, technologies of seeing form ways of grasping the world' (Crang, 1997: 362). Rather than mirroring or representing geographies, photographs partly create them, culturally, socially and materially. They produce what Said coined as 'imaginative geographies' (1995: 49–73).

The lust for 'mechanically reproduced' images represents, according to Benjamin, 'the desire of the contemporary masses to bring things closer spatially and humanly, which is just as ardent as their bent toward overcoming the uniqueness of every reality by accepting its reproduction. Every day the urge grows stronger to get hold of an object at very close range by way of its likeness, its reproduction' (1973: 225). For the majority not blessed with the means to travel, photographs provided world-tour tickets without the need for daunting and expensive physical travel:

> By our fireside we have the advantage of examining them, without being exposed to the fatigue, privation, and risks of the daring and enterprising artists who, for our gratification and instruction, have traversed lands and seas, crossed rivers and valleys, ascended rocks and mountains with their heavy and cumbrous photographic baggage. (Claudet, quoted in Gernsheim 1989: 66–7)

One nineteenth-century travel photographer stated the belief that 'the faithfulness of such pictures afford the nearest approach that can be made towards placing the reader actually before the scene which is represented' (quoted in Ryan, 1997: 25). Barthes argues that the photograph's 'ontological realism' invokes a sense of 'being there', of literally being transported 'back' to the pictured scene (2000). Thus photographs activate imaginative journeys. Yet the power to invoke a sense of 'being there' was also culturally constructed, animated by the faith in the medium's superior realism. Photography *seems* to be a means of transcribing reality. Photographs appear to be not statements about the world but pieces of it, even miniature slices of reality, without revealing its constructed nature or its ideological content. It seems that the camera does not lie. The realism of photographs made such travelling real and seductive. Visiting places through photographs was sometimes more or less as good as embodied gazing. Photography 'introduces us to scenes known only from the imperfect relations of travellers, it leads us before the ruins of antique architecture, illustrating the historical records of former and lost civilians; the genius, taste, and power of past ages, with which we have become *familiarized as if we had visited them*' (quoted in Schwartz, 1996: 16, our italics).

At this early stage, imaginative travelling satisfied, rather than promoted, desires for travelling, for bodily experiencing the 'real' thing (Schwartz, 1996). Sitting in the armchair, one's eyes could go sightseeing without being troubled by the body. The problem with corporeal tourism is the body, according to De Botton: 'it seems we may best be able to inhabit a place when we are not faced with the additional challenge of having to be there' (2002: 23).

More broadly, tourism places are affected by far-away place-myths. As Crang argues: 'tourism works as interplay of movement and fixity, absence and presence. That is, the tourist seeks to be present at a place, but as we examine those places we find that they are shot through by absences where distant others, removed in space and time, haunt the sites' (2006: 49, 55). This includes the ways of seeing that travel along with tourists. Duncan discusses how nineteenth-century British tourists constantly saw the Kandyan Highlands through tracing resemblances with their native landscapes. One tourist wrote home: 'In Kandy whether one will or not, the mind will go back to the Lake region in England' (1999: 156). Even when traversing land 7,000 miles away from home, tourists moved in the memories of domestic landscapes. The shock of the seeing the new was tamed by seeing it through a 'domestic' filter.

seductive commercial tactics

Travel photography was often asked to save 'vanishing' authentic cultures, primitive peoples and ancient traditions (Albers and James, 1993; Taylor, 1994; Schwartz, 1996; Gregory, 2003; Cohen and Manspeizer, 2009; Whittaker, 2009). Photographs serve this nostalgic desire to stop time and to conserve objects, as they freeze time and make a moment permanent; they document 'that has been' (Barthes, 2000). They are 'clocks for seeing' (Taylor, 1994).

Yet the 'objective' camera needed guiding in order to capture 'vanishing' landscapes and 'otherness'. Photographers turn a blind eye to certain features and shone a beautiful light upon others. Ironically, the camera-eye overlooked what the human eye at the scene could clearly see and captured what it could hardly see. By erasing contemporary signs, modern humans and connections elsewhere, western travel photography imprisoned the Orient in a timeless ancient space of architecture and monuments to produce the desired authentic Orient (Schwartz, 1996; Osbourne, 2000). Once fixed in the imagination, even when they encountered different realities, they photographed the imagination or subsequently airbrushed away undesired modern signs from the original photograph (Jackson, 1992: 95).

Photographs are thus the outcome of an active signifying practice in which photographers select, structure and shape what is going to be taken and how. In particular, there is the attempt to construct idealised images which beautify the object being photographed. Sontag summarises: 'the aestheticizing tendency of photography is such that the medium which conveys distress ends by neutralizing it' (1979: 109). To photograph is in some way to appropriate the object being photographed. It is a power/knowledge relationship. To have visual knowledge of an object is in part to have power, even if only momentarily, over it.

Photography thus tames the object of the gaze, some of the most striking examples being of exotic cultures. In the USA, the railway companies did much to create 'Indian' attractions to be photographed, carefully selecting those tribes with a particularly 'picturesque and ancient' appearance (Albers and James, 1988: 151). The rhetorical power of photography is grounded upon the ability to *naturalise*, to make innocent its cultural messages and connotations. Even though professional photographs are partial and constructed, they appear to have spontaneously drawn themselves (Barthes, 2000).

Pictures by such travel photographers can be regarded as 'real' and 'objective', *not* in the sense of mirroring the represented places' complex lived realities, but because they reflect and reinforce stereotypical western imaginations of these worlds. In other words, they were 'accurate' from a specific western perspective; far-away facts were transformed into western imaginative geographies. As a technology of cultural imperialism, the *photographer* employed the objective camera to picture or gaze upon the world through ethnocentric filters (Albers and James, 1983; Schwartz, 1996: 30–1; McQuire, 1998: 39).

Kodakisation

tourists can produce photog. produce

It was first in the late 1880s with Kodak's launching of user-friendly, lightweight and cheap Brownie cameras that photography undertaken by tourists themselves was born. Before then photography was something consumed rather than produced. Similar to Thomas Cook in relation to tourism generally, Kodak realised that photography required organisation by an institutional expert (Slater, 1991, 1999). The company targeted the new middle-class family and tourism as the agents and spaces where the power-knowledge relationships of 'Kodaking' could *produce* 'Kodak moments' and 'Kodak families'. In the USA and then in much of Europe, Kodak re-made and re-scripted photography as a leisurely family-centred performance. Kodak in effect invented *tourist* photography through developing a new system, assembling together a novel set of material and social relations.

As early as 1890, Kodak cameras were common among European tourists travelling in Egypt (Gregory, 2003: 211). *Photographic News* reported that in 1899 'thousands of Birmingham girls are scattered about the holiday resorts of Britain this month, and a very large percentage of them are armed with cameras' (quoted in Coe and Gates, 1977: 28). By 1910, one-third of American households owned a Kodak camera (West, 2000: 75). Kodak made cameras and picture-making 'mundane' and photographing a part of an emerging 'tourist habitus'.

One step in this was to mobilise and simplify photography *materially*. Since developing had to be executed on the spot, early photography required much knowledge and 'heavy travelling'. As Kodak's founder, Eastman, said in 1877: 'In those days, one did not "take" a camera: one accomplished the outfit of which the camera was only a part. ... I bought an outfit and learned that it took not only a strong but also dauntless man to be an outdoor photographer' (quoted in Ford and Steinorth, 1988: 14). Eastman foresaw that popular photography depended upon making photography 'light' in order to enrol people *without* prior photographic skills. Kodak achieved this through 'packaging'. Their 'Kodak system' consisted of a light, mobile hand-camera pre-loaded with a 100-frame roll film that Kodak then developed and re-loaded. Once cumbersome, technical demanding and messy, the making of photographs was reorganised as a straightforward, user-friendly practice. 'The Kodak system removes from the practice of Photography the necessity of exceptional facilities, so that *anyone* may take photographs without need of study, experiment, trouble, dark room, chemicals and without even soiling the fingers' and requires nothing but 'sufficient intelligence to point a small box straight and press a button' (quoted in West, 2000: 49, 51). As Kodak's slogan said: 'You Press the Button, We Do the Rest.'

Through marketing, Kodak scripted the cultural meanings and social performances of this new photography actor-network (Slater 1991, 1999; West, 2000). 'Loved ones' and tourism fitted Kodak's goal of teaching people and families 'to apprehend their experiences and memories as objects of nostalgia', especially avoiding painful and unpleasant experiences (West, 2000: 1; Hammond, 2001). Acts of overlooking and forgetting thus became integral to – the 'other' of – this photography while nostalgia became a defining character of its cultural viewpoint (see Taylor, 1994). Kodak stressed that the new simplicity made photography convenient and pleasurable. The 'Kodak Girl' – their advertising icon for almost eighty years – who was driving, riding on trains and gazing upon extraordinary landscapes and places promoted 'the sheer pleasure and adventure of taking photographs ... the delight of handling a diminutive camera, of not worrying about development and printing, of capturing subjects in candid moments, of recording travel to exotic places' (West, 2000: 13). She promoted cameras as standard equipment for touring and photographing as *the* touristic thing-to-do, while captions such as 'Take a KODAK with you', 'Kodak, as you go', 'Vacation Days are KODAK DAYS', 'All out-doors invites your Kodak' were common (West, 2000: plates 2, 8, 9, 16). Kodak's 'simplicity' motto signified freedom, ceaseless travelling and easy photography.

Kodak's advertising began to revolve around family life and memories (West, 2000: 13). The new slogan 'Let Kodak Keep The Story' discursively constructed Kodak memories as far superior to fragile human memory:

The only holiday that lasts forever is the holiday with a Kodak. ... Few memories are so pleasant as the memories of your holiday. And yet, you allow those memories to slip away! How little you remember, even of your happiest times! Don't let this year's holiday be forgotten – take a Kodak and save your happiness. Make Kodak snapshots of every happy scene. The little pictures will keep your holiday alive – they will carry you back again and again to sunshine and freedom. (Quoted in Holland, 2001: 145)

The camera became promoted as an indispensable tourist object because it enabled families to 'story' *their* experiences that can transport them back 'to the sunshine and freedom', again and again. Another ad instructed how 'the Kodak Story of summer days grows in charm as the months go by – it's always interesting – it's personal – it tells of the places, the people and the incidents from your point of view – just as *you* saw them' (quoted in West, 2000: 179). Kodak assured families that 'their' images will be unique and full of aura, no matter how similar they look to those of other tourists, because they show *their* 'loved ones' and the world through *their* eyes.

Kodak was powerful in re-making and re-imagining photography as a 'mundane' technology central to modern family life. Kodak 'taught modern Americans how to see, to remember, how to love' (West, 2000: xv) and, according to Chalfen, it formed a specific 'Kodak culture' that came to define the practices and meanings of private vernacular photography (1987). This photography network comprised families, consumerism and tourism. 'What holds these subjects together is the theme of domestic leisure: the modern family at play ... blind to the everyday life' (Slater, 1991: 57–8). Bourdieu highlights the intricate relations between photography and 'family life': '[P]hotographic practices only exist and subsist for most of time by the virtue of its family function' (1990: 14; Kuhn, 1995; Rose, 2003, 2004). Photography immortalises and celebrates the affective high points of family life. Much tourist photography takes place in the mobile space between home and away, of extraordinary places *and* familial faces. Tourist photography and family photography are thus not two separate worlds but bridges constantly traversed within and through the spaces of tourism (Haldrup and Larsen, 2003; Larsen, 2005).

Seductive Commercial Images

The longing provoked by the brochure was an example, at once touching and bathetic, of how projects (and even whole lives) might be influenced by the simplest and most unexamined images of happiness;

of how a lengthy and ruinously expensive journey might be set into motion by nothing more than the sight of a photograph of a palm tree gently inclining in a tropical breeze. I resolved to travel to the island of Barbados. (De Botton, 2002: 8–9)

This section examines how commercial photographs are desire-producing power-knowledge machines implicated in post-Fordist consumer capitalism. The knowledge-power art of commercial photography involves crafting images that stimulate – and not substitute – desires for 'transporting one's body' to the photographed place. Imaginative mobility is clearly poor business for the tourism industry. More broadly, following Foucault, we can see this making of seductive images and destinations as an institutional mediation by 'expert gazes' within which spectacle and surveillance intersect and power-knowledge relations are played out (Hollingshead, 1999; Cheong and Miller, 2000).

We explore how a 'photograph of a palm tree gently inclining in a tropical breeze' can trigger a 'lengthy and ruinously expensive journey'. Commercial photographs are assigned a twofold role by the tourism industries. They produce desires for bodily travel, and they script and stage destinations with extraordinary imaginative geographies. In other words, 'destination marketing is, therefore, simultaneously implicated in the construction of place imagery and the constitution of subjects who experience that image in specific ways' (Goss, 1993: 663).

Consumer capitalism 'invests' in photography to fabricate volatile consumer needs and desiring bodies, bodies we might say are disciplined to consume (Berger, 1972). Advertising promotes consumption. It exposes anxiety and shortcomings before offering instantaneous escape, relief and a road to betterment through consumption and the fantasy of other places. It shows people that consumption can make people happy, beautiful and fulfilled (Berger, 1972: 133).

Through embellishment, erasing, exaggeration, stereotyping and repetition, commercial photography produces the kind of imaginative geography that Shields calls 'place-myths' Here, Shields says, there are 'the various discrete meanings associated with real places or regions regardless of their character in reality. Images, being partial and often either exaggerated or understated, may be accurate or inaccurate. They result from stereotyping' (1990: 60). In the experience economy photographs stage and script scenes for experiences: 'Brochures become analogous to theatres; they image stage scenes through which consumers enter imaginative touristscapes and personally connect with place by creating performances through mindsets where consumer and product unite' (Scarles, 2004: 47, 2009). Commercial tourist photographs arouse desires by 'staging' geographies that thrill and seduce the eye. They create duplicate places aesthetically more compelling than those seen through mere human vision. They overpower human vision by being more theatrical, better lit, sharper and more highly coloured than seeing itself. Photographs do not only make places visible, perform-able, and memorable, places are also sculptured materially as simulations of idealised photographs as 'postcard places'. According to Osborne:

> All tourists, whether or not they take photographs, consume places and experiences which are photographic, as they have been made or have evolved to be seen, above all to be photographed. ... Such places are often photographs materialised in three-dimensional form. (2000: 79)

Crawshaw and Urry (1997) and Scarles (2004) examine many ways that professional photographers improve upon the appearance of place through 'gardening' and selective vision (see Feighery, 2009, for a Foucaultian interpretation of photo archives). Anticipating that potential tourists would consider them out-of-place, diluting its place-myth, photographers seek to avoid: 'vehicles, cars, anything that would date a picture. ... Anything that is obtrusive and jars. People with bright clothes on, people carrying plastic bags ... dead trees, barbed wire ... derelict buildings, scaffolding. Road signs, litter, car parks, crowds, traffic jams, low-flying planes, Bermuda shorts' (Crawshaw and Urry, 1997: 187). Professional photographers stage landscapes in the *right* light, frame and composition. Patience is crucial. While photographers turn a blind eye to undesired objects and people in the scene, the editor's 'computer hands' now greatly improve upon the reality of the place through digitisation. Elements within single images can be seamlessly deleted, moved, emphasised, juxtaposed and even joined with other photographic fragments. 'Surgery' and 'make-up' turn beaches crystal white, seas and skies deep blue and bodies tanned and trim. No eyesores spoil the paradise. Such photographic practices demonstrate how the environment is to be viewed, dominated by humans and subject to their possessive mastery (Taylor, 1994: 38–9).

Various discourses inform the professional tourist gaze. The romantic gaze frames the representational making of the Lake District, as well as many other landscapes, as picturesque or sublime 'timeless' scenery. This requires turning a blind eye to signs of modernity. The same process is visible in the staging of historical townscapes. The 'time machine' of the tourist industry and photography often freezes townscapes in an idyllic and untouched chocolate-box vision where time moves slowly if at all (Waitt and Head, 2002). Erased are modern artefacts and contemporary-looking humans. Places are presented as living museums where little life takes place. When 'locals' enter the scene their function is to signify authenticity, induce romanticism and bring life to the scene. The quest for picturesque townscapes is fuelled by a widespread desire to travel back in time, to a supposedly Golden Age of romanticised escapism (Taylor, 1994; Larsen, 2006a, 2006b).

Exoticism and the anthropological gaze are also popular lenses through which commercial tourism imagery produce extraordinary tourism geographies of mythic 'Otherness'. Various studies show how promotional images 'freeze' and stage ethnic Others, as premodern, exotic, sexual and available for visual consumption (Albers and James, 1983; Hollingshead, 1992; Goss, 1993; Selwyn, 1996; Dann, 1996a; Adams, 2004). Such images of exotic Others are traditionally produced and consumed by a well-off white gaze and pictures of a relatively impoverished black body.

Promotional images also stage alluring tourist places through collective and family gazes (Haldrup and Larsen, 2003). Dann's study of 'the people of the tourist brochures' in '11 representative summer holiday brochures targeted at the British public' shows that some 40 per cent of the photographs depict 'tourists only', often within clearly demarcated tourist ghettos. 'In such photos the emphasis was on the tourist group – eating together, on the beach together, relaxing by the communal pool together, enjoying themselves as one large happy family' (Dann, 1996a: 72). In contrast, some 24 per cent of photographs show places without people (predominately landscapes and sights) and locals appear in only 7 per cent (often working under the tourist gaze or reduced to cultural markers of locale-ness).

Commercial photographs are normally composed to make the viewer dream into the picture, which awaits the viewer's desires and pleasures in order to be completed. 'A typical example would show empty beaches where the waterline or a run of tress or a pier pass diagonally into and across the image. The diagonal introduces into the image the tourist's excited anticipation, a hedonistic rush, the line of the viewer's desire entering into, being entered by, the tourist scene and its pleasures' (Osborne, 2000: 85; Scarles, 2004). Other examples are photographs with tourists in them. These guide the reader's fantasies and make them seem realisable: this could be me! This is further underscored by how the written texts always focus upon 'you' (Scarles, 2004: 46). This could be an image of an exultant and affectionate youngish tourist couple whose bodies are tuned, tanned and attracted to each other. It shows how a holiday-in-the-sun transforms jaded and pale bodies into bronzed and attractive bodies.

Commercial tourist imagery achieves effects by provoking the viewer's unconscious. 'The photograph causes the viewer to, as it were, dream into it, causing it to become subjectivised by the viewer's desires, memories and associations' (Osborne, 2000: 77). 'It transports us in fantasy but to places that appear to exist' (Osborne, 2000: 88). While the power of commercial photography works through 'naturalisation', it also works through an economy of desires and imaginative geographies. People desire to be seduced and such images are artfully constructed to seduce. The contemporary consumer body is a seduced body and a body that *wants* to be seduced, restlessly searching for new sensations, experiences, identities and places (Bauman, 1999: 83; Elliott and Urry, 2010). 'Desire does not desire satisfaction. To the contrary, desire desires desire' (Taylor and Saarinen, quoted in Bauman, 1999: 83). Advertising images are structured around, and work through, mobilising and triggering the spectator's desires and fantasies through 'spatial fictions'. Commercial photographs are fictions and ask spectators to engage with them 'as if' they were real: to suspend disbelief and instead dream into their pictured heavens as if in the theatre or cinema (Osborne, 2000: 77). In order to seduce, they need people to buy into their fantasies and fictions; to accept them as 'real'. Fictions depend upon authenticity and reality, and the pleasures of fiction lies in accepting fantasies as real (Slater, 1995). Tourists can treat tourism's imaginative geographies as so real because they are built upon convictions of 'actualities' – views, national types and buildings. Tourism's desires and fantasies are located within a palpable visual grammar that looks real and invites identification. This is a seductive mix of reverie, reality and fiction – of simultaneous 'naturalisation' and 'fictionalisation'.

Photography and the Tourist Gaze

There has thus been an enormous proliferation of photographs since its invention. Over that century and a half there has been an utter insatiability of the photographing eye, an insatiability that teaches new ways of looking at and picturing the world, staging family life and new forms of authority for so doing. In nineteenth-century northern Europe the desire for and capacity to fix places of the 'other' dramatically developed. As we have seen, places came to be 'kodakised'. Such places of desire and fixing through the objects of the camera, tripod and photograph included the Mediterranean (Pemble, 1987), the Alps (Ring, 2000), the Caribbean (Sheller, 2003; Thompson, 2006), the Grand Canyon (Newmann, 1992, 1999), the exotic Nile (Gregory, 1999), stinking fishing villages (Lübbren, 2001) and water generally (Anderson and Tabb, 2002).

In nineteenth-century Egypt, Gregory describes how it became scripted as a place of constructed visibility, with multiple, enframed theatrical scenes set up for the edification, entertainment and visual consumption of 'European' visitors. As one Kodak-wearing *dahabeeah* passenger wrote: 'A vision of half-barbarous life passes before you all day and you survey it all in the intervals of French cooking: Rural Egypt at Kodak range – and you sitting in a long chair to look at it' (quoted in Gregory, 1999: 131). This produced a 'new Egypt' available for visually consuming visitors. Such an Egypt consisted of the Suez Canal, of 'Paris-on-the-Nile', of Thomas Cook and Sons, of a cleaned-up 'ancient Egypt', of the exotic oriental 'Other' and of convenient vantage-points and viewing platforms for the tourist gaze (see Brendon, 1991: 118).

Another example of 'Kodakisation' are the Kodak Hula Shows featuring 'traditional' Hula dancers. This Kodak-financed show has taken place on Hawaii since 1937. It is materially staged and corporeally performed so as to make the dancers photogenic and easily photograph-able (Hammond, 2001). Prior to the show tourists can photograph the performers close by or be photographed with them. The show takes place on an outdoor arena where the stands face the central stage with the sun facing the dancers (and not the 'camera-tourist') in order to secure optimal light conditions for photography. The show itself is choreographed to be photograph-able. Movements are not too rapid and dancers occasionally pause and freeze their posture for a prolonged moment or two so that tourists have time to capture the moment. The show is designed as a constant series of new Kodak moments, as dances, costumes and dancers relentlessly change (Hammond, 2001).

Photography thus overloads the visual environment. It involves the democratisation of many forms of human experience, both by turning everything into photographic images and enabling anyone to photograph them, especially with Kodak cameras and now with digital cameras, as we examine below. Photography, then, is part of the process of postmodernisation, a 'society of spectacles' where circulating and instantaneous images overpower reality; 'reality' becomes touristic, ready for visual consumption (Debord, 1983; see Chapter 6 above). The consumption and production of images become all-important, and participating in events is tantamount to seeing and capturing them as spectacular 'imagescapes' (Sontag, 1979). Sometimes it seems that each object or person photographed becomes equivalent to any other, equally interesting or uninteresting.

Barthes notes that photography began with photographs of the notable and has ended up making notable whatever is photographed (2000: 34; Sontag, 1979: 111). Photography is a promiscuous way of seeing which cannot be limited to an elite, as art. Sontag talks of photography's 'zeal for debunking the high culture of the past … its conscientious courting of vulgarity …. its skill in reconciling avant-garde ambitions with the rewards of commercialism … its transformation of art into cultural document' (1979: 131). As people become photographers, so they become amateur semioticians and competent 'gazers'. They learn that a thatched cottage with roses round the door represents 'ye olde England'; or that waves crashing onto rocks signifies 'wild, untamed nature'; or especially that a person with a camera draped around his/her neck is a 'tourist' (Hutnyk, 1996).

Much tourism becomes, in effect, a search for the photogenic. Sometimes it seem that tourist travel is a strategy for the accumulation of photographs and hence for the commodification and privatisation of personal and especially family memories. Photography has thus been enormously significant in democratising various kinds of mobilities, making notable whatever gets photographed rather than what elites might have specified. And photography gives shape to travel so that journeys consist of one 'good view' or family 'Kodak moment' to capture, to a series of others. Photography have been crucial in constituting the very nature of travelling and gazing, as sites turn into sights, they have constructed what is worth going to 'sightsee' and what images and memories should be brought back. Photography gives shape to much travel and gazing. It is the reason for stopping, to take (snap) a photograph, and then to move on. Photography involves obligations. People feel that they must not miss seeing particular scenes or 'Kodak moments' since otherwise the photo-opportunities will be missed and forgotten:

evidence that you went there

> It would not be wrong to speak of people having a *compulsion* to photograph: to turn experience itself into a way of seeing. Ultimately, having an experience becomes identical with taking a photograph of it, and participating in a public event comes more and more to be equivalent to looking at it in photographed form. ... Today everything exists to end in a photograph. (Sontag, 1979: 24)

We have argued that the tourist gaze is largely *preformed* by and within existing mediascapes. Hutnyk, in his ethnography of 'photogenic Calcutta' (1996), argues that tourists constantly picture the 'local poor' since this motif meets their media-generated geographies of Calcutta. Tourists not only frame and explore, they are also framed and fixed. Involved in much gazing and photographing is a hermeneutic circle. What is sought for in a holiday is a set of photographic images which have already been seen in brochures, TV programmes, blogs and social networking sites. Much tourist photography involves a ritual of 'quotation' (see Osborne, 2000: 81; see also Selwyn, 1996; Jenkins, 2003). While the tourist is away, this then moves to tracking down and capturing those images for oneself. And it ends up with travellers demonstrating that they really have been there by showing to friends and family their version of the images they had seen before they set off. A photograph thus furnishes evidence that someone really was there or that the mountain was that large or that the culture was indeed picturesque or that one really had a lovely family time. As Cohen et al. say:

> One the one hand, people tend to preserve in photos that which is closest to them: their children, spouses, friends, and relatives, as well as their most significant or enjoyable events in their lives. On the other hand, they also seek to retain strange, interesting, and exotic sights. (1992: 213–14)

The art of much tourist photography is to place one's 'loved ones' within an 'attraction' in such a way that both are represented aesthetically (see Larsen, 2005, for many ethnographic examples). Tourist places are woven into the webs of stories and narratives that people produce as they construct and sustain their social identities (Hsiu-yen Yeh, 2009). The family gaze highlights how much tourist photography engages significant others within significant places and is part of the 'theatre' that enables people to enact and produce their desired togetherness, wholeness and intimacy (Haldrup and Larsen, 2006: 283).

graspable objects

179

Elsewhere we examine the 'family gaze' within a Danish context (Bærenholdt et al., 2004: ch. 6). More than half the 1,000 tourist photographs collected from visitors to Bornholm (island in the Baltic sea) contain one or more family members or friends in the foreground while very few contain other 'tourists' or 'locals'. Holiday-makers desire 'private' photos. Yet their 'private' photographs reflect a socially and media-constructed notion of apparently 'loving' family life or friendship. Many photographs portray joyful moments and familial togetherness with traces of unhappiness or friction being absent. People are keen to photograph, for it is in the space of the photograph that they enjoy longed-for family happiness. People gaze at the holiday image – and the imaginary family or friendship of their holiday gazes back. The perfect social relationship and the perfect holiday may be a figment of the public imagination, but it stands for something that ought to exist. Tourist photography is not characterised by the suspension of norms but, like the everyday, is culturally informed by particular notions about what constitutes a loving social life.

Kodak taught us that non-recorded gazes and memories would evaporate, and studies show how the desire for capturing memories in image-form animates much tourist photography. Tourists anticipate that cameras will magically transform short-lived, fleeting gazes and events into durable artefacts that provide tickets to undying 'memory travel' (Haldrup and Larsen, 2003). In this sense, tourism is: 'not so much experienced in itself but for its future memory' (Crang, 1997: 366). Photographs extend the tourist gaze in time and space. Studies show that tourists regard their tourist photos as precious belongings destined for a long life. They are *material* objects full of life and emotion and not to be easily discarded (Haldrup and Larsen, 2003; Rose, 2010).

The camera effects all this by turning scenery and the 'gaze' into graspable objects (just as photography turns women into materialised objects on a page or video) that can have a long afterlife. Places and humans are transformed into objects passed from person to person. They are put on walls to decorate a house, structure reminiscences and create images of place (Spence and Holland, 1991; Taylor, 1994; on the afterlife of tourist photographs, see Haldrup and Larsen, 2010: ch. 7). Or so they were until digitisation.

Digitisation and Internetisation

The latest moment in this history of tourist photography is its recent digitisation and internetisation. Over the last century analogue photography more or less dies out as digital photography becomes commonplace. Photographs are now very widely produced, consumed and circulated upon computers, mobile phones and via the internet, especially through social-networking sites. There is the digitisation of images, media convergence and new performances of sociality reflecting broader shifts towards real-time, collaborative, networked sociality at-a-distance. Few tourists now take pictures with analogue cameras (Haldrup and Larsen, 2010). In 2004 Kodak stopped selling traditional cameras in North America and western Europe. At the same time, 68 million digital cameras and 246 million 'camera phones' (mobile phones with digital cameras) were sold world-wide (Larsen, 2008a). Many mobiles now produce good quality photographs and mobile-phone commercials (such as Nokia) increasingly highlight the functionality of the camera. In the UK, '448,962,359 MMS picture messages were sent in 2007, the equivalent of 19 million traditional (24 exposure) rolls of camera film' (www.themda.org/mda-press-releases/the-q1-2008-uk-mobile-trends-report.php; accessed 01.04.10).

Photography's networked convergence with mobiles and the internet means that the technical *affordances* of photography dramatically expand. Digital photography makes photographic images instantaneous, mobile and instantly consume-able on screens (Lister, 2007; Larsen, 2008a; Murray, 2008; Rubinstein and Sluis, 2008; see Figure 7.1). By contrast with the 'that has been' temporality of analogue photographs, digital camera screens show ongoing events right here, with the spaces of picturing, posing and consuming converged. Whereas 'analogue photography' was directed at a *future* audience, camera-phone photographs (and digital cameras with Wi-Fi technology) travel 'timelessly' so the receivers can gaze upon events unfolding more or less in real time (Gye, 2007; Hjorth, 2007; Villi, 2007; Larsen, 2008a; and see Figure 7.2). Here we can speak of 'live postcards' of happenings. Digital photography is typified by 'instantaneous time', the 'power of now' and what we term screen-ness.

One ethnography of digital photography show the significance of the *screen*; the camera screen is where most photographs are inspected *immediately* after springing into life as well as during their 'early days' (before 'uploading'). It has become a ritual to examine the digital-camera screen after a single shot or a longer series, at the very scene or somewhere with some shade, so that the image can be seen properly. 'Here you just take five [photos of everything] and then you can sit in the shadow and say: "this is crap, this is crap" and then there are two left ... there is so much *freedom* involved in this'

Figure 7.1   *Gazing on the screen*

Figure 7.2   Mobile phone photography

(Danish female, mid-20s, interviewed in Istanbul). In a short span of time, tourists have *learnt* to consume photographs instantly and digitally upon screens and to delete those deemed unappealing. They are less likely to be haunted by aesthetically unappealing images in the future. These practices are distinctive to digital photography. The 'magic' of digital cameras is that they make photographs and they do so instantly, thus photographs are widely consumed and erased on the screen (see Figure 7.1). Photographs that do not instantly charm are erased and retaken, which affords experimentation and control over how people and places are represented. Strikingly, few tourists express any emotional difficulties about deleting photographs even of loved ones. This delete-ness represents something radically new. Consuming and deleting photographs have become part of producing photographs, which make it easier (yet time-consuming because of *re*taking) to produce the anticipated images. The *flexible* digital camera represents a further twist to consumer society where 'the presentation of the self' takes a renewed importance (for details on this research, see Haldrup and Larsen, 2010).

Most images that survive deletion at this stage are uploaded to computers and viewed on yet another screen, the *computer* screen. From here, a small selection are mobilised and distributed, emailed to email boxes or uploaded to social-networking sites where they (hopefully) will be consumed upon further computer screens around the world. Whereas tourist photographs often used to be fixed material objects with a secure stable home in the bookshelf, most are today variable digital objects facing unpredictable afterlives in computer trash bins, folders, email boxes, blogs and social networking sites. Computer-networked photographs can be deleted, edited, distributed freely and timelessly as email attachments to and exhibited on family home pages, blogs, sites like Myspace and Facebook and photo/video sharing services such as Flickr and YouTube. All this illustrates how networked digital photography is a crucial component of Web 2.0 (see Chapter 3). Millions of personal photographs are daily uploaded on to user-generated social-networking sites such as www.virtualtourist, www.tripadvisor.co.uk, www.trekearth.com and www.flickr.com. It is estimated that 2–3 million photos are uploaded to the last of these, with four-fifths of people possessing open exhibition places (profiles) (Cox et al., 2008; Larsen, 2008a).

Indeed, many tourist sites examined in this book are Flickr-ised. Flickr contains 372,316 geo-tagged photographs of the Eiffel Tower, 170,966 of the Taj Mahal, 2,242,591 of Las Vegas, 364,841 of the

Lake District and 105,716 of the Bilbao Guggenheim (www.Flickr. com; accessed 27.04.10). Users of Facebook have uploaded more than 10 billion photographs, with the number increasing by an astonishing 700 million each month. Digitisation and internetisation mean that photographs travel faster and cheaper. They thus can be easily (re)distributed to significant others at-a-distance or exhibited in virtual space. Holiday photographs can be consumed without being co-present with the photographer.

Many personal photographic images are now destined to live, for shorter or longer periods, virtual, digital lives without material substance, in cameras, computers and on the internet. Emails, blogs and social-networking sites dislocate photographic memories from the fixed physical home and objectness and distribute them to selected email boxes from where they might travel to desktops, folders, printers, photo paper, frames – or trash bins. Moreover, some photographs have complex biographies because they materialise, dematerialise and rematerialise, take and retake various forms and inhabit different materialities over time. And their corporeal and facial look is also potentially transformable as the 'computer-hand' has the ability to reach into the guts of a photograph. Analogue photographs are inescapable as images and objects but this is not the case with digital photography. While camera screens have a material tactility, the photographs they display are images, not physical objects. And yet as camera screens increase in size and picture quality, they resemble more traditional albums. One example is the fashionable iPhone, perhaps the key gadget among the 'new petty bourgeoisie', which comes with a wide-screen where one can scroll from one photo to another by *touching* each image on the screen.

Unlike the traditional photo album, exhibitions of photographs on Flickr and Facebook are tied into the flow of the everyday and tend to reflect 'instantaneous time', a 'culture of instantaneity', where people expect 'rapid delivery, ubiquitous availability and the instant gratification of desires' (Tomlinson, 2007: 74). They do not so much share memories as ongoing or recent *experiences*. Photographs are less 'clocks for seeing' than performances of the now. While it is still early days, the lives of photographs on Facebook and Flickr tend to be short-lived; a stream of 'transitory, ephemeral, "throwaway"' images (Van House, 2007: 4; Murray, 2008). They are talked about today and forgotten tomorrow (Murray, 2008). Yet this does not make them insignificant and unnoticed. Given that the average Facebook-er has more than 100 'friends', Facebook-ing is an everyday practice, with its photographs much seen and commented upon. Such photographs now reach a wide audience (including 'weak' and 'old' ties) and have become part of the everyday life of the networked household and its face-to-screen sociality. Yet this also means that once a photographer lets loose a photograph on the internet, they lose control over its destiny as friends or strangers may use it in unforeseen contexts or distribute it yet further. As copy-able and timeless travelling bites of information, internet-residing photographs face unpredictable lives with multiple possible paths, with some of these being harmful and unpleasant (Dijck, 2008).

While their afterlife is uncertain, many tourist photographs are visible, mobile and tied up with everyday socialising upon various networked screens. And, we may add, disposable. Lack of an 'aura of thingness' partly explains why so many digital photographs are short-lived, but also why they are valued as a fast mobile form of communication. Digital photographs are a crucial component of mobile-networked societies of distanciated ties and screened sociality (Larsen et al., 2006). While many digital images exist virtually, digital photography is not without a material substance, and some digital images do materialise as objects with an 'aura of thingness' (Edwards and Hart, 2004: 9).

Conclusion

Photography has thus been crucial in developing the tourist gaze and tourism more generally; they are not separate processes but each derives from and enhances the other, as an 'ensemble'. If photography had not been 'invented' around 1840 and then enormously developed through the cheap Kodak camera, then contemporary tourist gazes would have been wholly different. Photography is evidently central to the tourist gaze and tourism more generally.

For some scholars this epitomises the 'alienating' nature of tourism (Albers and James, 1988: 136). Recalling his experience as a tour guide for a group of well-educated tourists that shortly after arriving at a ritual wished to move rapidly on, Bruner voices his contempt of modern tourism's visual nature:

> '*But we have seen it*'. These words still *haunt me*. The touristic mode of experiencing is primarily visual, and to have been there, to have 'seen' it, *only requires presence*. The tourist 'sees' enough of the Balinese ritual to confirm his prior images derived from the media. ... To 'see' a ritual

is comparable to collecting a souvenir. ... The tourist has 'seen' a strange thing, a token of the exotic, and there is no necessity to go further, to penetrate to any deeper level ... [than] to capture ... the ceremony in photographs. (1995: 235–6, our italics)

Photography is condemned for its refusing of experience. It is too visual, brief, image-driven and technological; too passive and impure (Osborne, 2000). Cameras and images have speeded up and mechanised the tourist's vision. Complex places are consumed as lightweight pre-arranged photo-scenes and experiencing is akin to seeing, seeing reduced to glancing and picture-making to clicking. Much of the normative critique of modern mass tourism, beginning with Boorstin (1964), revolves around scorning the camera-tourist's encounters with 'Otherness'. Therefore, it is unsurprising to see the unproductive tourist–traveller dichotomy positioned around photography. The Otherwise astute Taylor divides, out of the blue it seems, tourist photographers into 'travellers' (who gaze contemplatively), 'tourists' (who accumulate shallow glances), and 'trippers' (who see everything in blinks, blurs, or 'snaps') (1994: 14).

While we have argued that professional images are crucial in scripting the gazes and cameras of tourists and much tourism forms a hermeneutic circle, it is too simplistic to portray this as a one-way, pre-programmed flow of images from tourism and media organisations to tourists, who in turn *re*produce this received imagery. Instead tourist photographs can violate existing place-myths and contribute to new ones while commercial photographs mirror photographs by tourists rather than the other way round (Garrod, 2009; Scarles, 2009; Haldrup and Larsen, 2010). Indeed, marketing managers employ market research of ever-changing tourism preferences to obtain knowledge of how tourists do in fact gaze upon and experience places and what are its positive and negative place-myths (Scarles, 2004: 49).

And with Web 2.0, tourists increasingly produce and consume ordinary photographs placed upon 'public display'. These photographs by 'fellow tourists' may come to choreograph cameras as much as 'professional' images and TV programmes. As we discuss in the next chapter on performances, while tourism practices are scripted and 'choreographed' by commercial mediascapes, they are never entirely predetermined and predictable. As Foucault reminds us, power is distributed, ubiquitous and not a property of a group (1976). Power is everywhere and is exercised within relations of networks – and this is true also of tourism (Cheong and Miller, 2000). Locals and tourists also, from time to time, exercise power, performing and picturing against or bending the 'scripts' of those of tourism organisations and wider discourses. Tourists' practices are never completely determined by their 'framing' since there are, on occasions at least, unpredictability, creativity and embodied per-formances (Ek et al., 2008; Haldrup and Larsen, 2010).

8

Performances

Introduction

We have argued for understanding tourism through the lens of the tourist gaze. The previous chapters have examined the tourist gaze in relation to service work, the 'sign economy', contemporary mediatised culture, the built environment and the history of vision and photography. In this chapter we explore some contemporary practices of gazing, and we do so by considering the tourist gaze as *performance*. We believe that our loosely Foucault-inspired notion of the tourist gaze can be enlivened, made more bodily and theatrical, by incorporating Goffman's bottom-down approach to interaction. Here we follow Hacking's position that the top-down approach of Foucault and the bottom-up approach of Goffman are both necessary when analysing social interaction (2004).

In Chapter 1 we noted that a 'performance turn' examining the 'production of tourism, as a series of staged events and spaces and as an array of performative techniques and dispositions' (Edensor, 2001a: 61, 2001b), can be traced from the late 1990s within tourism theory, a move to which we contributed (Bærenholdt et al., 2004; Haldrup and Larsen, 2010). Goffman's dramaturgical metaphor inspired this turn. Franklin and Crang suggest that 'the cultural competencies and acquired skills that make up touristic culture themselves suggest a Goffmanesque world where all the world is indeed a stage' (2001: 17–18). This chapter rethinks the tourist gaze in the light of this performance turn and of a broader Goffmanian dramaturgical sociology. There are many similarities between the paradigms of the gaze and performance and they should 'dance together' rather than stare at each other at distance. We develop this further by examining the embodied and multi-sensuous nature of gazing as well as the complex social relations and fluid power geometries comprising performances of gazing. We end by illustrating the performative, embodied and relational gaze through the 'doing' of tourist photography.

In this sense, we respond to various authors who criticised the 'tourist gaze' thesis. It is said to neglect that most holiday experiences are physical or corporeal and not merely visual (Veijola and Jokinen, 1994). Female tourist writers argue that there is a *male* basis with the gaze and *flâneur*, signifying men's visual and voyeuristic mastery of women (Veijola and Jokinen, 1994; Wearing and Wearing, 1996; Pritchard and Morgan, 2000a, 2000b; Johnston, 2001). Some claim that female tourists derive pleasure from social *interaction* and from *touching* (Wearing and Wearing, 1996). Relatedly, it is argued that the notion of the gaze is too static and passive and ignores performance and adventure (Perkins and Thorns, 2001). Moreover, it is said to neglect some of the complex social relations of gazing, especially that by hosts (Maoz, 2006). MacCannell also argues that *The Tourist Gaze* fails to identify a kind of 'second gaze', which knows that looks deceive, that there are things unseen and unsaid, and that each gaze generates its own 'beyond' (2001).

We begin by outlining the 'performance turn' and how Goffman's sociology has influenced and shares commonalities with the gaze, and then clarify some elements of what the idea of the 'gaze' is meant to achieve (see Larsen, 2009, for more detail).

Performance Turn

ACTION / PARTICIPATION

First, the performance turn argues that 'tourism demands new metaphors based more on being, doing, touching and seeing rather than just "seeing"' (Perkins and Thorns, 2001: 189; Edensor, 2006). The performance turn highlights how tourists experience places in multi-sensuous ways that involve bodily sensations and affect. It is said that tourists have become bored of being mere spectators and that many tourism activities – adventure tourism – explicitly provide active, multi-sensuous bodily sensations, affect and actions (Cloke and Perkins, 1998; Franklin and Crang, 2001: 12; Bell and Lyall, 2002; Franklin, 2003). Some tourism spaces are 'playgrounds' where disciplined 'work-bodies', through engaging actively with humans, objects and places, transform into vibrant, playing and juvenile ones. Pons, for instance, discusses the ludic and haptic geographies of beach life in ethnographies of nude bathing and of the communal, processual and performative work of building a sandcastle with sculpturing hands, fine-grained sand, water, spades, buckets and so on (2007; on building a 'sandcastle', see Bærenholdt et al., 2004: ch. 1).

hosts are choreographed

① MANY AGENTS

② PERFS ARE PREDETERMINED

Second, the performance turn employs Goffmanian performative metaphors to conceptualise the themed and staged nature of tourist places as well as the scripted and theatrical corporealities and *embodied* actions of tourist bodies. It speaks of improvising performers, actors, cast members, sites as stages, guides as directors, stage management and so on (Edensor, 1998, 2000, 2001a). This is a perspective where situations, processes and performances are everything; there are no performances without doings. Through the lens of the performance turn, tourism is a doing, something accomplished *through* performances. By turning to ontologies of doing and acting (Franklin and Crang, 2001), Goffman lurks in the background. Goffman provides painstaking detail as to the embodied as well as the performed nature of interaction and social life in general within his micro-sociology of enacting, expressive, emotional and responsive bodies. These are bodies which pose, gesticulate, converse, apologise, blush, avoid eye contact and so on. The performance turn is Goffmanian in its portrayal of the tourist body as psychobiological, expressive and socialised.

Third, following on from Goffman's observation that teams are the basic unit, the performance turn discusses the many agents that make up particular tourism stages. There is a body of literature exploring the 'production-side' (similarly to the analysis in Chapter 4), examining how places are materially and symbolically staged and how key personnel perform the tourist product and maintain scripts. Edensor shows how tour guides choreograph tourists' spatial movements, their interpretation of places and appropriate behaviour. He says: 'The stage-management of tourist space, the directing of tourists and the choreographing of their movement can reveal the spatial and social controls that assist and regulate performance' (Edensor, 2001: 69). This turn, though, moves beyond Goffman in addressing the 'interaction order' in relation to power. As Weaver says in his ethnography of 'interactive service work' in the cruise industry: 'the importance of power, control and conflict is underestimated in Goffman's research' (2005: 8).

Some literature examines how tourists are not only audiences but also performers. Edensor explores how tourists at the Taj Mahal perform walking, gazing, photographing and remembering (1998), while Bærenholdt et al. examine performances of strolling, beach life and photography (2004). The performance turn builds upon Adler's 'Travel as a Performed Art', where she argues that 'the traveller's body, as the literal vehicle of travel art, has been subject to historical construction and stylistic constraint. The very senses through which

Ⓐ T'M is MORE THAN SEEING

Ⓑ PLACES ARE STAGED / BODIES EMBODY THIS REALITY

the traveller receives culturally valued experience have been moulded by differing degrees of cultivation and, indeed, discipline' (1989: 8). Tourists are not only choreographed by guides and visible signs, but also by absent or invisible cultural codes, norms and etiquettes for how to perceive and value tourist objects (Edensor, 2001a: 71). Just like Goffman, who stressed how styles of bodily idiom and self-presentation are specific to, learned through and regulated by 'cultural membership', the performance turn makes the case that tourist performances are in part *pre*formed. Performances are never for the first time because they require rehearsal, imitation of other performances and adjustment to norms and expectations to such extent that they appear natural and become taken-for-granted rituals. Performances are largely habitual and unplanned. As Goffman states:

> The legitimate performances of everyday life are not 'acted' or 'put on' in the sense that the performer knows in advance just what he is going to do, and does this solely because of the effect it is likely to have. The expressions it is felt he is giving off will be especially 'inaccessible' to him. ... The incapacity of the ordinary individual to formulate in advance the movements of his eyes and body does not mean that he will not express himself through these devices in a way that is dramatized and pre-formed in his repertoire of actions. In short, we all act better than we know how. (1959: 79–80; this prefigures aspects of Thrift's arguments in 2008)

Along the same lines, Edensor argues against the idea that tourism represents a break from the everyday: '[R]ather than transcending the mundane, most forms of tourism are fashioned by culturally coded escape attempts. Moreover, although suffused with notions of escape from normativity, tourists carry quotidian habits and responses with them: they are part of their baggage' (2001a: 61). Tourists never just travel *to* places: their mindsets, habitual practices and social relations travel unreflexively along *with* them (Larsen, 2008b; Haldrup and Larsen, 2010). Culturally coded patterns of tourist behaviour revolve around class, gender, ethnicity and sexuality, and they generate shared conventions about what should be seen and which actions are appropriate (Edensor, 2001a: 60).

Fourth, while performances are taught, learned and regulated, they are never completely predetermined. Goffman maintains that 'for interactants, rules are matters to be taken into consideration, whether as something to follow or carefully circumvent' (1963: 42). In contrast to studies portraying tourism as an overdetermined stage where tourists passively follow prescribed routes and scripts, the performance turn also uncovers creativity, detours and productive practices. Löfgren reminds us 'that standardized marketing does not have to standardize tourists. Studies of staging of tourist experience in mass tourism often reduce or overlook the uniqueness of all personal travel experience' (1999: 8). Tourists are not just written upon, they also enact and inscribe places with their own stories and can follow their own paths. Performances are never simply determined by their choreography (Larsen, 2005). Tourist performance is embodied practice and, therefore, as with 'any performance (indeed any performative activity), is inherently a contingent process' (Schieffelin, 1998: 197). Performative metaphors challenge ideas of complete standardisation and control and stress fluidity and malleability of human activity as well as the manifold roles that can be played (Weaver, 2005: 6). Edensor states that '[n]otions of tourism as performance indicate that a range of roles can be selected and enacted through experience, from disciplined rituals, to partially improvised performances to completely improvised enactions in unbounded spaces. Thus, the same tourist may act out a medley of roles during a single tour or holiday' (2000: 341). This allows space for tourist agency, struggle and resistance.

Fifth, tourist places are often presumed to be relatively fixed, given, passive and separate from those touring them. The performance turn destabilises such static and fixed conceptions of places and sites. Places and performances are conceived as non-stable and contingent enactments. As Edensor argues:

> The nature of the stage is dependent on the kinds of performance enacted upon it. For even carefully stage-managed spaces may be transformed by the presence of tourists who adhere to different norms. Thus, stages can continually change, can expand and contract. For most stages are ambiguous, sites for different performances. (2001a: 64)

Tourist places are continually reproduced and contested through being used and performed. Places only emerge as tourist places, stages of tourism, when and as they are performed (Bærenholdt et al., 2004).

Sixth, the performance turn emphasises how objects and technologies, such as cameras, tour buses and cars, are crucial for making tourism performances *happen*. They enhance the physicality of the body beyond its capabilities and enable it to do *new* things and sense *other* realities. And without material surfaces such as lawns, sand beaches and dance floors, which afford croquet, barbecuing,

tech. enHances body's interaction @ environment

tanning, beach volleyball, dancing and countless other performances, tourism would be 'lifeless' (Haldrup and Larsen, 2006, 2010: ch. 4). Crucial to analysing performances is the concept of 'affordance' (Gibson, 1986). Different surfaces and different objects, relative to the particular human organism and its technologies, provide affordances. These are objective *and* subjective, both part of the environment and of the organism. Affordances stem from their reciprocity through people's kinaesthetic movement within their particular world. Affordances constrain behaviour along certain possibilities: 'there are a range of options ... implicit within a physical milieu and this implicitness is directly connected to the bodily capacities and limits of the [human] organism' (Michael, 1996: 149). Given certain past and present social relations, then, particular 'objects' in the environment afford possibilities and resistances, given that humans are sensuous, corporeal, technologically extended and *mobile* beings.

Seventh, the performance turn does not see tourism as an isolated island but explores connections between tourism, the everyday and significant others, such as family members and friends. *Performing Tourist Places* (Bærenholdt et al., 2004) opens with a *private* photograph of two families posing with spades and buckets on a beach in front of their sandcastle. The communal performances of building a sandcastle and taking photographs show how people perform with other bodies as well. Most tourism performances are performed within teams, and this sociality is in part what makes them pleasurable *and* annoying. Tourism is not only a way of consuming (new) places, but also an emotional geography of sociability, of being together with close friends and family members from home (Haldrup and Larsen, 2010: ch. 2).

Lastly, the performance turn challenges representational and textual readings of tourism by making *ethnographies* of what humans and institutions enact and stage to make tourism and performances happen. It refuses 'to write or read off the feeling, style or atmosphere of a particular place as the 'effect' of some already determined relations' (Degen et al., 2008: 1909) and examines the 'tactics' (De Certeau, 1984) through which tourists perform out of tune with the officially inscribed signs, objects and places (Edensor, 1998; Cloke and Perkins, 2005).

Having outlined the main components of the performance turn, we now discuss it in relation to the tourist gaze *per se*. We begin with clarifying the relationship between the senses and the gaze and then we develop an embodied and multi-sensuous approach to gazing.

Embodied Gazing

We have brought out the crucially visual nature of tourist experiences. Yet it has never been the intention to argue that vision is the only sense through which tourists encounter places and that the tourist gaze can explain all aspects of tourism encounters. That would certainly be a one-sided and indeed perverse claim (see Urry, 1992). Tourists encounter places through a variety of senses. Saldanha asks: 'Don't tourists swim, climb, stroll, ski, relax, become bored perhaps, or all; don't they go to other places to taste, smell, listen, dance, get drunk, have sex?' (2002: 9). Yes, they do. Tourists eat exotic food, smell new odours, touch each other, are touched by the sun, dance to pulsating 'soundscapes', talk with friends and occasionally get drunk. Flavours, touches, smells and sounds, and doing and acting can also produce difference and the extraordinary (Franklin and Crang, 2001: 14). Kinaesthetic pleasures are omnipresent in tourism: walking a mountain, cycling in nature, diving in the sea, playing on the beach, skiing down the Alps, raving through the night. And tourists are not fixed but alternate between different roles. 'A main attraction of being on holiday', as Löfgren says more generally, 'is that there is a possibility to choose among a great many activities or mental states, between sightseeing, shopping, dozing on the beach, going for a walk, reading a novel, or having too many Tequila Sunrises' (1999: 267).

But many tourist buildings, objects, technologies and practices (as opposed to tourist motivations) are structured around visualism, as discussed in relation to cameras, photographs, advertising and themed spaces in previous chapters. While the visual sense is not the only sense, it is the organising sense. It organises the place, role and effect of the other senses. The unusualness of the visual sensations places these within a different frame (Rodaway, 1994). The distinctiveness of the visual is crucial for giving all sorts of practices and performances a special or unique character: the palm trees by the beach, the charming restaurant, the themed resort, the bedroom with a view, the sight of tropical birds, the colours of the exotic plants and so on. The most mundane of activities, such as shopping, strolling, having a drink, or swimming or river rafting appear extraordinary and become 'touristic' when conducted against a striking or unusual visual backcloth. As Bell and Lyall say with regard to adventure tourism: 'Nature tourism as kinaesthetic experience – paddled through, jumped into, trekked across – is still dependent on the glorious vista' (2002: 27).

While many tourist places are designed according to the logic of visualism, and in that process suppress or control the other senses, and the visual sense is normally the organising sense within tourist experiences, we now put forward a *relational* approach that acknowledges the complex intersections of the senses in people's encounters with places. We argue for a sensuous analysis of tourism and look at the relationship between the normally dominant visualism and other senses, including various kinds of movement. Gazing needs to be examined 'in relation to the moving, multi-sensuous bodies because this provide us with a scope for looking at the body that senses – sees, touches, smells, hears and tastes – and how all these senses are integrated by the way in which the living body moves' (Lund, 2006: 41).

In almost all situations different senses are interconnected with each other to produce a sensed environment of people and objects distributed across time and space. There are not only landscapes (and visual townscapes) but also associated soundscapes, as in Cuban tourism, especially following the film *Buena Vista Social Club* and raves in Goa, India (see Saldanha 2002); 'smellscapes', as experienced in walking through particular woods (see Macnaghten and Urry, 2000a) or heterogeneous tourist places in the third world (see Edensor, 1998; Dann and Jacobsen, 2003); 'tastescapes', especially following the late eighteenth-century invention of the restaurant (see Spang, 2000) and so-called food tourism (see Boniface, 2003; Everett, 2008); and geographies of touch, as with the hand of the climber: (see Lewis, 2000), the feet of mountaineers (see Lund, 2006), bronzing of the 'white' skin (see Ahmed, 2000) and building sandcastles (see Pons, 2009). As Lund says in her study of walking the Scottish hills, 'the sense of vision and the mountaineer's gaze cannot be separated from examining the body that moves and touches the ground' (2006: 40).

Bodies perform themselves in-between direct sensation of the 'other' and various sensescapes (Rodaway, 1994). Bodies navigate backwards and forwards between directly sensing the external world as they move bodily in and through it (or lie inertly waiting to be bronzed), and discursively mediated sensescapes that signify social taste and distinction, ideology and meaning. Such sensed and sensing bodies are concerned with various performativities. Bodies are not fixed and given but involve performances, especially to fold notions of movement, nature, taste and desire, into and through the body. There are thus complex connections between bodily sensations and socio-cultural 'sensescapes' mediated by discourse and language (see Crouch, 2000, and Macnaghten and Urry, 2000b, on embodied leisure-scapes). This can be seen in the case of much of tropical travel, such as to the Caribbean, where early visitors were able to taste new fruits, to smell the flowers, to feel the heat of the sun, to immerse one's body in the moist greenery of the rainforest, as well as to see astonishing new sights (Sheller, 2003).

There are also complex connections between bodily sensations and senses and various technologies (Ingold and Kurttila, 2000; Michael, 2000; Sheller and Urry, 2004). Michael brings out the 'agency' of walking boots in affording leisurely country walks and gazing (2000). They afford more pleasant walking *and* they make certain surfaces walk-able that would be painful if not impossible to traverse barefooted or even with ordinary shoes. Various technologies afford increased bodily capabilities, and as such they expand the affordances that nature permits the otherwise 'pure' body. While designed to be intangible, sometimes they are painful and therefore very tangible. Take the sightseeing bus. While on the move, eyes are stimulated and bodies relax in the 'comfort' of the seat. But because of the cramped and immobile viewing-position hindering proper blood circulation, the bus-chair is potentially 'a pain in the butt'. Just as it is difficult to experience nature as awe-inspiring if one's walking boots are aching, the 'cinematic shows' of the bus are ruined if one's legs or back are in pain. While places and the weather are experienced in a disembodied fashion, the experience of being in the bus is embodied. Whether they like it or not, people inescapably bring their long-suffering bodies into the bus.

Moreover, at times there is conflict between the visual sense or visualism, which may be the organising sense of a particular place and the specific ways tourists perform that particular place. They can resist the place, walk around in a way contrary to what the signs say and they can go to a place of visual beauty and make a lot of noise or come up with all sorts of protests. One example is Stonehenge. It is choreographed and represented through a 'preservation ethos' that privileges a swift visual museum-like engagement with the 'archaeological' stones. Yet some tourists try to touch them and undertake longer visits to connect physically and spiritually with the stones and its 'atmosphere' (Letcher et al., 2009). The systems of discourse, scripting and planning involved in the tourist gaze generate modes of resistance (as discussed below). We argue that there is a multiplicity of tourist gazes, and one way to approach this multiplicity is by examining the tastescapes, smellscapes, soundscapes, touchscapes involved in performances of the gaze.

Degen et al. interestingly develop a multi-sensuous, performative approach to vision in their ethnography of how 'designed urban environments', such as a shopping mall in Milton Keynes in the UK, are visually consumed. Their approach contains three components:

> The first is that experiences are theorised as *performative*. That is, visual experiences are generated through particular practices, at specific times and places, with constitutive consequences both for the object and for the subject involved. … Secondly, such experiences are *relational*: the interaction between spectator and object produces the qualities of the object, and vice versa. Thirdly, visuality is always *multimodal*: that is, visual experiences are almost always accompanied by aural, tactile, and oral experiences; and in the case of designed urban environments, by certain spatialities such as form, route, and volume. (2008: 1909, our italics)

Degen et al. unfold the 'performative', 'relational' and 'multimodal' nature of visual experiences through ethnographic vignettes of distinct ways of 'gazing' within the shopping centre. These include 'manoeuvring', the 'shopping look' and the 'parenting look'. All entail sensory engagements other than vision and complex intersubjective relations between people and objects.

Thus 'manoeuvring' highlights the intersections between walking and gazing. It enables people to 'manoeuvre and navigate a way through the mall. This is a broad, surveying gaze which is used to move around objects, which acknowledges objects but does not engage in any depth with them' (Degen et al., 2008: 1919). Touch, smell and immobility are pivotal to the 'shopping look'. 'When shopping, one's vision is more concentrated, actively searching for a desired product. As we look for it, we touch different materials. We sway from a "thinner", unfocused gaze that helps us to navigate around the shop to a "thicker", focused stare that involves touching and smelling, especially if the piece of clothing or perfume has a distinctive texture' (Degen et al., 2008: 1919). The 'parental look' accentuates the *relational*, communal nature of gazing. Most people perform gazing in the company of significant others and the social composition of one's 'team' affords some ways of seeing more than others. In particular, children influence the look of their parents:

When one is in the mall as a carer with children, eyes and bodies are responsively attuned to the bodies and movements of the children. The mall and its sensory stimuli (windows, music, street furniture) fall into the background as the children's bodies are followed and the mall's geography turns into a (sometimes dangerous, other times fun) playground ...with two mobile kids, enjoying being with them, my eyes and ears and hands were tuned into them, focused on them, and not so much on the wider space. Where were they, what were they saying, what were they doing. This was in relation to many material objects, of course, and also to other people. Sometimes it is possible almost to see and sense through the eyes of the children. We attune our perceptions to those of a child and read anew the affordances of a place as we learn that a public sculpture becomes a skeleton to climb on, the edge of a fountain a running track. (Degen et al., 2008: 1911)

This reformulation of seeing has significant implications for the tourist gaze. Throughout this book we have emphasised different modes of gazing and that the same sight in can be consumed in different ways according to the habitus and dispositions of tourists. The 'performed' tourist gaze involves other sensescapes; gazing is multimodal. People are never disembodied travelling eyes. Gazing upon a particular sight or objects in a museum depends upon people's bodily well-being. If a visitor is hung-over, hungry, thirsty, suffering from diarrhoea, or their shoes itch or the sun is too hot or the air-conditioning too cold, they may fail to be impressed. Similarly, impressive sight may be contradicted by inappropriate smells or noise. While sightseeing tours revolve around sights and seeing, tour guides provide 'soundtracks' to the passing scenery and attractions. Most sightseeing involves some modes of listening, sometimes involving audio technologies (see Figure 8.1).

Moreover, gazees often have a burning desire to touch, stroke, walk or climb upon and even collect the animals, plants, ruins, buildings and art objects that they lay their eyes upon. While most museums do not afford or permit such physical proximity between the gazer and the object of the gaze, in most other places gazing comprises seeing *and* touching. Lastly, tourists never just gaze upon places and things; they gaze upon them with known and/or unknown others. And who we gaze with is as important to the quality of the experience as is the object of the gaze. In the next section we discuss the multifaceted social relations of gazing, how they are tied up with relations between gazers, on the one hand, and hosts and guests, on the other.

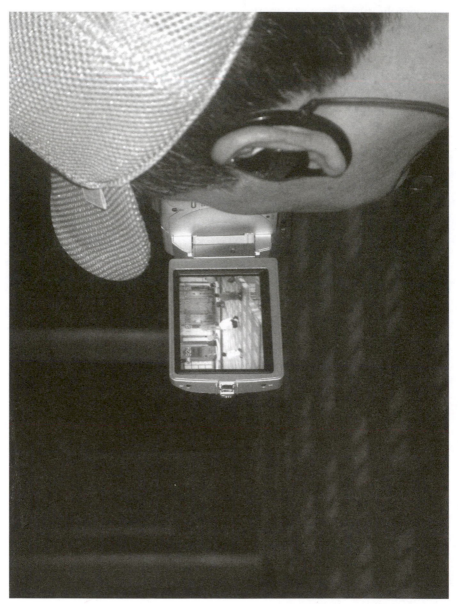

Figure 8.1 Sightseeing and soundscapes

Social Relations of Gazing

The 'parental look' specifies how children influence the rhythms and gazes of their parents. Their gaze lingers much on their children and they partly see an attraction through their eyes, with little time for sustained, contemplative gazing. And yet, from time to time, children are forced to follow in their parents' footsteps and see 'adult' things. Our argument is that gazing is a *relational* practice involving subtle bodily and verbal negotiations and interactions between 'team members'. Most tourists do not experience the world as a solitary *flâneur* but in 'teams' of colleagues, friends, family members and partners. Gazing almost always involves significant others. Gazing is an interactive, communal game where individual gazes are mediated and affected by the presence and gazes of others. Such social relations of gazing enable *and* constrain. As Crouch says more generally: 'By our own presence we have an influence on others, on their space and on their practice of that space, and vice versa, often considered as negative, as source of conflicts, but such a position overlooks its positive potential' (2005: 29).

Travelling with an affectionate partner makes it easy to fall in love with 'romantic Paris'. And yet 'romantic Paris' can taunt the single traveller with feelings of loneliness and lost love as well as the troubled couple with realising that not even *this* place can re-establish their affection for one another. Perhaps they secretly dream of gazing on 'romantic Paris' with someone else next time. The tourist's emotional and affective experiences with a given place depend as much upon the quality of their co-travelling social relations as upon the place itself.

Other tourists also influence and discipline the tourist gaze. Tourists spend much time gazing at fellow tourists. As Löfgren says more generally:

> tourists have ample time to observe other tourists and fellow travellers, while standing in line, sitting in a café or by the pool. Such situations may turn us into amateur sociologists, constantly observing and judging the behaviour of other tourists, but it also produces rich opportunities for daydreaming, fantasizing about the lives of the strangers surrounding you. What about the couple over there, the family down by the pool, the group of Japanese tourists crossing the piazza? We invent secret lives; compare our own situation with that of others. (2008: 94)

And we may also say that tourists turn into '*critical* sociologists', complaining about and mocking *other* tourists for their superficial, snobbish or boring behaviour. This status and taste game engulfs everyone. Tourists flag identity through separating them from co-present others. Dionysian tourists mock cultural tourists for missing out on fun, while the latter scorn 'lazy sun bathers' for lacking cultural capital. While they try to avoid each other, they rub shoulders at hotels, airports, sights and beaches and can destroy the experience for the other (Edensor, 1998).

'Collective gazers' upon package holidays and guided tours are subject to the disciplinary gaze of co-participants. *Others* restrict possible performances and show up conventions about 'appropriate' ways of being a tourist. Other key brokers in this network of social relations of the collective gaze are guides and tour reps who direct and frame gazes at sights: they suggest photo opportunities, provide scripted commentary, choreograph movements along prescribed paths and define normalising behaviour (Edensor, 1998; Cheong and Miller, 2000). In part, such rigid guiding makes enclavic tourist places resemble Goffman's 'total institution', where a group of people is 'cut off from the wider society for an appreciable period of time, together lead an enclosed formally administered round of life' (quoted in Ritzer and Liska, 1997: 106). The 'total institutions', or 'enclavic spaces', of modern tourism are typified by 'team performance', which is 'a highly directed operation, with guides and tour mangers acting as choreographers and directors, the performance is repetitive, specifiable in movement and highly constrained by time. Besides acting out there their own part in the drama by photographing, gazing and moving *en masse* according to well-worn precedent, the group also absorb the soliloquies of the central actor, the guides, who enact the same script at each performance' (Edensor, 1998: 65).

Larsen (2004a) ethnographically explores how the collective gaze is socially and materially orchestrated by guides upon sightseeing tours, in his case the 'Viking Land Tour' in and around Copenhagen and Roskilde in Denmark. While the bus takes the fastest way out of Copenhagen, the guide sets the scene:

> The 'Viking Land Tour'! This is an awful tour; it is a terrible tour. You won't see anything but tombs and graves and so on. But don't worry. At the end you'll love it. … We're taking you out in the beautiful Danish countryside showing you a bit around. Then we are going to the renowned Viking Ship Museum. That'll make you specialists in the Vikings. On the way to a 5000 years old dusky old passage-grave we're again taking you on a picturesque crosscutting tour through the countryside. … Before we're having a typical Danish buffet at an old

charming inn we are visiting the stunning cathedral of Roskilde. (Larsen, 2004a: 148–9)

Discourses of the sublime, picturesque and authenticity frame the tour and its landscapes and sights. After 20 minutes, the guide announces: 'Now we are going to be on the motorway for a couple of minutes. For the rest of the day we're going to drive along nice small roads with a view.' Then, with relief in his voice, the guide informs us that we have now reached our destination. Driving into the first village, the bus reduces speed while the guide's choreography intensifies:

Now we're in the village Sengeløse. Look left! Enjoy the old houses. Enjoy the village pond. Forget about the supermarket. Now please look in front of you! A typical country church again. It is about 800 years old. And look right! They're putting a new roof on the house. Look there on the right! That's the traditional way of doing it – old crafting skills. Now look to the left! Enjoy the neat churchyard. Each grave is like a small garden – well cared for and looked after. (Larsen, 2004a: 149)

By the means of verbal expression and body gestures, the guide – politely (please!) yet sternly – choreographs the consumption of what to see, how to see it and what not to see of the village. Everyone complies with his orchestratation; upper-bodies and heads move from side to side as one social body. The visions of 30–40 individually seated people are synchronised and choreographed into one 'collective gaze'.

Throughout the tour, but in particular when the guide instructs, the participants actively look – glancing out of the window with a concentrated fixed stare. When photography is intense or photo opportunities are around the corner, the bus slows down to give people time to focus and produce non-blurred images. Photography increases almost proportionally with the intensity of the guiding. When directing people to look to one or other side, the reaction is often a look *and* a 'click'. Typical 'time-killing' travel activities such as reading and listening to music rarely take place and even travel talk is rare. Those on the bus appear captivated by the storytelling guide and the scenic landscapes slowly passing by.

While consumed through a collective gaze, the guide scripts the villages as objects of the 'romantic gaze'. People are directed to look at the 'old houses', 'typical church villages', 'old crafting skills' and a 'neat churchyard'. Places and objects are scripted as 'typical',

'Danish' and 'ancient', reflecting how 'the rhetoric of tourism is full of manifestations of the importance of the authenticity of relationships between tourists and what they see' (MacCannell, 1999: 14). The guide also performs in a 'post-touristic' fashion on occasions. Jokingly, people are told not to worry about entering the dusky burial mound because he will lead them, and that visitors should 'forget about the supermarket'.

The guide provides an almost unending 'soundtrack' to the passing scenery. It is one-way communication (predominantly) that cannot be escaped at least while inside the bus. Since the guide constantly points out what to see and how to understand and value it, people are rarely left to draw their own interpretations. Outside the bus, they are also subject to 'soft control'. They are implicitly advised against individual exploration and explicitly asked to follow in his footsteps. And travelling as a team, they are 'monitored' by their co-participants. Thus, the rhythms and choreographies of this tour are characterised by a specific sociality of simultaneous autonomy, communality and social control.

Having discussed some relations between teams of gazers and guides and gazers, we now turn to relationships between gaz*ers* and the gaz*ees*, or guests and hosts. In previous writings we argued that hosts also contribute to the place ballets that make up tourism performances and stages, although we emphasised the former over the latter (see Bærenholdt et al., 2004; Sheller and Urry, 2004). This is normally described as an asymmetrical power relationship where the gaz*er* powerfully constructs and consumes the gaz*ee*, with little resistance from the powerless host. Similar to the performance turn that insists upon analysing resistance and creativity among tourists, we now discuss certain literature that brings out how gazees are not totally passive and powerless. Quinn argues: 'locals are implicated in complex ways of encountering, negotiating, controlling, and contesting the presence of tourists is as important as understanding the roles played by the latter' (2007: 461).

Maoz's concept of the 'mutual gaze' brings out the resistance and power of hosts when interacting face-to-face with tourists (2006). This notion is explicitly developed in relation to earlier formulations of the tourist gaze that mainly examined relations between the tourism industry and tourists while paying scant attention to the active, manipulating and resisting performances of 'hosts'. In fact, it was stressed that tourists exercised much power over the places and locals become the 'mad one' behind bars, relentlessly gazed upon and photographed (Urry, 1992). 'By contrast', Maoz says, 'the local gaze is based on a more complex, two-sided picture, where both the tourist and local gazes exist, affecting and feeding each other, resulting in what is termed "the mutual gaze"' (2006: 222). According to Maoz, *everyone* gazes at each other in the spaces of tourism; locals return the gaze of tourists and consequently tourists too can turn into the mad ones behind bars. Yet 'most tourists are hardly aware of this gaze, mainly because they arrogantly dismiss its presence. They rarely feel they are being watched, and thus act in what they perceive as a totally free and permissive environment' (Maoz, 2006: 229).

Maoz thus proposes a more complex and reciprocal power relation between hosts and guests where power is omnipresent and fluid, a situated outcome of performative interactions (see also Ateljevic and Doorne, 2005). In line with Foucault's power/resistance duality, 'the mutual gaze makes both sides seem like puppets on a string, since it regulates their behavior. It results in mutual avoidance, remoteness, and negative attitudes and behavior. There are no defined "dominators" and "dominated", as both groups simultaneously undergo and exercise power' (Maoz, 2006: 225).

Based upon ethnographic studies of interactions between backpackers from Israel and locals in India, Maoz outlines three modes of response to tourists that locals largely regard as 'shallow, hedonistic, and rude people, who are badly educated and can be easily deceived' (2006: 235). One mode is 'cooperation' where locals become the 'powerless' who always and unconditionally meet the needs of tourists, and they change their lifestyle and business according to satisfy these 'desires'. Some internalise the tourist gaze to the point where it becomes their own. But she also identifies two forms of resistance. There is a low-key form of 'veiled resistance', where locals laugh at and gossip about tourists as well as exploit that 'staged authenticity' of goods, services, spirituality and so on that can easily seduce the visitors. The authenticity seekers are not aware of the local gaze and are unlikely to notice the staging. Finally, there is 'open resistance', where locals 'strike back' at ignorant or obnoxious tourists' behaviour through verbal confrontations, written instructions about respectful behaviour, poor service to rude costumers and businesses banning tourists with signs saying 'no Israelis' (Maoz, 2006: 231). Maoz argues that the mutual gaze is *complementary* to the notion of the tourist gaze, which can be made more complex, performative and interactive by recognising that it is always a 'mutual gaze' with a multitude of intersecting, responsive gazes, between guests and guests, tourists and 'brokers' and between tourists themselves.

Gazes and Places

The performance turn brings forth how tourists are co-producers of tourist places and tourists can experience a given place through many different styles, senses and practices. While we have suggested that gazing is highly mediated and *pre*formed through circulating representations and architectural theming, it has also been noted that gazing is never predetermined and fully predictable. In Chapter 1 we listed several distinct ways of gazing, legitimated through different discourses and practices, and we did so in part to illustrate that any tourist attraction can be visually consumed in different ways despite that most are designed and regulated according to specific historic discourse or logic. The presence of different 'gazes' at a sight may cause conflict and turn it into a contested space, haunted by *other* tourists. Edensor shows how western tourists at Taj Mahal can perceive Indians as 'crappy tourists' while backpackers may complain that guided tourists spoil their prolonged, romantic visual encounter with this iconic sight (1998: ch. 4).

Visitors to heritage sites and shopping malls are not simply taken in by such sites and sightseeing tourists are not passive consumers of guided narratives and tours. Tourists are not cultural dopes. Following on from the performance turn, we need a *circuit* of performance model that blurs the distinction between production (choreographing) and consumption (acting) and instead see them as interrelated and overlapping in complex ways. 'Bodies are not only written upon but also write their own meanings and feelings upon space in a continual process of continual remaking' (Edensor, 2001a: 100). The act of 'consumption' is simultaneously one of production, of re-interpreting, re-forming, re-doing, of decoding the encoded in the present (Du Gay et al., 1997). Furthermore, tourists do not only decode past texts, but are part of creating new ones through ongoing interactions and performances with other tourists, guides, discourses, buildings and objects.

A key part of the argument against Hewison's *The Heritage Industry* (1987) was to show the diverse readings, responses and resistances to an imposed 'heritage-isation' (see Chapter 6). As Chronis concludes in his account of the co-construction of the Gettysburg storyscape of the American Civil War:

the narrative of the Civil War is not a result of an individual producer who introduces its meaning into society. The Gettysburg storyscape illustrates the interactive process through which a Civil War battle becomes a meaningful story through performance at a tourism space. As an event of the past, the battle of Gettysburg is a historical fact. Yet, as a cultural product, Gettysburg is a fluid narrative text staged by marketers and presented in multiple, heterogeneous forms. The resulting narratives are contested by tourists and become subject to negotiation. During the performance of the story, tourists are not passive readers of the text. Rather, they are actively engaged by using their prior background, negotiating, filling gaps, and imagining. Hence, service providers do not simply teach history and tourists do not only learn about the past. Rather, through their interaction, marketers and tourists perform history by means of negotiation, narrative completion, and embodiment. (2005: 400)

While much tourism is choreographed and tourists need to submit to its ordering, this does not rule out moments of resistance and post-tourist irony. Even shopping malls attract their share of 'post-shoppers', people who play at being consumers in complex, self-conscious mockery. Users should not be seen simply as victims of consumerism, as 'credit card junkies', but as being able to assert their independence from the mall developers. This is achieved by a kind of tourist *flânerie*, by continuing to stroll, to gaze, and to be gazed upon, '[t]heir wandering footsteps, the modes of their crowd practice constitute that certain urban ambiance: a continuous reassertion of the rights and freedoms of the marketplace, the *communitas* of the carnival' (Shields, 1989: 161). Fiske talks of a kind of sensuous consumption that does not create profit. The positive pleasure of parading up and down, of offending 'real' consumers and the gents of law and order, of asserting their difference within, and different use of, the cathedral of consumerism became an oppositional cultural practice (1989: 17).

Moreover, Edensor argues in relation to tours and enclavic spaces: 'taking these metaphors too literally creates a spatial determinism, erroneously suggesting that tourists are fully compelled to act out specific conformist performances' (2000: 330). Tucker's ethnography reveals resistance by the young participants on a longer guided tour as they toured through the 'natural wonderland' of Australia. Given that many regard the tour as an opportunity to meet new people (friends, partners and sexual partners) and have fun, they gazed and paid more attention to desired others rather than to the passing landscape and the narratives of the guides, they pulled faces when the guide became overly enthusiastic and they took silly photographs of each other when visiting the supposed highlights of the tour (Tucker, 2007).

Having discussed the tourist gaze as embodied, the social relations of gaze and forms of 'resistance', we now return to photography and discuss its varied performances.

Performing Tourist Photography

 Tourist photography is often seen as passive, superficial and disembodied, a discursively prefigured activity of 'quotation'. Some formulations of the 'hermeneutic circle' turn the photographic performances of *tourists* into a ritual of quotation by which tourists are framed and fixed by commercial images rather than framing and exploring themselves (Osborne 2000: 81). It is *pre*formed rather than *per*formed. This illustrates how analysing photography 'without looking for practices can only produce a mortuary geography drained of the actual life that inhabits these places' (Crang, 1999: 249). Writings about tourist photography have often produced lifeless tourists, eventless events and dead geographies. We discuss now how the performance turn 'enlivens' the analysis of tourist photography.

Performance theorists state that performances contain rituals but also play (see Haldrup and Larsen, 2010: ch. 7). In Chapter 7 we discussed how photography is a ritualised 'theatre' that people enact to produce their desired and expected self-image and togetherness, wholeness and intimacy with partner, family and friends. There is also a significant *play* element to photography, but this is so often drowned in writings highlighting the ritualised nature of photography and what it represents. Normally, photography is seen as a means to an end (photographs), but the play-aspect turns things on its head: photography can now also be an end in itself. Without neglecting the value of photographs, the play-aspect shows how photography can be a source of pleasure, creativity and sociability in itself and this explains its performances. Writing before digital cameras, Löfgren states:

> The critique of the urge to document misses an important point. The pleasure may not be in gathering up moments to display next winter but just in creating them: Letting the video roll … clicking through a roll of Kodachrome. However much energy goes into the production of these narratives and whatever their fate, producing them was an experience in its own right. … Here is an arena where nonartists …do not hesitate to try their hand at producing, a photo narrative … [or] video documentary. Here you may become your own director, scriptwriter or scenographer. (1999: 74)

Following on from this we shift from why to *how*, from studying functions of photography to doings and actions of photography (that might reproduce rituals and discourses of loving family life), and crucially, such performative actions are both representational (posing, self-representation and drawing on cultural discourses) *and* non-representational (involve interactions, work, sociability and so on). Photographic performances are always *more*-than-just representational.

We begin here with Said's statement that 'the very idea of representation is a theatrical one' (1995: 63). Grasping tourist photography as performance can highlight the embodied practices and social relations and its dramas. Photographing is not a performance of a single eye but of an engaged and multi-sensuous body. The practice of taking photographs is often conceived of as a visual practice that is rapid and does not require much more than 'clicking' but a performance approach can highlight the busy, active and playful 'bodies of photography'. When we conceive of photography as performance, it is a process over time. As Sather-Wagstaff says with regard to photographing the former World Trade Center: 'Tourists at the WTC simply do not all "picture" the site in the same way. They both see and experience the site through the lenses of their individual subjectivities, selectively choosing engagement with the objects and activities at the site that resonate for them, making prosthetic memories through such engagement, and capturing these different experiences photographically' (2008: 77). Or to cite Suonpää: 'When you find that you are watching the midnight sun at Nordkapp with hundreds of tourists jostling behind your back, the conveying of romantic experience calls for skilful use of the camera' (2008: 79).

Elsewhere we show how bodies of photographers are erect, or kneeling, or bending sideways, or forwards and backwards, leaning on ruins, lying on the ground and so on. Photographed tourists pose through composing their face and body as teams bond corporeally. Touch – body-to-body or what Goffman terms 'shoulder hold' and 'hand-holding' (1976: 55–6) – is an essential in relation to tourist photography enacted through the family gaze (see Figure 8.2). When cameras appear, people assume tender, desexualised postures such as holding hands, hugging and embracing. 'Arms around shoulders' or 'shoulder hold' is the common way of bonding friends and family members as one social body. Tourist photography simultaneously produces and displays bodily closeness. The proximity comes about because the camera event draws people together. To produce signs of loving and intimate family life, families need to enact it

Figure 8.2 Performing the family gaze

physically, to touch each other. Such 'group bonding' through photography also characterises the collective gaze of guided tours (see Figure 8.3.). Such staged intimacy tends to be put to an end when the shooting has finished (it would be rather inappropriate to carry on hugging even a good friend once the photo is taken!). This ties into Goffman's central idea that 'one of the most interesting times to observe impression management is the moment when a performer leaves the back region and enters the place where the audience is to be found, or when he returns therefrom, for at these moments one can detect a wonderful putting on and taking off of character' (1959: 123).

When faced by the camera-lens people become extraordinarily aware of their psychobiological and cultural body, its appearance and manner, and the setting they are part of, and they pose by reflex to 'give' an appropriate 'personal front'. Being photographed is one social situation where dramaturgical awareness always seems to arise; it is a form of bodily communication concerned with expression. As Barthes states, 'I have been photographed and I knew it. Now, once I feel myself observed by the lens, everything changes: I constitute myself in the process of "posing", I instantly make another body for myself, I transform myself in advance into an image' (2000: 10). Poses as one form of impression management are integral to photography. It seems to be a 'law' that people pose when the camera-face gazes at one. When being photographed, one cannot avoid 'giving off' information, but through posing one can try to convey a specific image for the future (Larsen, 2005). And yet this posing often goes unnoticed as 'expressive messages', as Goffman says, 'must often preserve the fiction that they are uncalculated, spontaneous and involuntary' (1963: 14).

In *Performing Tourist Places* we discuss the sustained efforts of two women to stage and photographically capture their children (Bærenholdt et al., 2004: ch. 7). First, there is the staging of the event. As if ill-clad for camera work, perhaps feeling too hot and stuffy, the camera-wearing woman takes off her jacket. Then, meticulously, one after another, she positions the boys. Next, the shooting begins. She squats so that the 'camera eye' is more level with the eyes of the children. Direct eye contact is established. Now the other woman joins in the action. Standing just behind the kneeling photographer with her eyes fixed on the boys, she waves vigorously with her arms in the air. Then a small break occurs and the photographer changes shooting position, straightening her body slightly. Now events intensify. For the next minute or so the photographer constantly frames and shoots, while the other woman's arms make all

Figure 8.3   *The collective gaze performed on a guided tour*

sorts of disco-aerobic moves and shakes – all acted out with a big smile on her face. Although the boys' arms are not 'joining in', their faces are probably laughing and a joyful holiday photo thankfully gets produced.

This ethnographic vignette illustrates some *social relations* of photography. Tourists enact photography bodily, creatively and multi-sensuously in teams of significant others (one's family, partner, friends, co-travelling tourists and so on) and with a (future) audience at hand or in mind. The performed aspects of tourist photography relates to practices of taking photos, posing for cameras, choreographing posing bodies, watching photographing tourists and consuming photographs. That photographing often involves 'teamwork' and 'audiences' also indicate the usefulness of studying it as performance. Photographing is typified by complex social relations between photographers, posers and present, imagined and future audiences. It is common that posers are instructed by photographers or other members of the team to bring into being certain appropriate fronts (the most common being 'Smile'!) or break off inappropriate activities.

This also illustrates how the camerawork of tourists is concerned not only with 'consuming places' (Urry, 1995a) or hegemonic 'place-myths' (Shields, 1990), but also with self-presentation and 'strategic impression management' enacted by teams of friends, couples and especially families through 'the family gaze' (Haldrup and Larsen, 2003; Larsen, 2005). Most tourists express a simultaneous desire to make pictures of and at destinations. They are looking out for 'physical settings' such as monuments, viewing-stations, beautiful spots and views within which to frame their team members.

The self is a 'dramatic effect' continuously created in public performances. Idealisation is a common dramaturgical practice (Goffman, 1959: 47). Much picturing amounts to a front-stage of encoded and enacted impression management. Frictions are almost automatically put on hold and even dull gatherings become full of life when the camera appears. Not all love for the camera is 'sincere' (Goffman, 1959: 28). Even families where little affection is shown can appear to perform affectionate family life for the camera (Kuhn, 1995).

Goffman once said that: 'we have party faces, funeral faces, and various kinds of institutional faces' (1963: 28). And to this list of faces we may add *tourist faces*. Tourist photography is intimately tied up with 'loving faces'. Stressed parents, bored teenagers and crying kids are instructed to put on a happy face and embrace one another before the camera begins to click. Careful impression management ensures returning home with photographic memories of apparently 'loving' family or friendship life. Many tourist teams co-produce *one* social body that is ceremoniously displayed. Everyone expresses respect for the photographic event by posing in a dignified way; gentle smiles are worn, bodies are straightened, hands are kept at sides. No one pokes fun or dominates (for ethnographic evidence of this, see Bærenholdt, et al., 2004: ch. 6). This is a *solemn gaze* celebrating both the social relation and the attraction. There may be mild contestations and what Goffman terms 'role distance' to such idealised family photography. Not everyone is always willing to 'fit in'. There are conflicts between the team members about what poses are appropriate. Examples include teenagers resisting their parents' instructions to look sweet because they desire to seem cool or blasé. Family members – especially fathers – can appear uncomfortable about staging the loving family at busy attractions.

There is also a 'playful pose' where tourists fool around and make humorous faces and obscene body gestures, playing to the camera. This anti-pose is particular widespread among youngish people and it has been popularised by digital cameras. Tucker shows the significance of this 'pose' on a guided tour where the young participants took silly photos of themselves and the places they visited so as to challenge the 'seriousness' that the guide tried to convey and inscribe the tour with (2007: 151). And somewhat similarly, there is the reflexive and mildly subversive 'post-tourist pose' where tourists playfully mock the conventional scripts of tourist photography. Edensor overheard a group of American tourists photographing and posing at the Taj Mahal:

TOURIST 1:   OK guys, line up and look astonished
TOURIST 2:   Yeah, but . . . it's great, I suppose – but what does it do?
TOURIST 3:   Bob had the best line – 'The Taj is amazing, but boring'
TOURIST 1:   Come on, let's do the photo so we can get outta here (1998: 133).

Finally, we return to the complex power relations between guests and hosts. While this relation is asymmetrical in terms of power, Gillespie's notion of the 'reverse gaze', inspired by Maoz's notions of the 'mutual gaze', interestingly brings out the shame and discomfort that tourist photographers experience when the photographee takes notice and gazes back at the photographer. Gillespie's argument is that this 'reverse gaze' wounds because self-proclaimed travellers, with their anthropological gaze, feel that it turns them into mere tourists and performers of voyeuristic gazing, precisely because photographing is a mocked and questionable tourist activity. By being caught by the reverse gaze the photographer 'loses face', even when the photographee does not mind being 'snapped'. As Gillespie says:

> The photographee, by a prolonged stare, a questioning look, or even just a raised eyebrow, can momentarily reverse the relationship between the photographer and photographee. In a glance the photographee can ... capture and objectify the tourist photographer as a particular type of tourist. That is to say, the reverse gaze, in its various forms, can mediate the emerging tourist self. (2006: 347)

Conclusion

We have thus seen many ways in which performances are central to tourism. We found Goffman a rich source of insight into the performative character of much tourism. We have also noted that social interaction in general is full of performances and that these will not easily go away or become less significant. This is very relevant to the final chapter when we examine some of the risks of tourism as an industry and as a core set of activities within the contemporary world, at least for those living in the rich North. And in that rich North it may turn out that the increasing scale and scope of leisurely travel under the regime of the tourist gaze actually turns out to be a somewhat limited period in human history. We consider the risks of that leisurely travel and note that it is destructive of the environments being visited, of long-term climates, and of the supplies of oil that 'fuelled' the tourist gaze over the mobile twentieth century.

And yet finding substitutions for such a modern mobile world is difficult to achieve for many reasons but partly because of this performative character. What kinds of performances we might ask could replace the performances of contemporary globalising tourism? Is it conceivable that performances could be re-localised? How can we imagine the tourist gaze being directed towards the very local and mundane? Is it necessary to travel long distances and to new places when we have seen that much tourism revolves around emotional geographies of performing family life and friendship with people that one is more or less proximate with on a daily basis? What indeed would digital photography be like if the objects photographed were all found within local neighbourhoods? Is it possible to imagine the performances of the tourist gaze being entirely based upon 'virtual sights' seen upon screens and never corporeally visited? Could the interactions of gazer and gaze be only virtual and never embodied and as such go against the whole thrust of argumentation derived from Goffman elaborated in this chapter? Or, will future tourist gazes be more 'local' and tied up with social relations rather than with long-distance travel and collecting faraway places?

9

Risks and Futures

Introduction

In this chapter we examine some contemporary and future developments within tourism. Especially significant are the interconnections between tourism and risk. When the first edition of this book appeared in 1990 there was little examination of risk except to consider the expert systems that Thomas Cook developed from the 1840s onwards. These were designed to offset some of the obvious risks of travel for each individual. However, since around 1990 there have been many new analyses of 'risk', mostly provoked by Beck's *The Risk Society* (2002, first published in English in 1992). In this book, Beck is concerned not with 'natural' disasters but with the 'person-made' risks of industrial society. The nuclear radiation blown across much of Europe that followed the explosions at Chernobyl nuclear plant in 1985 is seen as symptomatic of a shift from an industrial to a risk society. In the risk society there are not only goods, but also many 'person-made' 'bads'. This notion of the risk society and the spreading of multiple bads is applied to many of the environmental dangers of contemporary societies, of local pollution, of energy and resource constraints and changing climates. And especially from the September 11th terrorist attack onwards, part of the contemporary risk society is the bads and especially the fear of terrorism that generated much visual surveillance and control of mobile bodies in cities, resorts and airports.

We examine in particular whether and in what ways tourism itself is self-destructive, that it is using up or destroying the very preconditions of its own activity through generating powerful local or global risks or bads. These bads seem to stem from the exceptional development of tourism and travel from the early part of the nineteenth century onwards. Wordsworth's poem *The Brother* begins:

These Tourists, Heaven preserve us! needs must live
A profitable life: some glance along
Rapid and gay, as if the earth were air.
And they were butterflies to wheel about

Long as their summer lasted; some, as wise,
Upon the forehead of a jutting crag
Sit perch'd with book and pencil on their knee,
And look and scribble, scribble on and look,

Buzard argues that this poem from 1800 'signifies the beginning of modernity ... a time when one stops belonging to a culture and can only tour it' (1993: 27). So begins the processes of looking, comparing, contrasting and collecting places that has so marked the last two centuries. Many places are now global icons, wonders of the world, worth seeing for oneself through travelling there. Touring the world is how the world has been significantly experienced for the past two centuries and especially since its mobilisation commenced around 1840 in Europe. Schultz describes in a 972-page book *1000 Places To See Before You Die*, a thousand places to gaze upon for oneself (2003).

We examine in this book many different kinds of place that contemporary tourists seek to see for themselves. And tourists can collect and compare them with other places and obtain cultural capital from having been there and displaying this information increasingly via Web 2.0. Heaven preserve us, we might say, from all these tourists. Indeed, as the tourist gaze has gone global so it generates some powerful new configurations of risk in the contemporary world. These risks, or bads, include the effects upon the very places being visited, upon the supplies of oil that move people in and out of places, and upon the future conditions of life upon the planet. Before examining these risks we consider some strange intersections of risk and danger that stem from the proliferation of the tourist gaze and the many 'compulsions to consume' that it generates.

Risk and Danger

Although tourism is supposedly all about pleasure, this pleasure, this consuming of places around the world, often involves disease, danger and death (see Urry, 2004). There are often strange combinations of pleasure and pain, risk and danger. First, this is because tourist places are often full of the ill and the dying. We noted in Chapter 2 the early history of resorts as spas. Many resorts remain as places for the ill to take waters and the air, to receive treatment and to convalesce. There are often high concentrations of nursing homes, the retired and the infirmed, especially as medical and fitness tourism developed widely. Contemporary Cuba has an interesting comparative advantage in contemporary medical tourism because of the legacy of its good communist health service.

Second, consuming other places often involves gazing at and collecting places of violent death. We have discussed how dark tourist sites include jails, war memorials, castles, extermination camps, sites of deadly battles and disasters and fortresses. Examples include Changi Jail in Singapore, West African slave forts, Nazi-occupation sites in the Channel Islands, Glencoe, Falls Road Belfast, Ground Zero, Egyptian pyramids, Dachau, Hiroshima, Pearl Harbor, Hurricane Katrina in New Orleans and Sarajevo's 'massacre trail'. There are also places to commemorate the death of iconic individuals. These include the grassy knoll in Dallas where JFK was assassinated, Gracelands, Jim Morrison's grave in Paris and the underpass where Princess Diana died (Lennon and Foley, 2000). Furthermore, bloodthirsty cultures are often converted into cultures that can be consumed and played with, as Vikings, Incas or Zulu warriors (see Bærenholdt and Haldrup, 2004, on Vikings).

These places of death, disaster and suffering have come to be performed as places of leisure, often charging an entrance fee, providing interpretation and selling various other services and souvenirs. Many of these places developed and continue because of well-organised enthusiasts and fans (Bærenholdt and Haldrup, 2004; Hui, 2008). These enthusiasts perform 'work' involving reciprocity and mutual aid. Emphasis is placed upon acquiring through networks arcane forms of knowledge about that place or person. Enthusiasts seek to keep 'alive' the memories of their particular race, religion, star, culture or peoples. Organised fans or enthusiasts bring this experience of death and disaster into the public eye, to make the world witness it through a public memorial gazed upon by visitors who are thus key to this public commemoration. Also such tourist performances keep those memories in the public eye and hence reduce the likelihood of 'disaster fatigue', as Pezzullo shows well in the case of post-Katrina New Orleans (2009).

More generally, there are many connections between the mobilities of people and illnesses. High rates of international mobility have generated new risks, such as syphilis, AIDS or SARS, which are diseases of mobilities of travellers and tourists, modern plagues according to Farmer (1999). 'Sex tourism' and sexual encounters between 'guests' and 'hosts' discussed in Chapter 3 have contributed to the geographical spread of sexual diseases such as AIDS, while SARS resulted from particular patterns of travel within the Chinese diaspora. Places are immensely vulnerable to the movements of illnesses and especially to the fear of illness that can overnight turn a tourist place into a place fearing death. Panic can cause visitors to shun that place, as partially happened to the English Lake District in 2001 when the idyllic countryside was full of burning carcases of cattle that had been culled to slow down the spread of foot-and-mouth disease.

Third, tourist places have often been and imagined as places of danger, where crime and fears around personal safety are central. Rio shows such a hyper-concentration of tourism and criminality, where criminals from the favelas target tourists who provide a honeypot. There are many examples of the attraction of tourists for criminals, for mugging, prostitution, pickpocketing and illegal businesses relating to the addictions of visitors. Part the allure of the Caribbean is said to be that 'danger' is just around the corner, just beneath the veneer. Tales of pirates, Rastas, drugs and Yardies all contribute to the performing of 'dangerous tourism' in these paradise islands of the Caribbean (Sheller, 2003). There are various guidebooks for 'dangerous travel' (Schroeder, 2002: 73) as well as a BBC TV series called *Holidays in the Danger Zone*. And yet, as discussed in Chapter 6, enclavic tourist spaces such as tourist resorts, international hotels, shopping malls and theme parks represent an architecture of *security* explicitly designed to isolate consumers from places of danger and fear. In risky environments with many real or imagined bads, tourists often prefer the safety of the self-contained 'camp'.

Fourth, tourism performances often involve putting the body into other kinds of personal danger since, as Sennett says, 'the body comes to life when coping with difficulty' (1994: 310; Macnaghten and Urry, 2000b). As noted in previous chapters, adventure tourism has developed as new versions of the tourist gaze, involving distinctly dangerous and moving tourist performances. These performances of bodily extremes include bungee jumping, off-piste skiing, paragliding, skydiving, whitewater rafting and high-altitude walking. Thomas Mann once wrote that modernity, and especially those 'touring' this world, is in love with the abyss (quoted in Bell and Lyall, 2002: 23). New Zealand has especially developed new performances of the abyss. There is an accelerating sublime where it is said: 'Nature provides a site in which tourists indulge their dreams of mastery over the earth; of being adventure heroes starring in their own movies' as they seek to cheat death (Bell and Lyall, 2002: 22). New Zealand is where 'glorious vistas' provide appropriate locations for the dynamic consumption of the 'accelerated sublime'. This is how 'New Zealand packages landscape for consumption' (Bell and Lyall, 2002: 36). Other 'youngish' tourists put their body into 'playful risk' when chemically raving through the night and early morning (as in Goa and Ibiza) or drinking to excess (as in many package tours targeted at partying youths).

Finally, in this new century are the (imagined) risks and corporeal fears of terrorism and the widespread surveillance gaze that these risks and fears generate in the built environment. ETA terrorists in the Basque country especially targeted tourist areas such as their plan to bomb the Bilbao Guggenheim Museum. They used bombs directed against tourists as key in their campaign to secure Basque independence. But terrorism is increasingly global. Global terrorism seeks to challenge the global power of the USA and its allies, especially those in the Middle East. In this new world disorder, places that attract western tourists are the new target. Tourists are in the front line of this global warfare, as incidents in Cairo, Luxor, New York, Bali, Mombassa, Jakarta and Kashmir illustrate. Tourist places attract deadly visits from those seeking the mass sacrificial deaths of others. As one commentator wrote: 'The Bombs in Spain Fall Mainly on the Tourists' (http://slate.msn.com/id/112743/; accessed 02.12.10). Potential death and the fear of death now stalk many tourist places.

Tourist places can thus attract tourists *and* terrorists. Some of the time terrorists are tourists, intermittently transmuting into terrorists. The weapon of the weak is fear, to induce panic into those 'innocent tourists' playing away, doing what they are meant to do. 'The new fear is bound up with radical uncertainty. Terror hits randomly ... the new terror is blind and diffuse' (Diken and Laustsen, 2005: 2). And yet it often hits the spaces of travellers and tourists. The new fear is like an epidemic, potentially striking at the airport, on the plane, at the hotel, in the nightclub, on the beach, at the petrol station, on the tourist bus, in the underground. To be a tourist is to be in the front line of the war on terrorism, potentially to die. In some sense at least, 'Bin Laden has already won; his victory consists of creating an all-consuming fear' (Diken and Laustsen, 2005: 14). This all-consuming fear is particularly evident in airports, those gateways of international tourism.

This new invisible enemy generates new forms of sophisticated 'panoptic sorting'. International tourists need exceptionally refined systems of surveillance in order to keep them on the move. In the USA this requirement provoked an unprecedented event, the nationalising of airport security and the general development of control systems over the 550 million people who enter the USA *every* year (Diken and Laustsen, 2005: 3). The notion of inside and outside erodes; all are inside and outside simultaneously. Power, gazes and terror are everywhere. Indeed, tourists are now subject to the most intrusive monitoring, surveillance and regulation. In order to be a consumer in the global marketplace, tourists are subject to powerful and extensive systems and gazes of monitoring and regulation by the institutional gaze of corporations and states. Thus 'soft targets' of people 'playing' in tourist places are in the front line of the war on terror. And as both terrorists and tourists are 'on the move' and yet have to be kept 'apart', so gates, camps, sniffer dogs, cameras, face recognition biometric cameras, smart cards, iris recognition, satellites, listening bugs and Total Information Awareness are all part of the performances of contemporary travel and tourism. In order that one can enter paradise for a week, systems of personal security are morphing into a new Big Brother where gazing tourists are subject to omnipresent surveillance.

Cities and resorts increasingly share many characteristics with airports. New forms of surveillance, monitoring and regulation are being implemented as part of the global 'war on terror' in what has been called the 'frisk society'. Technologies trialled within airports move out to become mundane characteristics of cities and tourist resorts, places of fear and contingent ordering within the new world order. Hence, Martinotti writes that airports and the like 'are the places of the city we live in today. Non-places are nothing less than the typical places of the city of our times' (1999: 170; Cwerner et al., 2009). Airspaces are typical of those 'places' that the global order is ushering in, showing many overlaps and similarities with towns and cities around the world. It is increasingly difficult to distinguish between airspaces and other places. The exceptional camp of the airspace has become the rule. Not only do passengers increasing fly around the world but the systems of both movement and securitisation that make possible such travel also fly around, landing in many towns and cities. As Fuller and Harley state, 'the airport is the city of the future' especially when such cities are full of visitors, people from elsewhere who may or may not be 'just tourists' and need to be surveilled (2005: 48). It has been estimated that the average person in the UK is recorded over 300 times a day by CCTV cameras (Morgan and Pritchard, 2005). In Chapter 6 we argued that the *flâneur* was the forerunner of the tourist and that 'he' was able to be anonymous, to be in a liminal zone. But urban anonymity and liminality is now largely illusory in the face of the pervasive gaze of continuously running digitally based surveillance cameras:

> the all-seeing, pervasive gaze of the camera puts at risk the opportunities for anonymity that the public sphere has traditionally aimed to provide. Sophisticated CCTV systems ... coupled with databases and/ or automatic identification software, unobtrusively register individuals and their movements – even in spaces and situations wherein one may legitimately expect to be an anonymous, unidentified member of the public. (Dubbeld, 2003: 158)

Tourists are now routinely captured by and subject to a powerful digital panoptic machine justified by the perceived risks of crime, violence and terrorism.

And at the same time places of terror become new places upon which to gaze. So Ground Zero or the Falls and Shankhill Roads in Belfast are now on the tourist map, waiting for visitors to come (in Belfast there is a 'Troubles Tour'). Places of death transmute into places for visitors, appearing on ever-new tourist itineraries, part of the consumption practices of dark tourism. In the aftermath of September 11 there were calls for American 'patriotic tourism', to make sure that Americans got on those planes and went to places to play, to show the enemy that they could not win, that the fear of death could be defeated. As noted, a record number of tourists flocked to New York in the aftermath of September 11.

Positional Competition

We now turn to some other bads generated by the globalised tourist gaze. We consider first the generation of congestion, overcrowding and local environmental degradation, topics of debate since the 1960s in much of the 'west'. Mishan wrote of 'the conflict of interest … between, on the one hand, the tourists, tourist agencies, traffic industries and ancillary services … and all those who care about preserving natural beauty on the other' (1969: 140). He cites Lake Tahoe, whose plant and animal life was destroyed by sewage generated by the hotels built along its banks. There are countless other examples of such localised environmental damage caused by tourism development, especially documented by NGOs such as Tourism Concern (http://tourismconcern.org.uk/; accessed 11.06.10).

Mishan maintains that there is a conflict of interest between present and future generations stemming from how travel and tourism are costed. The cost of the marginal tourist takes no account of the additional congestion costs that they impose. These congestion costs include the generally undesirable effects of overcrowded beaches, a lack of peace and quiet, the noise of air flights, the destruction of the scenery, the damage to plant and animal life and so on (Verbeek, 2009). Moreover, many tourists will know that there is nothing to be gained from delaying a visit to the place in question. Indeed, there is a strong incentive to go as soon as possible – to enjoy the unspoilt gaze before the crowds get there. Thus 'the tourist trade, in a competitive scramble to uncover all places of once quiet repose, of wonder, beauty and historic interest to the money-flushed multitude, is in effect literally and irrevocably destroying them' (Mishan, 1969: 141). Especially, Mishan says the 'young and gullible' are taken in by fantasies dreamt up by the tourist industry (one wonders what his views of contemporary Ibiza or Goa might be: D'Andrea, 2007).

The spread of mass tourism does not democratise travel. Tourism is an illusion which destroys the very places being visited. This is because geographical space is limited. Mishan says: 'what a few may enjoy in freedom the crowd necessarily destroys for itself' (1969: 142). Unless international agreement is reached, the next generation will inherit a world almost bereft of places of 'undisturbed natural beauty' (1969: 142). Mishan perceptively advocated the banning of all international air travel! Allowing the market to develop without regulation destroys the very places which are the objects of the tourist gaze.

Beckerman clarified two points here (1974: 50–2). First, concern for the effects of mass tourism is basically a 'middle-class' anxiety (like much other environmental concern); and second, most groups affected by mass tourism do in fact benefit from some aspects of it, including pioneer visitors who find services available that would have been unobtainable.

However, key here is Hirsch's thesis on the social limits to growth and the positional economy (1978). He notes that individual liberation through the exercise of consumer choice does not make those choices liberating for all because of the positional economy. All aspects of goods, services, work, positions and other social relationships are scarce or subject to congestion or crowding. Competition is therefore zero-sum: as any one person consumes more of the good in question, so someone else consumes less or gains less satisfaction. Supply cannot be increased, unlike material goods where economic growth can generate more. People's consumption of positional goods is *relational*. The satisfaction derived by each individual is not infinitely expandable but depends upon one's own consumption compared with that of others. There is 'coerced competition' where people do not really have a choice. They have to participate and consume more even though at the end of the consumption process no one is better off; that is: 'one has to run faster in order to stay still' (see Schwartz, 2004).

Much tourism demonstrates this positional competition. The Mediterranean coastline is absolutely scarce and one person's consumption is at the expense of someone else. Also there are many holiday destinations which are consumed not because they are intrinsically superior but because they convey taste or superior status. For Europeans, the Far East would be current examples, although these will change as mass-tourist patterns themselves alter. Further, there are many tourist sites where people's satisfaction depends upon the degree of congestion. Hirsch quotes a middle-class professional who remarked that the development of cheap charter flights to such a previously 'exotic' country means that: 'Now that I can afford to come here I know that it will be ruined' (1978: 167).

However, in this book we have shown that it is unclear just what is meant by consumption in much tourism. Is it the ability to gaze at a particular object if necessary in the company of many others? Or is it to be able to gaze without others being present? Or is it to be able to rent accommodation for a short period with a view of the object close at hand? Or is it the ability to own property with a view of the object nearby? The problem arises because of the centrality of the 'gaze' within tourism. The scarcities involved in tourism are complex. One strategy of the tourism industry has been to build new developments which permit greatly increased numbers to gaze upon the same object, such as all bedrooms in a hotel having a 'sea view' or cruise ships redesigned so all rooms look outwards.

There is a further important distinction here relating to scarcity. We can distinguish between the physical carrying capacity of a tourist place and a place's visual capacity (Walter, 1982). With physical carrying capacity it is clear when a mountain path literally cannot take any more walkers since it erodes and disappears. Nevertheless, there are thousands of other mountain paths that can be walked along and so the physical scarcity only applies to *this* path leading to this view, not to all paths along all mountains.

The notion of visual capacity changes this. Walter is concerned here with the subjective quality of the tourist experience (1982: 296). Although the path may still be physically passable, it no longer signifies the pristine wilderness upon which the visitor had expected to gaze. Thus its visual carrying capacity has been reached, but not its physical capacity. Walter cites the example of an Alpine mountain. As a material good the mountain can be viewed for its grandeur, beauty and conformity to the idealised Alpine horn. There is almost no limit to this good. However, the same mountain can be viewed as a positional good, as a shrine to nature that people wish to enjoy in solitude or in a small team without other tourists being present. Such solitary 'consumption' demonstrates supposedly good taste (see Bourdieu, 1984). This is a 'romantic' tourist gaze in which people expect solitude, privacy and a personal, semi-spiritual relationship with the object of the gaze (see Chapters 2 and 8).

Barthes characterises this in the *Guide Bleu* as 'this bourgeois promoting of the mountains, this old Alpine myth ... only mountains, gorges, defiles and torrents … seem to encourage morality of effort and solitude' (1972: 74). Walter discusses a good example of the romantic gaze, namely, Stourhead Park in Wiltshire, which illustrates:

> the romantic notion that the self is found not in society but in solitudinous contemplation of nature. Stourhead's garden is the perfect romantic landscape, with narrow paths winding among the trees and rhododendrons, grottoes, temples, a gothic cottage, all this around a much indented lake. … The garden is designed to be walked around in wonderment at Nature and the presence of other people immediately begins to impair this. (1982: 298)

By contrast, the 'collective' tourist gaze is not like this. Walter describes a different Wiltshire house and garden, Longleat where there is:

> a large stately home, set in a Capability Brown park; trees were deliberately thinned … so that you can see the park from the house, and house from the park. Indeed the house is the focal point of the park … the brochure lists twenty-eight activities and facilities. … All this activity and the resulting crowds fit sympathetically into the tradition of the stately home: essentially the life of the aristocratic was public rather than private. (1982: 198)

This house was designed as a public place; other people make such a place. The collective gaze thus necessitates large numbers of other people, as were once found in the English seaside resorts discussed in Chapter 2. Other people provide atmosphere, indicating that this is *the* place to be. We have also noted that this is also the case in major cities, whose uniqueness is their cosmopolitan character. It is the presence of people from all over the world (tourists in other words) that gives capital cities their distinct excitement. Large numbers of other tourists do not only generate congestion, as the positional good argument would suggest (see Chapter 8).

Thus Hirsch's arguments about positional competition mainly apply to tourism characterised by the romantic gaze as well as the anthropological gaze. Where the mediatised gaze and collective gaze are to be found and performed there is less of a problem of crowding and congestion. And indeed Hirsch's argument rests on the notion that there are only a limited number of objects which can be viewed by the tourist. Yet in recent years, as described in this book, there has been an enormous increase in the objects of the tourist gaze, far beyond Mishan's 'undisturbed natural beauty'. Part of the reason for this increase is that contemporary tourists are often *collectors* of gazes and appear less interested in repeat visits to the same site.

We have discussed how the contemporary tourist gaze is increasingly signposted, identifying the things and places worthy of one's gaze. Such signposting identifies a relatively small number of tourist nodes so concentrating most tourists within limited areas. Walter says 'the sacred node provides a positional good that is destroyed by democratisation' (1982: 302). He favours the view that there are 'gems to be found everywhere and in everything ... there is no limit to what you will find' (Walter, 1982: 302). We should, he says, get away from the tendency to construct the tourist gaze at a few selected sacred sites, and be more catholic in the objects at which we gaze. This has somewhat occurred in recent years, particularly with the development of industrial, rural and heritage tourism, film-induced tourism and adventure tourism, as examined above. However, Walter's analysis of the class character of the romantic gaze is persuasive:

> professional opinion-formers (brochure writers, teachers, Countryside Commission staff, etc.) are largely middle class and it is within the middle class that the romantic desire for positional goods is largely based. Romantic solitude thus has influential sponsors and gets good advertising. By contrast, the largely working class enjoyment of conviviality, sociability and being part of a crowd is often looked down upon by those concerned to conserve the environment. This is unfortunate, because it ... exalts an activity that is available only to the privileged. (Walter, 1982: 303; see also Butcher, 2003)

So there are complex connections between congestion, taste and place. Those who value solitude and a romantic gaze do not see this as merely *one* way of regarding nature. Rather they attempt to make everyone sacralise nature in the same way (see Wood and House, 1991, on the 'good tourist' and, by contrast, Butcher's critique of the 'new moral tourism': 2003). Romanticism involved in the early emergence of mass tourism has become widespread and generalised. The more its adherents proselytise its virtues to others, the more this in effect undermines the romantic gaze: 'the romantic tourist is digging his [*sic*] own grave if he seeks to evangelize others to his own religion' (Walter, 1982: 301). The romantic gaze is an important mechanism thus helping to spread tourism on a global scale, drawing almost every country into its ambit as the romantic seeks ever-new objects of that solitary and lonely gaze. This includes more recently eco-tourism developments, such as eco-lodges located within virgin rainforests or upon islands in the Great Barrier Reef, which demonstrate 'environmental good taste'. Positional competition is thus a powerful mechanism for spreading tourism worldwide.

In the next section we turn to a different critique of tourism and a different set of risks. Positional competition and the romantic gaze are part of the process by which another risk is being generated, a risk that may turn out to be very powerful in its effects. This is that global tourism is centrally implicated in the using up of a crucial resource, not of 'natural beauty', but of the energy used to move, build, heat, cool and entertain all those billions of visitors moving around the world. Those visitors do not pay the full costs of the oil especially, or its carbon consequences, which actually seem to make the world go round (see Elliott and Urry, 2010).

Oil

Today's global economy and society is deeply dependent upon, and embedded into, abundant cheap oil. Most industrial, agricultural, commercial, domestic and consumer systems are built around the plentiful supply of oil that is remarkably versatile, convenient and was, during the twentieth century, cheap. Without it there would be no global tourism and corporeal tourist gaze. 'Oil powers virtually all movement of people, materials, foodstuffs, and manufactured goods – inside our countries and around the world' (Homer-Dixon, 2006: 81). It became vital to virtually everything that *moves* on the planet (Kunstler, 2006). The world-wide transport sector has a dependency on oil of at least 95 per cent. There has been an annual average growth rate of oil production of more than 2 per cent (Leggett, 2005: 21). 'Cheap' oil lubricates most areas of social, industrial, military and commercial life. Oil is, moreover, bound up with dirty politics (Bower, 2009). Central to its development has been the power of its vested interests. Leggett describes the 'Empire of Oil' as more powerful than most nation-states (2005: 12, 15; Bower, 2009). We can talk of the 'carbon military-industrial complex' that seeks to develop and extend major carbon-based systems, such as the car system; the developing of distant, specialised leisure and tourism sites visited from afar; and aeromobility with its multiple airspaces. These complex interests directly and indirectly fund climate change scepticism and lobbying against regulation and intervention in energy markets (Urry, 2011). Apart from Norway, most oil states are authoritarian, corrupt and highly unequal. Such states are the indirect source of much terrorism throughout the world and especially in the Middle East.

Oil was central to the twentieth century, but it is now both running out and contributes massively to rising carbon emissions and hence to changing climates. The peak oil hypothesis states that extracting oil reserves has a beginning, a middle and an end. And at some point it reaches a maximum, with the peak occurring when around half the potential oil has been extracted. After this peak, oil becomes more difficult and expensive to extract. Oil production typically follows a bell-shaped curve. This does not mean that oil suddenly runs out, but the supply of oil drops and prices rise, sometimes dramatically in the form of spikes as in the middle years of the 2000s. After peak oil, the extraction process within a particular field becomes very much less profitable. Some suggest that global peak oil occurred as early as the late 1990s. Others estimate that it peaked in 2004 or 2005 (Deffeyes, 2005; Strahan, 2007). More optimistic predictions, such as that of the International Energy Agency, locate peak oil in the 2020s.

The largest oilfields were discovered over half a century ago, with the peak of oil *discovery* being 1965. There have been no really vast discoveries since the 1970s. Three to four barrels of oil are now consumed for every new one that is discovered. The peaking of oil in the USA, which is where the global addiction to oil-based car and air transport first developed, occurred in 1970. So over the long term oil will be increasingly expensive and there will be frequent shortages because of falls in its *per capita* availability. There is not enough oil to fuel worldwide systems of global travel and consumption that need, with 'business as usual', to double by 2050 (Homer-Dixon, 2006: 174). Thus 'industrial civilization is based on the consumption of energy resources that are inherently limited in quantity, and that are about to become scarce ... in the end, it may be impossible for even a single nation to sustain industrialism as we have known it during the twentieth century' (Heinberg, 2005: 1).

Thus the 'petroleum interval' in human history could turn out to be only a brief (twentieth) century or so of Easy Oil. Oil supplies are concentrated among few countries and this increases the likelihood of uneven and problematic supplies. And oil interests, both corporations and states, consistently exaggerate the size of their reserves, upon whose estimates official global figures depend. And there is the fastest-growing economy in the world. From 1999 to 2004 China's oil imports doubled. Peak-oil researcher Kunstler estimates that at the current rate of growth in demand China will consume 100 per cent of the currently available world exports of oil within ten years. And this assumes no growth in demand elsewhere in the world and no fall off in global production (Kunstler, 2006: 84).

Not having sufficient oil to sustain rising levels of global economic growth, travel and consumption will generate significant economic downturns, resource wars and lower population levels. The probable peaking of oil has *already* had major economic and social consequences that could be a harbinger of the future. The worldwide economic and financial crash of 2008 was partly activated by the speculative building and risky funding of extensive tracts of 'marginal' suburbs and related shopping and leisure developments within the USA. The oil-surplus period of the late 1980s and early 1990s led to oil trading at only $10 per barrel (in 1998). But by mid-2008, the price per barrel of oil rose to over $135. This led many of those suburbs and related leisure facilities to be no longer viable since residents could not continue to live there; and this flight from the suburbs had the direst of knock-on effects upon the financial system worldwide.

As oil prices peaked banks collapsed and had to be bailed out. Various consequences for travel were that airlines began to file for bankruptcy, car manufacturers recorded reduced sales, especially of larger models (13 per cent decline in 2009), the USA was no longer the world's largest car market as iconic firms filed for bankruptcy, slower driving speeds were recorded around the world, Detroit looked increasingly like a bombed-out city, many speculative leisure and tourism developments folded, and international travel and tourism plummeted (see Dennis and Urry, 2009; Urry, 2011).

The main exception to this is China as both destination and as source of both domestic and especially international tourist. Here, in 2006, an editorial in the *China Daily* exhorted the Chinese to 'unleash consumption' and this not only generated the world's largest car market, but also hugely increased the number of Chinese visitors worldwide. China has in 30 years come to be central to global tourism, although during the Maoist period up to the mid-1970s mobility was seen as a bourgeois vice. Many destinations across the globe report that they are redesigning themselves to cater for Chinese visitors, the numbers having increased fivefold since the beginning of the new century. Such developments can be seen in Bali where the carvings on statues are now of Buddhist rather than Hindu gods, in France where Chinese tourists are the largest category of visitors, in the USA where Marriott hotels are introducing Chinese breakfasts, and especially in Hong Kong and Macao where post-socialist Chinese tourists are learning to develop consuming bodies within hotels, casinos, shopping centres, arcades and so on (see Simpson, 2009; Anderlini, 2010; Nyíri, 2010, on the new cultures of Chinese mobility).

So tourism uses much oil, this oil props up unequal and corrupt regimes, such regimes generate terrorism, and so the tourists are at risk of being bombed in those tourist sites that are intermittently visited by terrorists. Oil makes the world go round, but this is a world of both tourism and terrorism. And that lubrication of the world through oil may well be slowing down. Travel is likely to become increasingly expensive, which makes the long-term growth in international tourism less likely.

Climate Change

On top of the peaking of oil there are the likely future consequences of climate change. Twentieth-century capitalism seems to have resulted in global temperatures rising by at least 0.8°C. This appears to result from higher levels of greenhouse gases in the earth's atmosphere (IPCC, 2007; Stern, 2007). Greenhouse gases trap the sun's rays. As a result of this 'greenhouse' effect the earth warms. Moreover, such greenhouse gas levels and world temperatures will significantly further increase over the next few decades. With 'business as usual' and no significant reductions in high carbon systems, especially of travel, the stock of greenhouse gases could treble by the end of the century. The Stern Review states that average temperatures may rise within a few decades from between 3°C and a staggering 10°C (rather than the 6°C most analysts suggest). There could be a 5–20 per cent reduction in world consumption levels (Stern, 2007: 3). Even a temperature worldwide increase of 3°C overall is beyond human experience and would change temperature patterns, rainfall, crops, animals and life worldwide.

The scientific evidence for climate change is less uncertain than when the first Intergovernmental Panel on Climate Change (IPCC) Report appeared in 1990. By the 2007 Report the IPCC declared that the warming of the world's climate is now 'unequivocal', based upon extensive observations of increases in global average air and ocean temperatures, widespread melting of snow and ice and rising global average sea levels. The Report further shows that carbon dioxide is the most important of the human-produced or anthropogenic greenhouse gases. Its concentration levels exceed by far the natural range identified over the past 650,000 years. Carbon dioxide's high and rising levels thus stem from 'non-natural' causes. There are many elements of global warming: an increase in arctic temperatures, the reduced size of icebergs, the melting of icecaps and glaciers, a reduced permafrost, changes in rainfall, reduced bio-diversity, new wind patterns, droughts, heat waves, tropical cyclones and other extreme weather events (Lovelock, 2006; Pearce, 2006; Lynas, 2007; Monbiot, 2007).

Through the IPCC, the organised actions of thousands of scientists around the globe have transformed public debate and this is even reflected in various movies, including *The Day after Tomorrow* (2004), *An Inconvenient Truth* (2006) and *The Age of Stupid* (2009). The Pentagon announced that climate change will result in a global catastrophe, costing millions of lives in wars and natural disasters and is a much greater threat to global stability than terrorism.

However, there is still significant uncertainty as to the scale, impact and speed of future climate change over the next century. The Global Climate Models used to predict rates of greenhouse gases and temperature increases contain many 'unknowns'. The IPCC Reports are based on reaching a complex scientific and political consensus and thus do not factor in all the potential and uncertain feedback effects. These feedback effects in turn depend upon whether people will fly, drive cars, travel in high-speed trains, go to mega-events such as World Cups, heat/air condition their homes/ hotels, desalinate their water or develop space tourism (see recent carbon footprint calculations of all these in Berners Lee, 2010). If they do, temperatures will increase; and as temperatures increase over the next few decades, these will probably trigger *further* temperature rises as the earth's environmental systems cannot absorb the original increases. The most dramatic of these positive feedbacks would involve the whole or partial melting of Greenland's ice cap. Climate change thus produces further climate change. Recent ice core research shows that in previous glacial and inter-glacial periods abrupt and rapid changes occurred in the earth's temperature. Earth does not engage in gradual change (Pearce, 2007). Rapid changes have been the norm not the exception. Moreover, temperatures at the time of the last Ice Age were only 5°C colder than they are now. And in the Arctic recent increases in temperature have been really marked, with feedbacks creating local warming of 3–5°C over the past thirty years.

Thus various diverse yet interconnected changes within the earth's environmental systems could create a vicious circle of accumulative disruption. The World Health Organization calculated as early as 2000 that over 150,000 deaths are caused each year by climate change. The planet will endure, but many forms of human habitation, especially those that involve being regularly and extensively 'on the move', may not. And the first places to disappear may be those tourist resorts built on or by the beach, including the Maldives where plans to relocate their population from the islands are already advanced (Amelung, Nicholls and Viner, 2007; Becken and Hay, 2007).

In the next section we briefly consider what the world and tourism may be like in 2050, given the interdependence between declining availability of oil (and gas), changing climates and continued huge growth in population. Will there still be a powerful tourist gaze by the middle of this century (see Smart, 2010; Urry, 2011: ch. 9)? We consider three scenarios for 2050.

Futures

The first possibility for 2050 is a future of hypermobility and hyper-tourist consumption. Resource shortages and the effects of climate change actually turn out to be less significant, at least for those in the rich North whose patterns of movement and consuming food, objects, places and services gets even more extensive, frequent and utterly part of their 'persona'.

This is a 'hyper' world, people are 'always on', with messages and individual media continuously streamed to miniature intelligent devices, especially when 'on the move', which people would be much of the day and night. Average citizens are travelling four to five hours a day, so overcoming the notion of a constant and limited travel time. New kinds of fuel and vehicles overcome limits of space and time. Personalised air travel would be common through the use of third-generation biofuels or hydrogen. Cars would be unfashionably stuck on the ground as a Corbusier-inspired future beckons everyone to the skies, including regular flights into space with Virgin Galactica. Regular trips into at least inner space would be common. The final frontier would indeed be overcome as space tourism is privatised and the long decline of the idea of space travel comes to be reversed (Dickens and Ormrod, 2007: ch. 5).

In this scenario most people study elsewhere, they migrate frequently, they regularly meet and re-meet with family, they often see long lost friends, they go shopping on the other side of the world, and some go on holidays to the moon. Because people seek to do these things with other people who are geographically distant and are themselves constantly moving, so they travel and communicate very frequently and over very long distances. There is an enormous burden of fast travel and constant communications in order to keep up with colleagues, friends and family. Underlying this scenario is the way that social status is derived from high levels of extraordinary consumerism and especially from long-distance machine-based movement and the discovery of new tourist sites. It is presumed here that fast travel and the tourist gaze remain powerful 'positional goods'. Consumption here is conspicuous so that the fast car, access to a private plane or ownership of a holiday apartment are meant to be seen, commented upon and generative of status. Travelling long distances and having far-flung connections with those in other societies are the major bases of status, except of course for those who are forced to be migrants or exiles.

Electronic communications do not *substitute* for physical travel but enhance it and provide further ways in which consumption is made conspicuous and enhancing of status. In this highly connected world, social life and work are intense, and the boundaries between them blurred. Even low-paid service workers are so used to being 'always available' and holidays are no longer a break. This is a 'Star Trek' vision of the future with many on 'holiday' much of the time.

The second scenario is what many environmentalists argue for, namely a worldwide reconfiguration of economy and society around the idea of 'local sustainability'. This Schumacher model would involve a network of self-reliant (and probably also semi-isolated) communities in which most people would live, work and mostly recreate. This involves a dramatic global shift towards lifestyles more local and smaller in scale. Friends would have to be chosen from neighbouring streets, families would not move away at times of new household composition, work would be found nearby, walking, cycling and public transport replace cars and planes, education would be sought only in local schools and colleges, the seasons would determine which and when foodstuffs were produced and consumed, most goods and services would be simpler and produced nearby, and almost all travel would be localised with very little 'tourism' as such.

It would be unfashionable to live and bring up children in anything apart from such 'compact cities' or undertake travel to faraway places, especially for tourist pleasure. Status attributions would be re-localised and long-distance mobility would be a positional bad, not a good. This scenario depends upon new kinds of 'friendship', on choosing to know mostly those who live close by and can be walked or cycled to. People would be unperturbed by a lack of long-distance travel and connection. Long-distance travel and forms of mass tourism based on 'choice' and 'convenience', cars and planes, would be uncommon and a source of low status.

Kunstler predicts that the twenty-first century will be much more about staying put than about going to other places (2006). In an extreme post-peak oil scenario, cars would be a luxury, creating resentment among those unable to drive. This could lead to vehicles being vandalised or drivers subject to abuse. Kunstler maintains that the future will involve comprehensive downscaling, downsizing, re-localising and the radical reorganisation of lifestyles. He states that:

> Anyway one might imagine it, the transportation picture in the mid-twenty-first century will be very different from the fiesta of mobility we have enjoyed for the past fifty years. It will be characterized by austerity and a return to smaller scales of operation in virtually every respect of travel, tourism and transport. It will compel us to make the most of our immediate environments. (Kunstler 2006: 270)

Many forms of life are locally centred and concentrated. Because much movement is local, so feet, the bicycle and new low-carbon forms of transport are found alongside some motorised forms.

This scenario could develop in response to dramatically decreased availability of cheap energy and increased global contestation. Intense economic crisis could generate a global push towards local sustainability and a local sense of place with a marked *de*-globalisation of the tourist gaze except through virtual travel on the internet. Values of community and eco-responsibility could come to be viewed as more valued than those of consumerism and unrestrained tourism mobility. As a result, many international tourism systems, of places and transport, would fade away.

In the third scenario, climate change, oil, gas and water shortages and intermittent wars would lead to the substantial breakdown of many of the mobility, energy and communication connections that now straddle the world and are the ambivalent legacy of the twentieth century. In this decivilising future there would be a plummeting standard of living, a re-localisation of mobility patterns, an increasing emphasis upon local 'warlords', relatively weak national or global forms of governance and little tourist travel because of risks and environmental and cultural bads. There would be no monopoly of physical coercion in the hands of legitimate national states. Tribal and other wars within countries would be increasingly common, making travel and tourism hazardous.

It is likely that many infrastructural systems would begin to collapse and there would be increasing separation of production and consumption between different regions. These 'warlords' would control recycled forms of mobility and weaponry, with increasingly localised recycling of bikes, cars, trucks and phone systems. Much of the time they would not be working. Cars and trucks would rust away in the deserts or would be washed away in floods. Certain consequences of climate change may partially rectify themselves as oil and other resource use declines and overall world population would plummet (see recent post-oil 'warlord' dystopias Sarah Hall's *The Carhullan Army*, 2007, and Marcel Theroux's *Far North*, 2009).

Systems of secure long-range mobility and tourism would disappear except for the super-rich who will congregate in 'policed' enclaves or camps. As in the medieval epoch, long-distance travel would be risky and probably not undertaken unless armed. Mass tourism would disappear. The rich would travel mainly in the air in armed helicopters or light aircraft. Each warlord-dominated region would potentially be at war with their neighbours, especially for control of water, oil and gas. With extensive flooding, especially of the seaside places of twentieth-century excess, extreme weather events and the break-up of long-distance oil and gas pipelines, these resources would be fought over and defended by armed gangs. Some cars and trucks will remain but they would mainly be rusting versions from previous decades. Enormous efforts and skills need to be deployed to keep these wrecks moving and to stop them being commandeered. The use and re-use of cars in current developing societies indicates the kind of improvisational, tinkering car culture that would probably develop.

The movie *Mad Max 2* depicts this future of a bleak, dystopian, impoverished society facing a breakdown of civil order resulting from oil shortages and where power rests with those able to improvise new mobilities, including short-term flight. Under this scenario, life, as already prefigured in parts of the poor South of the world, would be less mobile, and nasty, brutish and 'shorter'.

None of these scenarios is simply desirable and without cost for the tourism industry and especially for the wider society. The perpetual-motion future is rendered doubtful because of the lack of future energy source and the many dire consequences of carbon emissions. The second future could only support a much smaller population worldwide, while the third would involve many lives that would be nasty, brutish and short. In order to overcome deficiencies of each of these scenarios there are various strategies that should be developed (see Smart, 2010, for related arguments).

First, we need somehow to dispense with the 'exotic gaze' which drives so much contemporary tourism and instead favour discourses, schemes and funding which develop what we might term a 'local gaze', to keep people *in* places rather than roaming across the globe. And when people do travel longer distances, this need to be undertaken collectively and where possible by sustainable higher-speed trains. Relatedly, we need to reduce the scale of signposting so that people instead search out and find 'treasures' that are within their 'backyard', not imagining that the exotic and distant is necessarily better. Somehow the effects of the internet need to be focused upon revealing the pleasures of the nearby and yet also developing software and experiences that can substitute corporeal travel with virtual travel. Overall, localised patterns of visiting and meetings should be rediscovered and this would be facilitated by a more general rejection of the idea of the tourist gaze, or what Heidegger refers to as an object 'ready to hand for the viewer' (Smith, 2009: 627). Also what needs development are forms of virtual meetingness that effectively substitute all or at least most of the emotional pleasures of being present with others face-to-face, body-to-body, or being in some other place or event. The internet and Web 2.0 need to strengthen localness and no longer global choice and corporeal travel. Further, the power of carbon interests needs to be radically offset through taxing and regulation while 'public' transport and new sustainable forms of 'personal' transport needs much funding and subsidising. This is probably the most challenging of requirements in a world of enduring neo-liberal capitalism. And paralleling this would be, for planning and architectural guidelines, to favour place distinctiveness and low-carbon, bicycle- and pedestrian-friendly cities rather than placelessness, de-localised postmodern theming (discussed in Chapter 6) and 'automobility dominated cities' within contemporary design and planning (Dennis and Urry, 2009, develops this kind of innovation in detail).

But it could just be that the perpetual-motion future is already on a slippery slope to something else. In the twentieth century one place in particular symbolised such a place of motion and excessive consumption and its rise and it potential fall may index something important about the future of tourist places and the tourist gaze worldwide (although it may just be like the normal rise and fall of tourists resorts, as discussed in Chapter 2).

Dubai

In the epoch since the 1980s, what some call neo-liberalism, many new design- and-themed places of tourism and consumption excess developed, some of which were examined in Chapter 6. Davis and Monk (2007) provocatively refer to these places as 'evil paradises', examples including Arg-e Jadid, a Californian oasis in the Iranian desert; the $40 billion 2008 Olympics in Beijing; Palm Springs gated community in Hong Kong; Sandton in Johannesburg; Dubai; Las Vegas; and Macao. The last of these involves a $25 billion investment oriented to providing leisured gambling for the 1.3 billion Chinese (Simpson, 2010).

These are places of high carbon 'consumption'. Their speculative development is often only made possible by large infrastructural projects involving celebrity architects. The associated new transport systems are typically paid for by public money. Building such places involves the profligate consumption of water, oil, power and building materials in order to build on reclaimed land (Macao, Dubai) or in the desert (Las Vegas, Gran Scala, Abu Dhabi). Such sites are highly commercialised with many simulated environments, more 'real' than the original from which they are copied. Gates, often digitised, prevent the entry and exit of local people and those visitors who do not have signs of good credit. Norms of behaviour are unregulated by family/neighbourhood with bodies being subject to many forms commodifying experience. Such themed places are beyond control by the neighbourhood with unregulated modes of consumption and only pleasure and not guilt unless insufficient consumption occurs. Indeed, these places are sites of potential mass addiction of especially gambling, alcohol, over-eating and related forms of criminality. Such zones come to be globally known for their consumption excess and for the huge flows of visitors and often workers.

In the last years of the last century and in the early years of this century Dubai has been the leading exemplar of such excess. Drilling for oil began there in 1966 but relatively soon the oil began to run out and a gigantic tourist, leisure, sporting, real-estate and consumption economy replaced it. Instead of being an oil producer, over 90 per cent of Dubai's revenue is now non-oil related (Davidson, 2008: 1). It is a huge consumer of oil. This is used to build islands, hotels and attractions in what has been the world's largest building site, to transport in and out very large numbers of visitors and workers, and to provide spectacular cooled environments for visitors where average temperatures are over 40°C. Dubai thus consumes energy, including for the air conditioners blowing full blast into the open air to make gardens cooler and for the indoor ski resort where sub-zero temperatures are maintained in the middle of a desert, even in summer. Not surprisingly, Dubai ranks just second in the global league table of per capita carbon emissions, beaten only by its neighbour, Qatar (see Schmid, 2009, for much detail here).

The Dubai skyline reveals dozens of megaprojects on the go. These include two palm-island developments extending the coastline by

120 kilometres; a string of new islands shaped like the world; vast shopping complexes; a domed ski resort and other major sports venues; the world's tallest building, the Burj Khalifa; the world's largest hotel, the Asia-Asia with 6,500 rooms; and the world's first 7-star hotel, the Burj Al Arab with 100-mile views (Davis and Monk, 2007; Davidson, 2008; Schmid, 2009). This is a place of monumental excess needing massive amounts of oil. It had been Dubai's ambition to be the number one luxury-consumer paradise, especially for Middle Eastern and South Asian visitors. As such, 'it must ceaselessly strive for visual and environmental excess' (Davis, 2007: 52). Dubai has achieved this through architectural gigantism and perfectibility, with many massive simulacra for play, the Hanging Gardens of Babylon, the Taj Mahal, the Pyramids, and a snow mountain, simulacra more perfect than any original. This is a place of over-consumption, of shopping, eating, drinking, prostitution and gambling. Guilt in what is nominally an Islamic country is not to consume to the 'limit'. And as befits a paradise of consumption, its official national holiday is the celebrated Shopping Festival, a month-long extravaganza. It is the iconic place of consumption excess for visitors and also rich locals. This was a place where nature could not be allowed stand in the way. If there were no beaches, beaches were made, crafting them so that the Gods could see the shape of a palm tree or a map of the world. So much money, so fast, it was impossible to keep up with Dubai and its overcoming the limits of nature in the most inhospitable of environments.

But the peaking of oil and the effects of climate change, with rising sea levels and turbulent weather, may mean that this Arabian Las Vegas will slide back into the sand from where it had come. This is like many other beach locations and resorts which also depend upon massive energy use but which could be washed away by rising sea levels and floods (Amelung, Nicholls and Viner, 2007). This was close to occurring in the highly successful if unequal tourist city of New Orleans in September 2005, a place also built by the sea and partially below sea level and threatened by extreme weather events. Hurricane Katrina showed what happens to those living in a major rich city when an extreme event washes away many resources of those forced to live near the sea. TV pictures showed how whole populations are 'disposable', with bloated corpses of the black poor displayed on the billion or so TV screens around the world. Katrina also showed the vulnerability of oil supply to localised flooding. The world's refineries were already working to maximum capacity and so were unable to raise production when the Mississippi refineries shut down and so shortages were common and oil prices soared. This in turn contributed to oil-price spikes in the mid-2000s that brought down many sub-prime mortgages and related financial instruments during 2008; and this meant that many real-estate tourist developments around the world stalled towards the end of the decade. It is typical of the tourist industry, however, that some of the locations of financial collapse are new sights of the tourist gaze, with one firm running a 'Scandals and Scoundrels Tour' around Wall St (Clark, 2010).

In that financial collapse the hubris that is Dubai would seem to be leading the way. Its astonishing growth has gone into reverse. Dubai did not actually make anything. Its money for all that building had been borrowed. The luxury was built on the backs of foreign workers, toiling away in forms of modern bondage hidden away from the tourist gaze. Over a million men and women from across Asia turned Dubai from a sleepy village into a shimmering Arabian Las Vegas. Expats now are fleeing and leaving their cars bought on credit at the airport, thousands of construction workers have been laid off, there is a predicted 60 per cent fall in property values, half the construction projects are on hold or cancelled, the population is shrinking and Dubai needed to be bailed out by a $10 billion loan from Abu Dhabi (www.cnn.com/2009/BUSINESS/12/14/dubai.10.billion.bailout/index.html; accessed 05.03.10). Journalist Paul Lewis pronounced: 'Too high, too fast: the party's over for Dubai' (2009; Schmid, 2009).

Is this history of the rise and fall of Dubai a forerunner of the history of the global present as in the next few decades the spreading of the tourist gaze comes to a shuddering halt or even a reversal beginning in an Arabian desert? Was the tourist gaze on a mass scale a feature of the twentieth-century hubris that will gradually disappear once the oil begins to run down and sea levels rise further? The decline and fall of Dubai may thus be the start of a much more general decline in the significance of the tourist gaze. Will there still be a relatively widespread and common 'tourist gaze' operating away in 2050?

Bibliography

Abercrombie, N. and Longhurst, B. (1998) *Audiences*. London: Sage.

Adams, M. K. (2004) 'The genesis of touristic imagery: politics and poetics in the creation of a remote Indonesian island destination', *Tourist Studies*, 4: 115–35.

Adey, P. (2006) 'Airports and air-mindednesss: spacing, timing and using Liverpool airport, 1918–39', *Social and Cultural Geography*, 7: 343–63.

Adey, P. (2010) *Aerial Life: Spaces, Mobilities, Affects*. London: Wiley-Blackwell.

Adkins, L. (1995) *Gendered Work*. Buckingham: Open University Press.

Adler, J. (1989) 'Origins of sightseeing', *Annals of Tourism Research*, 16: 7–29.

Ahmed, S. (2000) *Strange Encounters*. London: Routledge.

Albers, P. and James, W. (1983) 'Tourism and the changing photographic image of the Great Lakes Indians', *Annals of Tourism Research*, 10: 123–48.

Albers, P. and James, W. (1988) 'Travel photography: a methodological approach', *Annals of Tourism Research*, 15: 134–58.

Amelung, B., Nicholls, S. and Viner, D. (2007) 'Implications of global climate change for tourism flows and seasonality', *Journal of Travel Research*, 45: 285–96.

Anderlini, J. (2010) 'Chinese travellers change the face of tourism', *Financial Times*, 8 June.

Anderson, S. and Tabb, B. (eds) (2002) *Water, Leisure and Culture: European Historical Perspectives*. Oxford: Berg.

Andrews, H. (2005) 'Feeling at home: embodying Britishness in a Spanish charter tourist resort', *Tourist Studies*, 5: 247–66.

Andrews, M. (1989) *The Search for the Picturesque: Landscape, Aesthetics and Tourism in Britain, 1760–1800*. Aldershot: Scolar Press.

Arellano, A. (2004) 'Bodies, spirits and Incas: performing Machu Picchu', in M. Sheller and J. Urry (eds), *Tourism Mobilities*. London: Routledge. pp. 67–77.

Ateljevic, I. and Doorne, S. (2005) 'Dialectics of authentication: performing "exotic otherness" in a backpacker enclave of Dali, China', *Journal of Tourism and Cultural Change*, 3: 1–17.

Atkinson, J. (1984) 'Manpower strategies for flexible organisations', *Personnel Management*, August: 28–31.

Augé, M. (1995) *Non-Places*. London: Verso.

Bærenholdt, J. O. and Haldrup, M. (2004) 'On the track of the Vikings', in M. Sheller and J. Urry (eds), *Tourism Mobilities*. London: Routledge. pp. 78–89.

Bærenholdt, J. O., Haldrup, M., Larsen, J. and Urry, J. (2004) *Performing Tourist Places*. Aldershot: Ashgate.

Bagguley, P. (1991) 'Gender and labour flexibility in hotel and catering', *Services Industries Journal*, 10: 737–47.

Bagguley, P., Mark-Lawson, J., Shapiro, D., Urry, J., Walby, S. and Warde, A. (1989) 'Restructuring Lancaster', in P. Cooke (ed.), *Localities*. London: Unwin Hyman. pp. 129–65.

Bagguley, P., Mark-Lawson, J., Shapiro, D., Urry, J., Walby, S. and Warde, A. (1990) *Restructuring Place, Class and Gender*. London: Sage.

Ball, R. (1988) 'Seasonality: a problem for workers in the tourism labour market', *Service Industries Journal*, 8: 501–13.

Barnes, J. (1999) *England, England*. London: Picador.

Barrett, F. (1989a) *The Independent Guide to Real Holidays Abroad*. London: Independent.

Barrett, F. (1989b) 'Why the tour operators may face their last supper', *Independent*, 7 November.

Barthes, R. (1972) *Mythologies*. London: Jonathan Cape.

Barthes, R. (2000) *Camera Lucida*. London: Vintage.

Batchen, G. (1999) *Burning with Desire: The Conceptions of Photography*. London: MIT Press.

Bate, J. (1991) *Romantic Ecology: Wordsworth and the Environmental Tradition*. London: Routledge.

Baudrillard, J. (1983) *Simulations*. New York: Semiotext(e).

Baudrillard, J. (1985) 'The ecstacy of communication', in H. Foster (ed.), *Postmodern Culture*. London: Pluto Press. pp. 126–34.

Baudrillard, J. (1988) *America*. London: Verso.

Baum, T. (2007) 'Human resource in tourism: still waiting for change', *Progress in Tourism Management*, 28: 1383–99.

Bauman, Z. (1987) *Legislators and Interpreters*. Cambridge: Polity.

Bauman, Z. (1993) *Postmodern Ethics*. London: Routledge.

Bauman, Z. (1999) *Globalization: The Human Consequences*. Cambridge: Polity.

Bauman, Z. (2000) *Liquid Modernity*. Cambridge: Polity.

Bauman, Z. (2003) *Liquid Love*. Cambridge: Polity.

Beardsworth, A. and Bryman, A. (2001) 'The wild animal in late modernity: the case of the Disneyization of zoos', *Tourist Studies*, 1: 83–104.

Beaverstock, J., Derudder, B., Falconbridge, J. and Witlox, F. (eds) (2010) *International Business Travel in the Global Economy*. Aldershot: Ashgate.

Beck, U. (2002) *Risk Society*. London: Sage.

Beck, U. and Beck-Gernsheim, E. (1995) *The Normal Chaos of Love*. Cambridge: Polity.

Becken, S. and Hay, J. (2007) *Tourism and Climate Change*. London: Channel View.

Beckerman, W. (1974) *In Defence of Economic Growth*. London: Jonathan Cape.

Beer, D. and Burrows, R. (2007) 'Sociology and, of and in Web 2.0: some initial considerations', *Sociological Research Online*, 12(5), www.socresonline.org.uk/12/5/17.html (accessed 22.11.10).

Beeton, S. (2005) *Film-induced Tourism*. Chichester: Channel View.

Bell, C. and Lyall, J. (2002) 'The accelerated sublime: thrill-seeking adventure heroes in the commodified landscape', in S. Coleman and M. Crang (eds), *Tourism: Between Place and Performance*. New York: Berghahn. pp. 21–37.

Bell, D. (2007) 'The hospitable city: social relations in commercial spaces', *Progress in Human Geography*, 31: 7–22.

Benjamin, W. (1973) 'The work of art in the age of mechanical reproduction', in T. Bennett (ed.), *Illuminations*. London: Fontana. pp. 219–54.

Berger, J. (1972) *Ways of Seeing*. Harmondsworth: Penguin.

Berman, M. (1983) *All that is Solid Melts into Air*. London: Verso.

Berners Lee, M. (2010) *How Bad are Bananas?* London: Profile Books.

Bhabha, H. (ed.) (1990) *Nation and Narration*. London: Routledge.

Bianchi, V. R. (2000) 'Migrant tourist-workers: exploring the "contact zones" of post-industrial tourism', *Current Issues in Tourism*, 33: 107–37.

Billig, M. (1997) *Banal Nationalism*. London: Sage.

Blackbourn, D. (2002) 'Fashionable spa towns in nineteenth century Europe', in S. Anderson and B. Tabb (eds), *Water, Leisure and Culture*. Oxford: Berg. pp. 9–22.

Blau, J. (1988) 'Where architects work: a change analysis 1970–80', in P. Knox (ed.), *The Design Professions and the Built Environment*. London: Croom Helm. pp. 127–46.

Boden, D. and Molotch, H. (1994) 'The compulsion to proximity', in R. Friedland and D. Boden (eds), *Now/Here: Time, Space and Modernity*. Berkeley, CA: University of California Press. pp. 257–86.

Boniface, P. (2003) *Tasting Tourism: Travelling for Food and Drink*. Aldershot: Ashgate.

Boon, B. (2007) 'Working with the front-of-house/back-of-house boundary: room attendants in the hotel guest room space', *Journal of Management and Organization*, 13: 160–74.

Boorstin, D. (1964) *The Image: A Guide to Pseudo-Events in America*. New York: Harper.

Boswell, D. and Evans, J. (eds) (1999) *Representing the Nation: A Reader*. London: Routledge.

Bourdieu, P. (1984) *Distinction*. London: Routledge and Kegan Paul.

Bourdieu, P. (1990) *Photography: A Middle-brow Art*. London: Polity.

Bower, T. (2009) *The Squeeze: Oil, Money and Greed in the Twenty First Century*. London: Harper Press.

Brendon, P. (1991) *Thomas Cook: 150 Years of Popular Tourism*. London: Secker & Warburg.

Brunner, E. (1945) *Holiday Making and the Holiday Trades*. Oxford: Oxford University Press.

Bruner, E. (1994) 'Abraham Lincoln as authentic reproduction: a critique of post-modernism', *American Anthropologist*, 96: 397–415.

Bruner, E. (1995) 'The ethnographer/tourist in Indonesia', in M.-F. Lanfant, J. Allcock and E. Bruner (eds), *International Tourism*. London: Sage. pp. 224–41.

Bryman, A. (1995) *Disney and His Worlds*. London: Routledge.

Bryman, A. (2004) *The Disneyization of Society*. London: Sage.

Bryson, N. (1983) *Vision and Painting*. London: Macmillan.

Buhalis, D. and Law, R. (2008) 'Progress in information technology and tourism management: 20 years on and 10 years after the Internet: the state of eTourism research', *Tourism Management*, 29: 609–23.

Butcher, J. (2003) *The Moralisation of Tourism*. London: Routledge.

Butler, T. and Savage, M. (eds) (1995) *Social Change and the Middle Classes*. London: UCL Press.

Buzard, J. (1993) *The Beaten Track*. Oxford: Clarendon Press.

Callan, R. (1989) 'Small country hotels and hotel award schemes as a measurement of service quality', *Service Industries Journal*, 9: 223–46.

Campbell, C. (1987) *The Romantic Ethic and the Spirit of Modern Consumerism*. Oxford: Basil Blackwell.

Campbell, M. (1989) 'Fishing lore: the construction of the "Sportsman"', *Annals of Tourism Research*, 16: 76–88.

Carlzon, J. (1987) *Moments of Truth*. Cambridge, MA: Ballinger.

Casey, M. (2009) 'Tourist gay(ze) or transnational sex: Australian gay men's holiday desires', *Leisure Studies*, 28: 157–72.

Cass, J. (2004) 'Egypt on steroids: Luxor Las Vegas and postmodern orientalism', in D. Medina Lasanky and B. McLaren (eds), *Architecture and Tourism: Perception, Performance and Place*. Oxford: Berg. pp. 241–64.

Castells, M. (1996) *The Rise of the Network Society*. London: Blackwell.

Chalfen, R. (1987) *Snapshot Versions of Life*. Bowling Green, OH: Bowling Green State University Popular Press.

Chan, W. Y. (2006) 'Coming of age of the Chinese tourists: the emergence of non-Western tourism and host–guest interactions in Vietnam's border tourism', *Tourist Studies*, 6: 187–213.

Chandler, P. (2000) 'The UK outbound tour operating market: changing patterns of distribution', *ETC Insights*, London: English Tourism Council.

Cheong, M. S. and Miller, L. M. (2000) 'Power and tourism: a Foucauldian observation', *Annals of Tourism Research*, 27: 371–90.

Chhabra, D. (2010) 'How they see us: perceived effects of tourist gaze on the Old Order Amish', *Journal of Travel Research*, 49: 93–105.

Chronis, A. (2005) 'Coconstructing heritage at the Gettysburg storyscape', *Annals of Tourism Research*, 32(2): 386–406.

Clark, A. (2010) 'Financial crisis: walk this way', *Guardian*, 29 May.

Clark, P. (1983) *The English Alehouse: A Social History, 1200–1830*. London: Longman.

Clark, T. J. (1984) *The Painting of Modern Life*. London: Thames & Hudson.

Clarke, J. and Critcher, C. (1985) *The Devil Makes Work*. London: Macmillan.

Clifford, J. (1997) *Routes*. Cambridge, MA: Harvard University Press.

Clift, S. and Carter, S. (eds) (1999) *Tourism, Travel and Sex*. London: Cassell.

Clift, S. and Carter, S. (2000) *Tourism and Sex: Culture, Commerce and Coercion*. London: Cassell.

Cloke, P. and Perkins, H. (1998) 'Cracking the canyon with the awesome foursome: representations of adventure tourism in New Zealand', *Environment and Planning D: Society and Space*, 16: 185–218.

Cloke, P. and Perkins, H. C. (2005) 'Cetacean performance and tourism in Kaikoura, New Zealand', *Environment and Planning D: Society and Space*, 23: 903–24.

Cloke, P., Phillips, M. and Thrift, N. (1995) 'The new middle classes and the social constructs of rural living', in T. Butler and M. Savage (eds), *Social Change and the Middle Classes*. London: UCL Press. pp. 220–38.

Coe, B. and Gates, P. (1977) *The Snapshot Photograph: The Rise of Popular Photography, 1888–1939*. London: Ash and Grant.

Cohen, B. and Manspeizer, I. (2009) 'The accidental tourist: NGOs, photography, and the idea of Africa', in M. Robinson and D. Picard (eds), *The Framed World: Tourism, Tourists and Photography*. Aldershot: Ashgate. pp. 79–94.

Cohen, C. (1995) 'Marketing paradise, making nation', *Annals of Tourism Research*, 22: 404–21.

Cohen, E. (1972) 'Towards a sociology of international tourism', *Social Research*, 39: 164–82.

Cohen, E. (1979) 'A phenomenology of tourist types', *Sociology*, 13: 179–201.

Cohen, E. (1988) 'Traditions in the qualitative sociology of tourism', *Annals of Tourism Research*, 15: 29–46.

Cohen, E., Nir, Y. and Almagor, U. (1992) 'Stranger–local interaction in photography', *Annals of Tourism Research*, 19: 213–33.

Coleman, S. and Crang, M. (eds) (2002a) *Tourism: Between Place and Performance*. Oxford: Berghahn Books.

Coleman, S. and Crang, M. (2002b) 'Grounded tourists, travelling theory', in S. Coleman and M. Crang (eds), *Tourism: Between Place and Performance*. Oxford: Berghahn Books. pp. 1–17.

Comolli, J.-L. (1980) 'Machines of the visible', in D. T. Lauretis and S. Heath (eds), *The Cinematic Apparatus*. London: Palgrave Macmillan. pp. 121–42.

Cooper, R. (1997) 'The visibility of social systems', in K. Hetherington and R. Munro (eds), *Ideas of Difference: Social Spaces and the Labour of Division*. Oxford: Blackwell and Sociological Review. pp. 32–41.

Corbin, A. (1992) *The Lure of the Sea: The Discovery of the Seaside in the Modern World, 1750–1840*. Cambridge: Polity.

Cosgrove, D. (1984) *Social Formation and Symbolic Landscape*. London: Croom Helm.

Couldry, N. (2005) 'On the actual street', in D. Crouch, R. Jackson and F. Thompson (eds), *The Media and the Tourist Imagination: Converging Cultures*. London: Routledge. pp. 60–75.

Cox, A. M., Clough, P. D. and Marlow, J. (2008) 'Flickr: a first look at user behaviour in the context of photography as serious leisure', *Information Research*, 13(1): paper 336, http://informationr.net/ir/13-1/paper336.html (accessed 22.11.10).

Crang, M. (1997) 'Picturing practices: research through the tourist gaze', *Progress in Human Geography*, 21: 359–73.

Crang, M. (1999) 'Knowing, tourism and practices of vision', in D. Crouch (ed.), *Leisure/Tourism Geographies*. London: Routledge. pp. 238–56.

Crang, M. (2006) 'Circulation and emplacement: the hollowed out performance of tourism', in C. Minca and T. Oakes (eds), *Travels in Paradox: Remapping Tourism*. Lanham, MD: Rowman & Littlefield. pp. 47–64.

Crang, M. and Travlou, P. (2009) 'The island that was not there: producing Corelli's island, staging Kefalonia', in P. Obrador, M. Crang and P. Travlou (eds), *Cultures of Mass Tourism: Doing the Mediterranean in the Age of Banal Mobilities*. Aldershot: Ashgate. pp. 75–90.

Crang, P. (1994) 'It's showtime: on the workplace geographies of display in a restaurant in Southeast England', *Environment and Planning D: Society and Space*, 12: 675–704.

Crang, P. (1997) 'Performing the tourist product', in C. Rojek and J. Urry (eds), *Touring Cultures*. London: Routledge, pp. 137–54.

Crawshaw, C. and Urry, J. (1997) 'Tourism and the photographic eye', in C. Rojek and J. Urry (eds), *Touring Cultures*. London: Routledge. pp. 176–95.

Cresswell, T. (2006) *On the Move: Mobility in the Modern Western World*. London: Routledge.

Crick, M. (1988) 'Sun, sex, sights, savings and servility', *Criticism, Heresy and Interpretation*, 1: 37–76.

Crouch, D. (ed.) (2000) *Leisure/Tourism Geographies*. London: Routledge.

Crouch, D. (2005) 'Flirting with space: tourism geographies as sensuous/expressive practice', in C. Cartier and A. Lew (eds), *Seductions of Place*. London: Routledge. pp. 23–35.

Culler, J. (1981) 'Semiotics of tourism', *American Journal of Semiotics*, 1: 127–40.

Cunningham, H. (1980) *Leisure in the Industrial Revolution*. London: Croom Helm.

Cuthill, V. (2007) 'Consuming Harrogate: performing Betty's Café and Revolution Vodka Bar', *Space and Culture*, 10: 64–76.

Cwerner, S. (2001) 'The times of migration', *Journal of Ethnic and Migration Studies*, 27: 7–36.

Cwerner, S., Kesselring, S. and Urry, J. (eds) (2009) *Aeromobilities*. London: Routledge.

D'Andrea, A. (2007) *Global Nomads: Techno and New Age as Transnational Countercultures in Ibiza and Goa*. London: Routledge.

Daniels, S. and Cosgrove, D. (1988) 'Introduction: iconography and landscape', in D. Cosgrove and S. Daniels (eds), *The Iconography of Landscape*. Cambridge: Cambridge University Press. pp. 1–10.

Dann, G. (1996a) 'The people of tourist brochures', in T. Selwyn (ed.), *The Tourist Image: Myths and Myth Making in Tourism*. Chichester: John Wiley & Sons. pp. 61–81.

Dann, G. (1996b) *The Language of Tourism: A Social Linguistic Perspective*. Wallingford: CAB International.

Dann, G. and Jacobsen, J. K. S. (2003) 'Tourism smellscapes', *Tourism Geographies*, 5: 3–25.

Davidson, C. (2008) *Dubai: The Vulnerability of Success*. London: Hurst and Company.

Davis, M. (2007) 'Sand, fear, and money in Dubai', in M. Davis and D. Monk (eds), *Evil Paradises*. New York: The New Press. pp. 48–68.

Davis, M. and Monk, D. (eds) (2007) *Evil Paradises*. New York: The New Press.

De Botton, A. (2002) *The Art of Travel*. New York: Pantheon Books.

De Certeau, M. (1984) *The Practice of Everyday Life*. Berkeley, CA: University of California Press.

Deane, P. and Cole, W. A. (1962) *British Economic Growth, 1688–1959*. Cambridge: Cambridge University Press.

Debord, G. (1983) *Society of the Spectacle*. Detroit, IL: Black & Red.

Deffeyes, K. (2005) *Beyond Oil: The View from Hubbert's Peak*. New York: Hill & Wang.

Degen, M. (2004) 'Barcelona's games: the Olympics, urban design, and global tourism', in M. Sheller and J. Urry (eds), *Tourism Mobilities*. London: Routledge. pp. 131–42.

Degen, M. (2008) *Sensing Cities*. London: Routledge.

Degen, M., DeSilvey, C. and Rose, G. (2008) 'Experiencing visualities in designed urban environments: learning from Milton Keynes', *Environment and Planning A*, 40: 1901–20.

della Dora, V. (2007) 'Putting the world into a box: a geography of nineteenth-century "travelling landscapes"', *Geografiska Annaler*, 89B: 287–306.

della Dora, V. (2009) 'Travelling landscape-objects', *Progress in Human Geography*, 33: 334–54.

Denison-Edson, P. W. (1967) 'Some aspects of a historical geography of Morecambe', BA dissertation, University of Cambridge, Cambridge.

Dennis, K. and Urry, J. (2009) *After the Car*. Cambridge: Polity.

Dent, K. (1975) 'Travel as education: the English landed classes in the eighteenth century', *Educational Studies*, 1: 171–80.

Derrida, J. (2000) *Of Hospitality*. Stanford, CA: Stanford University Press.

Desforges, L. (1998) '"Checking out the planet": global representations/local identities and youth travel', in T. Skelton and G. Valentine (eds), *Cool Places*. London: Routledge. pp. 175–92.

Desmond, J. (1999) *Staging Tourism*. Chicago, IL: University of Chicago Press.

Devine, F., Savage, M., Crompton, R. and Scott, J. (eds) (2005) *Rethinking Class: Identities, Cultures and Lifestyles*. London: Palgrave.

Dickens, P. and Ormrod, J. (2007) *Cosmic Society*. London: Routledge.

Dicks, B. (2000) *Heritage, Place and Community*. Cardiff: University of Wales Press.

Dijck, V. J. (2008) 'Digital photography: communication, identity, memory', *Visual Communication*, 7: 57–76.

Diken, B. and Laustsen, C. (2005) *The Culture of Exception: Sociology Facing the Camp*. London: Routledge.

Dillard, C., Browning, L., Sitkin, S. and Sutcliffe, K. (2000) 'Impression management and the use of procedures at the Ritz-Carlton: moral standards and dramaturgical discipline', *Communication Studies*, 51: 404–14.

Drachman, H. (1881) *Skraaplaner: Vildt og Tæmmet. Fortællinger og Naturstudier*. Copenhagen: Gyldendahl.

Du Gay, P., Hall, S., James, L., Mackey, H. and Negus, K. (1997) *Doing Cultural Studies: The Story of the Sony Walkman*. London: Sage.

Dubbeld, L. (2003) 'Observing bodies: camera surveillance and the significance of the body', *Ethics and Information Technology*, 5: 151–62.

Duncan, J. (1999) 'Dis-orientation: on the shock of the familiar in a far-away place', in J. Duncan and D. Gregory (eds), *Writes of Passage: Reading Travel Writing*. London: Routledge. pp. 151–63.

Duncan, T., Scott, D. G. and Baum, T. (2009) 'Mobilities and hospitality work', in *27th International Labour Process Conference*, Edinburgh, April 2009.

Eade, J. and Sallnow, M. (eds) (1991) *Contesting the Sacred: The Anthropology of Christian Pilgrimage*. London: Routledge.

Eco, U. (1986) *Travels in Hyper-Reality*. London: Picador.

Edensor, T. (1998) *Tourists at the Taj*. London: Routledge.

Edensor, T. (2000) 'Staging tourism: tourists as performers', *Annals of Tourism Research*, 27: 322–44.

Edensor, T. (2001a) 'Performing tourism, staging tourism: (re)producing tourist space and practice', *Tourist Studies*, 1: 59–81.

Edensor, T. (2001b) 'Walking in the British countryside: reflexivity, embodied practices and ways to escape', in P. Macnaghten and J. Urry (eds), *Bodies of Nature*. London: Sage. pp. 81–106.

Edensor, T. (2002) *National Identity, Popular Culture and Everyday Life*. Oxford and New York: Berg.

Edensor, T. (2006) 'Sensing tourist places', in C. Minca and T. Oaks (eds), *Travels in Paradox: Remapping Tourism*. Lanham, MD: Rowman & Littlefield. pp. 23–46.

Edensor, T. and Kothari, U. (2004) 'Sweetening colonialism: a Mauritian themed resort', in D. Medina Lasanky and B. McLaren (eds), *Architecture and Tourism: Perception, Performance and Place*. Oxford: Berg. pp. 189–206.

Edgar, D. (1987) 'The new nostalgia', *Marxism Today*, March: 30–5.

Edwards, E. and Hart, J. (2004) 'Introduction: photographs as objects', in E. Edwards (ed.), *Photographs Objects Histories: On the Materiality of Images*. London: Routledge. pp. 1–15.

Ehrenreich, B. (1983) *The Hearts of Men*. London: Pluto Press.

Ehrenreich, B. (1989) *Fear of Falling*. New York: Pantheon.

Ek, R., Larsen, J., Hornskov, B. S. and Mansfeldt, O. (2008) 'A dynamic framework of tourist experiences: space-time and performances in the experience economy', *Scandinavian Journal of Hospitality and Tourism*, 8: 122–40.

Elliott, A. and Urry, J. (2010) *Mobile Lives*. London: Routledge.

English Tourism Council (2000/2001) *ETC Insights*. London: ETC.

Enloe, C. (1989) *Bananas, Beaches and Bases*. London: Pandora.

Everett, S. (2008) 'Beyond the visual gaze? The pursuit of an embodied experience through food tourism', *Tourist Studies*, 8: 337–58.

Fainstein, S. and Judd, D. (eds) (1999) *The Tourist City*. New Haven, CT: Yale University Press.

Farmer, P. (1999) *Infections and Inequalities: The Modern Plagues*. Berkeley, CA: University of California Press.

Farrant, S. (1987) 'London by the sea: resort development on the south coast of England, 1880–1939', *Journal of Contemporary History*, 22: 137–62.

Faulks, S. (1988) 'Disney comes to Chaucerland', *Independent*, 11 June.

Featherstone, M. (1987) 'Consumer culture, symbolic power and universalism', in G. Stauth and S. Zubaida (eds), *Mass Culture, Popular Culture, and Social Life in the Middle East*. Frankfurt: Campus. pp. 17–46.

Febvre, R. (1982) *Problems of Unbelief in the Sixteenth Century*. Cambridge, MA: Harvard University Press.

Feifer, M. (1985) *Going Places*. London: Macmillan.

Feighery, W. (2009) 'Tourism, stock photography and surveillance: a Foucauldian interpretation', *Journal of Tourism and Cultural Change*, 7: 161–78.

Finkelstein, J. (1989) *Dining Out: A Sociology of Modern Manners*. Cambridge: Polity.

Fiske, J. (1989) *Reading the Popular*. Boston, MA: Unwin Hyman.

Fjellman, S. (1992) *Vinyl Leaves: Walt Disney World and America*. Boulder, CO: Westview Press.

Ford, C. and Steinorth, K. (eds) (1988) *You Press the Button, We Do the Rest: The Birth of Snapshot Photography*. Bradford: Dirk Nissen Publishing/National Museum of Photography, Film and Television.

Forster, E. M. (1955) *A Room with a View*. Harmondsworth: Penguin (orig. 1908).

Foster, H. (1985a) 'Postmodernism: a preface', in H. Foster (ed.), *Postmodern Culture*. London: Pluto Press. pp. ix–xvi.

Foster, H. (ed.) (1985b) *Postmodern Culture*. London: Pluto Press.

Foster, H. (ed.) (1988) *Vision and Visuality*. Seattle, WA: Bay Press Seattle.

Foucault, M. (1970) *The Order of Things*. London: Tavistock.

Foucault, M. (1976) *The Birth of the Clinic*. London: Tavistock.

Foucault, M. (1979) *Discipline and Punish: The Birth of the Prison*. Harmondsworth: Penguin.

Frampton, K. (1988) 'Place-form and cultural identity', in J. Thackara (ed.), *Design After Postmodernism*. London: Thames & Hudson. pp. 51–66.

Franklin, A. (1999) 'Zoological gaze', in A. Franklin (ed.), *Animals and Modern Cultures: A Sociology of Human–Animal Relations in Modernity*. London: Sage. pp. 62–83.

Franklin, A. (2003) *Tourism: An Introduction*. London: Sage.

Franklin, A. and Crang, M. (2001) 'The trouble with tourism and travel theory', *Tourist Studies*, 1: 5–22.

Franklin, S., Lury, C. and Stacey, J. (2000) *Global Nature, Global Culture*. London: Sage.

Freire-Medeiros, B. (2011) *Touring Poverty*. London: Routledge.

Frieden, B. and Sagalyn, L. (1989) *Downtown, Inc.: How America Rebuilds Cities*. Cambridge, MA: MIT Press.

Frisby, D. and Featherstone, M. (eds) (1997) *Simmel on Culture*. London: Sage.

Fuller, G. and Harley, R. (2005) *Aviopolis: A Book about Airports*. London: Black Dog Publishing.

Gabriel, Y. (1988) *Working Lives in Catering*. London: Routledge.

Garrod, B. (2009) 'Understanding the relationship between tourism destination imagery and tourist photography', *Journal of Travel Research*, 47: 346–58.

Germann Molz, J. and Gibson, S. (2007a) 'Introduction: mobilizing and mooring hospitality', in J. Germann Molz and S. Gibson (eds), *Mobilizing Hospitality*. Aldershot: Ashgate. pp. 1–25.

Germann Molz, J. and Gibson, S. (eds) (2007b) *Mobilizing Hospitality*. Aldershot: Ashgate.

Gernsheim, H. (1982) *The Origins of Photography*. London: Thames & Hudson.

Gernsheim, H. (1989) *The Rise of Photography 1850–1880: The Age of Collodion*. Volume 2. London: Thames & Hudson.

Gibson, C. and Kong, L. (2005) 'Cultural economy: a critical review', *Progress in Human Geography*, 29: 541–61.

Gibson, J. (1986) *The Ecological Approach to Visual Perception*. Hillsdale, NJ: Lawrence Erlbaum Associates.

Giddens, A. (1992) *The Transformation of Intimacy*. Cambridge: Polity.

Gil, J. (1998) *Metamorphoses of the Body*. Minneapolis, MN: University of Minneapolis Press.

Gillespie, A. (2006) 'Tourist photography and the reverse gaze', *Ethos*, 34: 343–66.

Goffman, E. (1959) *The Presentation of Self in Everyday Life*. Garden City, NY: Doubleday Anchor.

Goffman, E. (1963) *Behavior in Public Places: Notes on the Social Organization of Gatherings*. New York: Free Press.

Goffman, E. (1976) *Gender Advertisements*. London: Harper.

Goodwin, A. (1989) 'Nothing like the real thing', *New Statesman and Society*, 12 August.

Goss, J. (1993) 'Placing the market and marketing place: tourist advertising of the Hawaiian Islands, 1972–92', *Environment and Planning D: Society and Space*, 11: 663–88.

Gottdiener, M. (2001) *Life in the Air: Surviving the New Culture of Air Travel*. Lanham, MD: Rowman & Littlefield.

Gottlieb, A. (1982) 'Americans' vacations', *Annals of Tourism Research*, 9: 165–87.

Goulborne, H. (1999) 'The transnational character of Caribbean kinship in Britain', in S. McRae (ed.), *Changing Britain: Families and Households in the 1990s*. Oxford: Oxford University Press. pp. 176–97.

Grass, J. (1972) 'Morecambe: the people's pleasure. The development of a holiday resort, 1880–1902', MA dissertation, University of Lancaster, Lancaster.

Graves, R. (1965) *Majorca Observed*. London: Cassell.

Green, N. (1990) *The Spectacle of Nature*. Manchester: Manchester University Press.

Greene, M. (1982) *Marketing Hotels into the 1990s*. London: Heinemann.

Gregory, D. (1994) *Geographical Imaginations*. Cambridge, MA: Blackwell.

Gregory, D. (1999) 'Scripting Egypt: Orientalism and the cultures of travel', in J. Duncan and D. Gregory (eds), *Writes of Passage*. London: Routledge, pp. 114–50.

Gregory, D. (2001) 'Performing Cairo: Orientalism and the City of the Arabian Nights'. Paper presented at the 'Space Odyssey' Conference, Roskilde University.

Gregory, D. (2003) 'Emperors of the gaze: photographic practices and productions of space in Egypt, 1839–1914', in J. Schwartz and J. Ryan (eds), *Picturing Place: Photography and the Geographical Imagination*. London: I.B. Tauris. pp. 195–225.

Grenblatt, S. (1991) *Marvellous Possessions: The Wonder of the New World*. Oxford: Clarendon Press.

Guerrier, Y. and Adib, A. (2003) 'Work at leisure and leisure at work: a study of the emotional labour of tour reps', *Human Relations*, 56: 1399–417.

Gye, L. (2007) 'Picture this: the impact of mobile camera phones on personal photographic practices', *Continuum*, 21: 279–88.

Hacking, I. (2004) 'Between Michel Foucault and Erving Goffman: between discourse in the abstract and face-to-face interaction', *Economy and Society*, 3: 277–302.

Haldrup, M. and Larsen, J. (2003) 'The family gaze', *Tourist Studies*, 3: 23–46.

Haldrup, M. and Larsen, J. (2006) 'Material cultures of tourism', *Leisure Studies*, 25: 275–89.

Haldrup, M. and Larsen, J. (2010) *Tourism, Performance and the Everyday: Consuming the Orient*. London: Routledge.

Hall, M. (1994) 'Gender and economic interests in tourism prostitution: the nature, development and implications of sex tourism in south-east Asia', in V. Kinnaird and D. Hall (eds), *Tourism: A Gender Analysis*. Chichester: John Wiley, pp. 142–63.

Hall, S. (2007) *The Carhullan Army*. London: Faber & Faber.

Halsall, M. (1986) 'Through the valley of the shadow', *Guardian*, 27 December.

Hammond, D. J. (2001) 'Photography, tourism and the Kodak Hula Show', *Visual Anthropology*, 14: 1–32.

Hannam, K. and Knox, D. (2010) *Understanding Tourism*. London: Sage.

Harris, H. and Lipman, A. (1986) 'Viewpoint: a culture and despair: reflections on "post-modern" architecture', *Sociological Review*, 34: 837–54.

Harrison, B. (1971) *Drink and the Victorians*. London: Faber & Faber.

Harvey, D. (1989) *The Condition of Postmodernity*. Oxford: Blackwell.

Harvey, P. (1996) *Hybrids of Modernity*. London: Routledge.

Hawken, P., Lovins, A. and Lovins, L. H. (1999) *Natural Capitalism*. London: Earthscan.

Hayes, D. and MacLeod, N. (2007) 'Packaging places: designing heritage trails using an experience economy perspective to maximize visitor engagement', *Journal of Vacation Marketing*, 13: 45–58.

Hebdige, D. (1986–7) 'A report from the Western Front', *Block*, 12: 4–26.

Hebdige, D. (1988) *Hiding in the Light*. London: Routledge.

Heidegger, M. (1993) 'Building dwelling thinking', in *Basic Writings*. London: Routledge. pp. 347–63.

Heidegger, M. (2005) *Sojourns*. Albany, NY: State University of New York Press.

Heinberg, R. (2005) *The Party's Over: Oil, War and the Fate of Industrial Society*. New York: Clearview Books.

Hendry, J. (2000) *The Orient Strikes Back: A Global View of Cultural Display*. Oxford: Berg.

Hern, A. (1967) *The Seaside Holiday*. London: Cresset Press.

Hetherington, K. (2000a) 'Museums and the visually impaired: the spatial politics of access', *Sociological Review*, 48: 444–63.

Hetherington, K. (2000b) *New Age Travellers: Vanloads of Uproarious Humanity*. London: Cassell.

Hewison, R. (1987) *The Heritage Industry: Britain in a Climate of Decline*. London: Methuen.

Hirsch, F. (1978) *Social Limits to Growth*. London: Routledge and Kegan Paul.

Hjorth, L. (2007) 'Snapshots of almost contact: the rise of camera phone practices and a case study in Seoul, Korea', *Continuum*, 2: 227–38.

Hochschild, A. (1983) *The Managed Heart: Commercialization of Human Feeling*. Berkeley, CA: University of California Press.

Hoffman, M. L. and Musil, J. (1999) 'Culture meets commerce: tourism in postcommunist Prague', in D.R. Judd and S. Fainstein (eds) *The Tourist City*. New Haven and London: Yale University Press. pp. 179–97.

Holderness, G. (1988) 'Bardolatry: or, the cultural materialist's guide to Stratford-upon-Avon', in G. Holderness (ed.), *The Shakespeare Myth*. Manchester: Manchester University Press. pp. 1–15.

Holland, P. (2001) 'Personal photography and popular photography', in L. Wells (ed.), *Photography: A Critical Introduction*. London: Routledge. pp. 117–62.

Hollingshead, K. (1992) '"White" gaze, "red" people – shadow visions: the disidentification of "Indians" in cultural tourism', *Leisure Studies*, 11: 43–64.

Hollingshead, K. (1999) 'Surveillance of the worlds of tourism: Foucault and the eye-of-power', *Tourism Management*, 20: 7–23.

Hollinshead, K. (2009) 'Theme parks and the representation of culture and nature: The consumer aesthetics of presentation and performance', in T. Jamal and M. Robinson (eds) (2009) *The Sage Handbook of Tourism Studies*. London: Sage.

Homer-Dixon, T. (2006) *The Upside of Down: Catastrophe, Creativity, and the Renewal of Civilization*. London: Souvenir.

Hooper-Greenhill, E. (1988) 'Counting visitors or visitors who count', in R. Lumley (ed.), *The Museum Time-Machine*. London: Routledge. pp. 213–32.

Horne, D. (1984) *The Great Museum*. London: Pluto Press.

Hsiu-yen Yeh, J. (2009) 'The embodiment of sociability through the tourist camera', in M. Robinson and D. Picard (eds), *The Framed World: Tourism, Tourists and Photography*. Aldershot: Ashgate. pp. 199–216.

Hui, A. (2008) 'Many homes for tourism: re-considering spatializations of home and away in tourism mobilities', *Tourist Studies*, 8: 291–311.

Hutnyk, J. (1996) *The Rumour of Calcutta*. London: Zed Books.

Ibelings, H. (1998) *Supermodernism: Architecture in the Age of Globalisation*. Rotterdam: NAI Publishers.

Ingold, T. and Kurttila, T. (2000) 'Perceiving the environment in Finnish Lapland', *Body and Society*, 6: 183–96.

IPCC (2007) *Climate Change 2007: Synthesis Report*. Geneva: IPCC.

Jackson, P. (1992) 'Constructions of culture, representations of race: Edward Curtis's "way of seeing"', in K. Anderson and F. Gale (eds), *Inventing Places: Studies in Cultural Geography*. London: John Wiley & Sons. pp. 89–106.

Jacobsen, S. K. J. (2003) 'The tourist bubble and the Europeanization of holiday travel', *Tourism and Cultural Change*, 1: 71–87.

Jakle, J. (1985) *The Tourist*. Lincoln, NB: University of Nebraska Press.

Jamal, J. and Robinson, M. (eds) (2009) *The Sage Handbook of Tourism Studies*. London: Sage.

James, N. (1989) 'Emotional labour: skill and work in the social regulation of feelings', *Sociological Review*, 37: 15–42.

Jameson, F. (1985) 'Postmodernism and consumer culture', in H. Foster (ed.), *Postmodern Culture*. London: Pluto Press. pp. 111–25.

Januszczak, W. (1987) 'Romancing the grime', *Guardian*, 2 September.

Jarvis, R. (1997) *Romantic Writing and Pedestrian Travel*. London: Macmillan.

Jay, M. (1993) *Downcast Eyes*. Berkeley, CA: University of California Press.

Jeffreys, S. (1999) 'Globalizing sexual exploitation: sex tourism and the traffic in women', *Leisure Studies*, 18: 179–96.

Jencks, C. (1977) *The Language of Post-Modern Architecture*. New York: Academy.

Jenkins, O. H. (2003) 'Photography and travel brochures: the circle of representation', *Tourism Geographies*, 5: 305–28.

Jenkins, S. (1987) 'Art makes a return to architecture', *Sunday Times*, 15 November.

Jenks, C. (1995) 'The centrality of the eye in western culture: an introduction', in C. Jenks (ed.), *Visual Culture*. London: Routledge. pp. 1–25.

Johnson, J. and Pooley, C. (eds) (1982) *The Structure of Nineteenth Century Cities*. London: Croom Helm.

Johnson, K. and Mignot, K. (1982) 'Marketing trade unionism to service industries: an historical analysis of the hotel industry', *Service Industries Journal*, 2: 5–23.

Johnston, L. (2001) '(Other) bodies and tourism studies', *Annals of Tourism Research*, 28: 180–201.

Jokinen, E. and Veijola, S. (1997) 'The disoriented tourist: the figuration of the tourist in contemporary cultural critique', in C. Rojek and J. Urry (eds), *Touring Cultures*. London: Routledge. pp. 23–51.

Jones, A. (1987) 'Green tourism', *Tourism Management*, December: 354–6.

Jordan, F. and Aitchison, C. (2008) 'Tourism and the sexualisation of the gaze: solo female tourists' experiences of gendered power, surveillance and embodiment', *Leisure Studies*, 27: 329–49.

Kaplan, C. (1996) *Questions of Travel*. Durham, NC: Duke University Press.

King, A. (1984) *The Bungalow*. London: Routledge.

Kinnaird, V. and Hall, D. (eds) (1994) *Tourism: A Gender Analysis*. Chichester: John Wiley.

Kirshenblatt-Gimblett, B. (1998) *Destination Culture: Tourism, Museums and Heritage*. Berkeley, CA: University of California Press.

Klein, N. (2000) *No Logo*. London: Flamingo.

Klingmann, A. (2007) *Brandscapes*. Cambridge, MA: MIT Press.

Knox, P. (1987) 'The social production of the built environment', *Progress in Human Geography*, 11: 354–77.

Knox, P. (1988) 'The design professions and the built environment in a postmodern epoch', in P. Knox (ed.), *The Design Professions and the Built Environment*. London: Croom Helm. pp. 1–11.

Krier, L. (1984) '"Berlin-Tagel" and "building and architecture"', *Architectural Design*, 54: 87–119.

Kroker, A. and Cook, D. (1986) *The Postmodern Scene*. New York: St. Martin's Press.

Kuhn, A. (1995) *Family Secrets: Acts of Memory and Imagination*. London: Verso.

Kunstler, J. (2006) *The Long Emergency: Surviving the Converging Catastrophes of the 21st Century*. London: Atlantic Books.

Landry, C. (2006) *The Art of City Making*. London: Earthscan.

Landry, C., Montgomery, J., Worpole, K., Gratton, C. and Murray, R. (1989) *The Last Resort*. London: Comedia Consultancy/SEEDS (South East Economic Development Strategy).

Larkham, P. (1986) *The Agents of Urban Change*. University of Birmingham, Department of Geography, Occasional Publication No. 21.

Larsen, J. (2000) 'The Trafford Centre: a modern machine for consumption and postmodern spectacle', *Travel and Destination*. Proceedings of a conference held at Roskilde University, 17 February. Department of Geography, Roskilde University. pp. 39–61.

Larsen, J. (2001) 'Tourism mobilities and the travel glance: experiences of being on the move', *Scandinavian Journal of Hospitality and Tourism*, 1: 80–98.

Larsen, J. (2004a) 'Performing tourist photography'. PhD, Roskilde University, Department of Geography.

Larsen, J. (2004b) '(Dis)connecting tourism and photography: corporeal travel and imaginative travel', Journeys: International Journal of Travel and Travel Writing, 5: 19–42.

Larsen, J. (2005) 'Families seen photographing: the performativity of tourist photography', Space and Culture, 8: 416–34.

Larsen, J. (2006a) 'Geographies of tourism photography: choreographies and performances', in J. Falkheimer and A. Jansson (eds), Geographies of Communication: The Spatial Turn in Media Studies. Göteborg: Nordicom. pp. 241–57.

Larsen, J. (2006b) 'Picturing Bornholm: the production and consumption of a tourist island through picturing practices', Scandinavian Journal of Hospitality and Tourism, 6: 75–94.

Larsen, J. (2008a) 'Practices and flows of digital photography: an ethnographic framework', Mobilities, 3: 141–60.

Larsen, J. (2008b) 'De-exoticizing tourist travel: everyday life and sociality on the move', Leisure Studies, 27: 21–34.

Larsen, J. (2009) 'Goffman and the tourist gaze: a performativity approach to tourism mobilities', in M. H. Jacobsen (ed.), Contemporary Goffman. London: Routledge, pp. 313–32.

Larsen, J., Urry, J. and Axhausen, K. (2006) Mobilities, Networks, Geographies. Aldershot: Ashgate.

Larsen, J., Urry, J. and Axhausen, K. (2007) 'Networks and tourism: mobile social life', Annals of Tourism Research, 34: 244–62.

Lasanky, M. (2004) '"Tourist geographies": remapping old Havana', in D. Medina Lasanky and B. McLaren (eds), Architecture and Tourism: Perception, Performance and Place. Oxford: Berg. pp. 165–88.

Lash, S. (1990) Sociology of Postmodernism. London: Routledge.

Lash, S. and Urry, J. (1987) The End of Organized Capitalism. Cambridge: Polity.

Lash, S. and Urry, J. (1994) Economies of Signs and Space. London: Sage.

Latour, B. (1991) 'Technology is society made durable', in J. Law (ed.), A Sociology of Monsters: Essays on Power, Technology and Domination. London: Routledge.

Lawson, A. and Samson, C. (1988) 'Age, gender and adultery', British Journal of Sociology, 39: 409–40.

Lea, J. (1988) Tourism and Development in the Third World. London: Routledge.

Leadbetter, C. (1988) 'Power to the person', Marxism Today, October: 14–19.

Leggett, J. (2005) Half Gone: Oil, Gas, Hot Air and Global Energy Crisis. London: Portobello Books.

Leheny, D. (1995) 'A political economy of Asian sex tourism', Annals of Tourism Research, 22: 367–84.

Lencek, L. and Bosler, G. (1998) The Beach: The History of Paradise on Earth. London: Secker & Warburg.

Lennon, J. and Foley, M. (2000) Dark Tourism. London: Continuum.

Letcher, A., Blain, J. and Wallis, J. R. (2009) 'Re-viewing the past: discourse and power in images of prehistory', in M. Robinson and D. Picard (eds), The Framed World: Tourism, Tourists and Photography. Aldershot: Ashgate. pp. 169–84.

Lett, J. (1983) 'Ludic and liminoid aspects of charter yacht tourism in the Caribbean', Annals of Tourism Research, 10: 35–56.

Levitt, T. (1981) 'Marketing intangible products and product intangibles', Cornell HRA Quarterly, August: 37–44.

Lewis, N. (2000) 'The climbing body: nature and the experience of modernity', *Body and Society*, 6: 58–80.

Lewis, P. (2009) 'Too high, too fast: the party's over for Dubai', *Guardian*, 14 February: 28–9.

Ley, D. and Olds, K. (1988) 'Landscape as spectacle: world's fairs and the culture of heroic consumption', *Environment and Planning D: Society and Space*, 6: 191–212.

Lickorish, L. J. and Kershaw, A. G. (1975) 'Tourism between 1840 and 1940', in A. J. Burkart and S. Medlik (eds), *The Management of Tourism*. London: Heinemann. pp. 11–26.

Light, A. (1991) *Forever England: Femininity, Literature and Conservatism between the Wars*. London: Routledge.

Light, D. (2001) 'Gazing on communism: heritage tourism and post-communist identities in Germany, Hungary and Romania', *Tourism Geographies*, 2: 157–76.

Lisle, D. (2004) 'Gazing at Ground Zero: tourism, voyeurism and spectacle', *Journal for Cultural Research*, 88: 3–21.

Lister, M. (2007) 'A sack in the sand: photography in the age of information', *Convergence*, 13: 251–74.

Littlewood, I. (2001) *Sultry Climates: Travel and Sex since the Grand Tour*. London: John Murray.

Litvin, W. S., Goldsmith, E. R. and Pan, B. (2008) 'Electronic word-of-mouth in hospitality and tourism management', *Tourism Management*, 29: 458–68.

Lodge, D. (1991) *Paradise News*. London: Secker & Warburg.

Löfgren, O. (1999) *On Holiday: A History of Vacationing*. Berkeley, CA: University of California Press.

Löfgren, O. (2003) 'The new economy: a cultural history', *Global Networks*, 3: 239–54.

Löfgren, O. (2008) 'The secret lives of tourists: delays, disappointments and daydreams', *Scandinavian Journal of Hospitality and Tourism*, 8: 85–101.

Lovelock, J. (2006) *The Revenge of Gaia*. London: Allen Lane.

Lowe, P. and Goyder, J. (1983) *Environmental Groups in Politics*. London: Allen & Unwin.

Lowenthal, D. (1985) *The Past is a Foreign Country*. Cambridge: Cambridge University Press.

Lübbren, N. (2001) *Rural Artists' Colonies in Europe, 1870–1910*. Manchester: Manchester University Press.

Lukas, S. (2007) *The Themed Space*. Lanham, MD: Lexington Books.

Lukas, S. (2008) *Theme Park*. London: Reaktion Books.

Lumley, R. (ed.) (1988) *The Museum Time-Machine*. London: Routledge.

Lund, K. (2006) 'Seeing in motion and the touching eye: walking over Scotland's mountains', *Etnofoor: Antropological Journal*, 18: 27–42.

Lunn, T. (1989) 'How to swing unused talent into action', *Sunday Times*, 20 August.

Lynas, M. (2007) *Six Degrees*. London: Fourth Estate.

Lynch, K. (1960) *The Image of the City*. Cambridge, MA: MIT Press.

Lynch, K. (1973) *What Time is This Place?* Cambridge, MA: MIT Press.

MacCannell, D. (1973) 'Staged authenticity: arrangements of social space in tourist settings', *American Sociological Review*, 79: 589–603.

MacCannell, D. (1999) *The Tourist*. New York: Schocken (orig. 1976).

MacCannell, D. (2001) 'Tourist agency', *Tourism Studies*, 1: 23–38.

Macdonald, S. (1995) 'Consuming science: public knowledge and the dispersed politics of reception among museum visitors', *Media, Culture and Society*, 17: 13–29.

Macdonald, S. (1997) 'A people's story: heritage, identity and authenticity', in C. Rojek and J. Urry (eds), *Touring Cultures*. London: Routledge. pp. 155–75.

Macnaghten, P. and Urry, J. (1998) *Contested Natures*. London: Sage.

Macnaghten, P. and Urry, J. (2000a) 'Bodies in the woods', *Body and Society*, 6: 166–82.

Macnaghten, P. and Urry, J. (eds) (2000b) *Bodies of Nature*, double issue of *Body and Society*, 6: 1–202.

Macnaghten, P. and Urry, J. (2000c) 'Introduction', *Body and Society*, 6: 1–11.

Maoz, D. (2006) 'The mutual gaze', *Annals of Tourism Research*, 33: 221–39.

Markwick, M. (2001) 'Postcards from Malta: image, consumption, context', *Annals of Tourism Research*, 28: 417–38.

Mars, G. and Nicod, M. (1984) *The World of Waiters*. London: Allen & Unwin.

Marshall, G. (1986) 'The workplace culture of a licensed restaurant', *Theory, Culture and Society*, 3: 33–48.

Martin, B. (1982) *A Sociology of Contemporary Popular Culture*. Oxford: Blackwell.

Martin, B. and Mason, S. (1987) 'Current trends in leisure', *Leisure Studies*, 6: 93–7.

Martinotti, G. (1999) 'A city for whom? Transients and public life in the second-generation metropolis', in R. Beauregard and S. Body-Gendrot (eds), *The Urban Moment: Cosmopolitan Essays on the Late-20th-century City*. London: Sage. pp. 155–84.

Mason, J. (2004) 'Managing kinship over long distances: the significance of "the visit"', *Social Policy & Society*, 3: 421–9.

Massey, D. (1994) *Space, Place and Gender*. Cambridge: Polity.

Mazierska, E. and Walton, K. J. (2006) 'Tourism and the moving image', *Tourist Studies*, 6: 5–11.

McClintock, A. (1995) *Imperial Leather*. New York: Routledge.

McCrone, D. (1998) *The Sociology of Nationalism*. London: Routledge.

McCrone, D., Morris, A. and Kiely, R. (1995) *Scotland – the Brand*. Edinburgh: Edinburgh University Press.

McKay, I. (1988) 'Twilight at Peggy's Cove: towards a genealogy of "maritimicity" in Nova Scotia', *Borderlines*, Summer: 29–37.

McQuire, S. (1998) *Visions of Modernity: Representation, Memory, Time and Space in the Age of the Camera*. London: Sage.

Mellinger, W. M. (1994) 'Toward a critical analysis of tourism representations', *Annals of Tourism Research*, 21: 756–79.

Mellor, A. (1991) 'Enterprise and heritage in the dock', in J. Corner and S. Harvey (eds), *Enterprise and Heritage*. London: Routledge. pp. 93–115.

Mennell, S. (1985) *All Manners of Food*. Oxford: Blackwell.

Mercer, C. (1983) 'A poverty of desire: pleasure and popular politics', in T. Bennett (ed.), *Formations of Pleasure*. London: Routledge and Kegan Paul. pp. 84–101.

Merriman, N. (1989) 'Museum visiting as a cultural phenomenon', in P. Vergo (ed.), *The New Museology*. London: Reaktion. pp. 149–71.

Metcalf, H. (1988) 'Careers and training in tourism and leisure', *Employment Gazette*, February: 84–93.

Meyrowitz, J. (1985) *No Sense of Place: The Impact of Electronic Media on Social Behaviour*. New York: Oxford University Press.

Michael, M. (1996) *Constructing Identities*. London: Sage.

Michael, M. (2000) *Reconnecting, Culture, Technology and Nature*. London: Routledge.

Miller, D. and Slater, D. (2000) *The Internet*. London: Berg.

Mills, C. A. (1988) '"Life on the upslope": the postmodern landscape of gentrification', *Environment and Planning D: Society and Space*, 6: 169–89.

Milton, K. (1993) 'Land or landscape: rural planning policy and the symbolic construction of the countryside', in M. Murray and J. Greer (eds), *Rural Development in Ireland*. Aldershot: Avebury. pp. 120–50.

Mishan, E. (1969) *The Costs of Economic Growth*. Harmondsworth: Penguin.

Mitchell, T. (1989) 'The world as exhibition', *Comparative Studies in Society and History*, 31: 217–36.

Mitter, S. (1986) *Common Fate, Common Road*. London: Pluto Press.

Monbiot, G. (2006) *Heat*. London: Allen Lane.

Mordue, T. (2001) 'Performing and directing resident/tourist cultures in *Heartbeat* country', *Tourist Studies*, 1: 233–52.

Mordue, T. (2009) 'Television, tourism and rural life', *Journal of Travel Research*, 47: 332–45.

Morgan, N. and Pritchard, A. (2005) 'Security and social "sorting": traversing the surveillance–tourism', *Tourist Studies*, 5: 115–32.

Morris, M. (1988) 'At Henry Parkes Motel', *Cultural Studies*, 2: 1–47.

Munt, I. (1994) 'The other postmodern tourist: culture, travel and the new middle classes', *Theory, Culture and Society*, 11: 101–24.

Murray, S. (2008) 'Digital images, photo-sharing, and our shifting notions of everyday aesthetics', *Journal of Visual Culture*, 7: 147–63.

Myerscough, J. (1974) 'The recent history of the use of leisure time', in I. Appleton (ed.), *Leisure Research and Policy*. Edinburgh: Scottish Academic Press. pp. 3–16.

Neumann, M. (1992) 'The travelling eye: photography, tourism and ethnography', *Visual Sociology*, 7: 22–38.

Newmann, M. (1999) *On the Rim: Looking for the Grand Canyon*. Minneapolis, MN: University of Minnesota Press.

Norman, P. (1988) 'Faking the present', *Guardian*, 10–11 December.

Nyri, P. (2010) *Mobility and Cultural Authority in Contemporary China*. Seattle, WA: University of Washington Press.

O'Dell, T. (2007) 'Hospitality, kinesthesis, and health: Swedish spas and the market for well-being', in J. Germann Molz and S. Gibson (eds), *Mobilizing Hospitality*. London: Ashgate. pp. 103–20.

O'Dell, T. and Billing, P. (eds) (2005) *Experiencescapes: Tourism, Culture and Economy*. Copenhagen: Copenhagen Business School.

O'Rourke, P. J. (1988) *Holidays in Hell*. New York: Atlantic Monthly Review.

Obrador, P., Crang, M. and Travlou, P. (eds) (2009) *Cultures of Mass Tourism*. Aldershot: Ashgate.

Ockman, J. (2004) 'New politics of the spectacle: "Bilbao" and the global imagination', in D. Medina Lasanky and B. McLaren (eds), *Architecture and Tourism: Perception, Performance and Place*. Oxford: Berg. pp. 189–206.

Ong, A. and Nonini, D. (eds) (1997) *Ungrounded Empires*. London: Routledge.

Oppermann, M. (1999) 'Sex tourism', *Annals of Tourism Research*, 26: 251–66.

Osborne, P. (2000) *Travelling Light: Photography, Travel and Visual Culture*. Manchester: Manchester University Press.

Ostling, S. (2007) 'The global museum and the orbit of the Solomon R. Guggenheim Museum New York', *Internatiomal Journal of Humanities*, 5: 87–94.

Ousby, I. (1990) *The Englishman's England*. Cambridge: Cambridge University Press.

Pan, B. and Fesenmaier, R. D. (2006) 'Online information search: vacation planning process', *Annals of Tourism Research*, 33: 809–32.

Pan, B., MacLaurin, T. and Crotts, C. J. (2007) 'Travel blogs and the implications for destination marketing', *Journal of Travel Research*, 46: 35–45.

Papastergiadis, N. (2000) *The Turbulence of Migration*. Cambridge: Polity.

Parr, M. (1995) *Small World*. Stockport: Dewi Lewis Publishing.

Parr, M. (1999) *Boring Postcards*. London: Phaidon Press.

Pearce, F. (2007) *With Speed and Violence: Why Scientists Fear Tipping Points in Climate Change*. Boston, MA: Beacon Press.

Pearce, P. and Moscardo, G. (1986) 'The concept of authenticity in tourist experiences', *Australian and New Zealand Journal of Sociology*, 22: 121–32.

Pelizzari, A. M. (2003) 'Retracing the outlines of Rome: intertextuality and imaginative geographies in nineteenth-century photographs', in J. Schwartz and J. Ryan (eds), *Picturing Place: Photography and the Geographical Imagination*. London: I.B. Tauris. pp. 55–73.

Pemble, J. (1987) *The Mediterranean Passion*. Oxford: Clarendon Press.

Perkin, H. (1976) 'The "social tone" of Victorian seaside resorts in the north-west', *Northern History*, II: 180–94.

Perkins, H. and Thorns, D. (2001) 'Reflections on Urry's tourist gaze in the context of contemporary experience in the antipodes', *International Sociology*, 16: 185–204.

Pezzullo, P. (2009) 'Tourists and/as disasters: rebuilding, remembering, and responsibility in New Orleans', *Tourist Studies*, 9: 23–41.

Pfeil, F. (1985) 'Makin' flippy-floppy: postmodernism and the baby-boom PMC', in M. Davis, F. Pfeil and M. Spinker (eds), *The Year Left: An American Socialist Yearbook 1985*. London: Verso. pp. 263–95.

Phelps-Brown, E. H. (1968) *A Century of Pay*. London: Macmillan.

Pillsbury, R. (1990) *From Boarding House to Bistro*. Boston, MA: Unwin Hyman.

Pimlott, J. (1947) *The Englishman's Holiday*. London: Faber & Faber.

Pine, B. J. and Gilmore, H. J. (1999) *The Experience Economy*. Boston, MA: Harvard Business School Press.

Pine, R. (1987) *Management of Technological Change in the Catering Industry*. Aldershot: Avebury.

Piore, M. and Sabel, C. (1984) *The Second Industrial Divide*. New York: Basic Books.

Pollard, S. (1965) *The Genesis of Modern Management*. London: Edward Arnold.

Pons, O. P. (2007) 'A haptic geography of the beach: naked bodies, vision and touch', *Social and Cultural Geography*, 8: 123–41.

Pons, O. P. (2009) 'Building castles in the sand: re-positioning touch on the beach', *Senses and Society*, 4: 195–210.

Pons, O. P., Crang, M. and Travlou, P. and (eds) (2008) *Doing Tourism: Cultures of Mediterranean Mass Tourism*. Aldershot: Ashgate.

Poon, A. (1989) 'Competitive strategies for a "new tourism"', in C. Cooper (ed.), *Progress in Tourism, Recreation and Hospitality Management Vol. 1*. London: Belhaven Press. pp. 91–102.

Poon, A. (1993) *Tourism, Technology and Competitive Strategies*. Wallingford: CAB International.

Pratt, M. (1992) *Imperial Eyes*. London: Routledge.

Pritchard, A. and Morgan, N. (2000a) 'Privileging the male gaze: gendered tourism landscapes', *Annals of Tourism Research*, 27: 884–905.

Pritchard, A. and Morgan, N. (2000b) 'Constructing tourism landscape: gender, sexuality and space', *Tourism Geographies*, 2: 115–39.

Pritchard, A. and Morgan, N. (2000c) *Advertising in Tourism and Leisure*. London: Butterworth-Heinemann.

Pritchard, A. and Morgan, N. (2006) 'Hotel Babylon? Exploring hotels as liminal sites of transition and transgression', *Tourism Management*, 27: 762–72.

Quick, R. C. (1962) *The History of Morecambe and Heysham*. Morecambe: Morecambe Times.

Quinn, B. (2007) 'Performing tourism: Venetian residents in focus', *Annals of Tourism Research*, 34: 458–76.

Raban, J. (1986) *Coasting*. London: Picador.

Raento, P. and Flusty, S. (2006) 'Three trips to Italy: deconstructing the New Las Vegas', in C. Minca and T. Oakes (eds), *Travels in Paradox: Remapping Tourism*. Oxford: Rowman & Littlefield. pp. 97–124.

Retzinger, J. (1998) 'Framing the tourist gaze: railway journeys across Nebraska, 1866–1906', *Great Plains Quarterly*, 18: 213–26.

Richards, J. and MacKenzie, J. (1986) *The Railway Station*. Oxford: Oxford University Press.

Richards, J., Wilson, S. and Woodhead, L. (eds) (1999) *Diana: The Making of a Media Saint*. London: I.B. Tauris.

Riley, R., Baker, B. and Van Doren, S. (1998) 'Movie-induced tourism', *Annals of Tourism Research*, 25: 919–35.

Ring, J. (2000) *How the English Made the Alps*. London: John Murray.

Ritzer, G. (2008) *The McDonaldization of Society*. Thousand Oaks, CA: Pine Forge Press.

Ritzer, G. and Liska, A. (1997) 'McDisneyization and post-tourism: complementary perspectives on contemporary tourism', in C. Rojek and J. Urry (eds), *Touring Cultures*. London: Routledge, pp. 96–112.

Roche, M. (2000) *Mega-Events and Modernity*. London: Routledge.

Rodaway, P. (1994) *Sensuous Geographies*. London: Routledge.

Rojek, C. (1993) *Ways of Escape*. London: Sage.

Rojek, C. (1997) 'Indexing, dragging and the social construction of tourist sights', in C. Rojek and J. Urry (eds), *Touring Cultures*. London: Routledge. pp. 52–74.

Rojek, C. (2004) *Celebrity*. London: Reaktion Books.

Rojek, C. and Urry, J. (eds) (1997) *Touring Cultures*. London: Routledge.

Rose, G. (2003) 'Family photographs and domestic spacings: a case study', *Transactions of the Institute of British Geographers*, 28: 5–18.

Rose, G. (2004) 'Everyone's cuddled up and it just looks really nice: an emotional geography of some mums and their family photos', *Social & Cultural Geography*, 5: 549–64.

Rose, G. (2010) *Doing Family Photography*. Aldershot: Ashgate.

Rose, M. (1978) *The Gregs of Styal*. Cheshire: Quarry Bank Mill Development Trust.

Rubinstein, D. and Sluis, K. (2008) 'A life more photographic', *Photographies*, 1: 9–28.

Ryan, C. and Hall, M. (2001) *Sex Tourism*. London: Routledge.

Ryan, J. (1997) *Picturing Empire: Photography and the Visualisation of the British Empire*. London: Reaktion Books.

Said, E. (1995) *Orientalism: Western Conceptions of the Orient*. Harmondsworth: Penguin.

Saldanha, A. (2002) 'Music tourism and factions of bodies in Goa', *Tourist Studies*, 2(1): 43–63.

Samuel, R. (1994) *Theatres of Memory*. London: Verso.

Samuel, R. (1998) *Island Stories*. London: Verso.

Sasser, W. and Arbeit, S. (1976) 'Selling jobs in the service sector', *Business Horizons*, 19: 61–5.

Sather-Wagstaff, J. (2008) 'Picturing experience: a tourist-centred perspective on commemorative historical sites', *Tourist Studies*, 8: 77–103.

Savage, M. (1988) 'The missing link? The relationship between spatial mobility and social mobility', *British Journal of Sociology*, 39: 554–77.

Savage, M., Barlow, J., Dickens, P. and Fielding, T. (1992) *Bureaucracy, Property and Culture: Middle-Class Formation in Contemporary Britain*. London: Routledge.

Scarles, C. (2004) 'Mediating landscapes: the processes and practices of image construction in tourist brochures of Scotland', *Tourist Studies*, 4: 43–67.

Scarles, C. (2009) 'Becoming tourist: renegotiating the visual in the tourist experience', *Environment and Planning D: Society and Space*, 27: 465–88.

Schama, S. (1995) *Landscape and Memory*. London: HarperCollins.

Schieffelin, E. (1998) 'Problematizing performance', in F. Hughes-Freeland (ed.) *Ritual, Performance, Media*. ASA Monograph 35. London: Routledge. pp. 194–208.

Schivelbusch, W. (1986) *The Railway Journey: Trains and Travel in the Nineteenth Century*. Oxford: Blackwell.

Schmallegger, D. and Carson, D. (2008) 'Blogs in tourism: changing approaches to information exchange', *Journal of Vacation Marketing*, 14: 99–110.

Schmid, H. (2009) *Economy of Fascination*. Berlin: Gebrüder Borntraeger.

Schroeder, J. (2002) *Visual Consumption*. London: Routledge.

Schultz, P. (2003) *1000 Places To See Before You Die*. New York: Workman Publishing.

Schwartz, B. (2004) *The Paradox of Choice*. New York: HarperCollins.

Schwartz, J. (1996) 'The geography lesson: photographs and the construction of imaginative geographies', *Journal of Historical Geography*, 22: 16–45.

Schwartz, J. and Ryan, J. (eds) (2003a) *Picturing Place: Photography and the Geographical Imagination*. London: I.B. Tauris.

Schwartz, J. and Ryan, J. (2003b) 'Introduction: photography and the geographical imagination', in J. Schwartz and J. Ryan (eds), *Picturing Place: Photography and the Geographical Imagination*. London: I.B. Tauris. pp. 1–18.

Scruton, R. (1979) *The Aesthetics of Architecture*. Princeton, NJ: Princeton University Press.

Selwyn, T. (ed.) (1996) *The Tourist Image*. Chichester: John Wiley.

Sennett, R. (1994) *Flesh and Stone*. London: Faber & Faber.

Shaw, G., Agarwal, S. and Bull, P. (2000) 'Tourism consumption and tourist behaviour: a British perspective', *Tourism Geographies*, 2: 264–89.

Sheller, M. (2003) *Consuming the Caribbean*. London: Routledge.

Sheller, M. and Urry, J. (eds) (2004) *Tourism Mobilities*. London: Routledge.

Shields, R. (1989) 'Social spatialization and the built environment: the West Edmonton Mall', *Environment and Planning D: Society and Space*, 7: 147–64.

Shields, R. (1990) *Places on the Margin*. London: Routledge.

Shoard, M. (1987) *The Land is Our Land*. London: Paladin.

Simpson, T. (2010) 'Materialist pedagogy: the function of themed environments in post-socialist consumption in Macao', *Tourist Studies*, 9: 60–80.

Slater, D. (1991) 'Consuming Kodak', in J. Spence and P. Holland (eds), *Family Snaps: The Meanings of Domestic Photography*. London: Virago. pp. 45–59.

Slater, D. (1995) 'Photography and modern vision: the spectacle of natural magic', in C. Jenks (ed.), *Visual Culture*. London: Routledge. pp. 218–37.

Slater, D. (1999) 'Marketing mass photography', in J. Evans and S. Hall (eds), *Visual Culture: The Reader*. London: Sage. pp. 289–306.

Smart, B. (2010) *Consumer Society*. London: Sage.

Smith, M. (2009) 'Ethical perspectives exploring the ethical landscape of tourism', in J. Jamal and M. Robinson (eds), *The Sage Handbook of Tourism Studies*. London: Sage. pp. 613–30.

Smith, V. (1989) *Hosts and Guests: The Anthropology of Tourism*. Philadelphia, PA: University of Pennsylvania Press (orig. 1978).

Sontag, S. (1979) *On Photography*. Harmondsworth: Penguin.

Spang, L. (2000) *The Invention of the Restaurant*. Cambridge, MA: Harvard University Press.

Special Projects Group, Lancaster City Council (1987) *Lancaster – Heritage City: Position Statement*. Lancaster: Lancaster City Council.

Spence, J. and Holland, P. (1991) *Family Snaps: The Meanings of Domestic Photography*. London: Virago.

Spillman, L. (1997) *Nation and Commemoration*. Cambridge: Cambridge University Press.

Sprawson, C. (1992) *The Black Masseur*. London: Jonathan Cape.

Stallinbrass, C. (1980) 'Seaside resorts and the hotel accommodation industry', *Progress in Planning*, 13: 103–74.

Stamp, G. (1987) 'A right old Roman carry-on', *Daily Telegraph*, 28 December.

Stanley, J. (2005) 'Wanted: adventurous girls, ships' stewardesses, 1919–1939'. PhD Lancaster University, Lancaster.

Stauth, G. and Turner, B. (1988) 'Nostalgia, postmodernism and the critique of mass culture', *Theory, Culture and Society*, 2/3: 509–26.

Stern, N. (2007) *The Economics of Climate Change: The Stern Review*. Cambridge: Cambridge University Press.

Strahan, D. (2007) *The Last Oil Shock*. London: John Murray.

Strange, C. and Kempla, M. (2003) 'Shades of dark tourism: Alcatraz and Robben Island', *Annals of Tourism Research*, 30: 386–405.

Suonpää, J. (2008) 'Blessed be the photograph: tourism choreographies', *Photographies*, 1: 67–86.

Szerszynski, B. and Urry, J. (2002) 'Cultures of cosmopolitanism', *Sociological Review*, 50: 461–8.

Szerszynski, B. and Urry, J. (2006) 'Visuality, mobility and the cosmopolitan: inhabiting the world from afar', *British Journal of Sociology*, 57: 113–31.

Tagg, J. (1988) *The Burden of Representation: Essays on Photographies and Histories*. Amherst, MA: University of Massachusetts Press.

Talbot, H. F. (1839) 'Some account of the art of photogenic drawing, or, the process by which natural objects may be made to delineate themselves without the aid of the artist's pencil', in B. Newhall (ed.), *Photography: Essays and Images*. New York: Museum of Modern Art. pp. 23–30.

Talbot, H. F. (1844–46) *The Pencil of Nature*. London: Longman, Brown, Green (unpaginated).

Taylor, J. (1994) *A Dream of England: Landscape, Photography and the Tourist's Imagination*. Manchester: Manchester University Press.

Tester, K. (ed.) (1994) *The Flâneur*. London: Routledge.

Theroux, M. (2009) *Far North*. London: Faber & Faber.

Thompson, E. P. (1967) 'Time, work-discipline, and industrial capitalism', *Past and Present*, 38: 56–97.

Thompson, G. (1981) 'Holidays', Unit 11 of *Popular Culture and Everyday Life* (2). Milton Keynes: Open University Press.

Thompson, G. (1983) 'Carnival and the calculable: consumption and play at Blackpool', in T. Bennett (ed.), *Formations of Pleasure*. London: Routledge. pp. 124–36.

Thompson, K. (2006) *An Eye for the Tropics: Tourism, Photography, and Framing the Caribbean Picturesque*. Durham, NC: Duke University Press.

Thrift, N. (1989) 'Images of social change', in C. Hamnett, L. McDowell and P. Sarre (eds), *The Changing Social Structure*. London: Sage. pp. 12–42.

Thrift, N. (1996) *Spatial Formations*. London: Sage.

Thrift, N. (2008) *Non-Representational Theory*. London: Routledge.

Tomlinson, T. (2007) *The Culture of Speed: The Coming of Immediacy*. London: Sage.

Tooke, N. and Baker, M. (1996) 'Seeing is believing: the effect of film on visitor numbers to screened locations', *Tourism Management*, 17: 87–94.

Towner, J. (1985) 'The Grand Tour: a key phase in the history of tourism', *Annals of Tourism Research*, 12: 297–33.

Towner, J. (1988) 'Approaches to tourism history', *Annals of Tourism History*, 15: 47–62.

Travel Alberta (n.d.) *West Edmonton Mall*. Edmonton: Alberta Tourism.

Tucker, H. (2007) 'Performing a young people's package tour of New Zealand: negotiating appropriate performances of place', *Tourism Geographies*, 9: 139–59.

Turner, C. and Manning, P. (1988) 'Placing authenticity – on being a tourist: a reply to Pearce and Manning', *Australian and New Zealand Journal of Sociology*, 24: 136–8.

Turner, L. and Ash, J. (1975) *The Golden Hordes*. London: Constable.

Turner, V. (1973) 'The center out there: pilgrim's goal', *History of Religions*, 12: 191–230.

Turner, V. (1974) *The Ritual Process*. Harmondsworth: Penguin.

Turner, V. and Turner, E. (1978) *Image and Pilgrimage in Christian Culture*. New York: Columbia University Press.

Tzanelli, R. (2008) *The Cinematic Tourist*. London: Routledge.

UNDP (1999) *Human Development Report*. New York: UNDP and Oxford University Press.

Urry, J. (1992) 'The tourist gaze "revisited"', *American Behavioral Scientist*, 36: 172–86.

Urry, J. (1995a) *Consuming Places*. London: Routledge.

Urry, J. (1995b) 'A middle class countryside?', in T. Butler and M. Savage (eds), *Social Change and the Middle Classes*. London: UCL Press. pp. 205–19.

Urry, J. (1996) 'How societies remember the past', in S. Macdonald and G. Fyfe (eds), *Theorizing Museums*. Oxford: Sociological Review Monographs and Blackwell, pp. 45–65.

Urry, J. (2000) *Sociology Beyond Societies*. London: Routledge.

Urry, J. (2003) *Global Complexity*. Cambridge: Polity.

Urry, J. (2004) 'Death in Venice', in M. Sheller and J. Urry (eds), *Tourism Mobilities*. London: Routledge, pp. 205–15.

Urry, J. (2007) *Mobilities*. Cambridge: Polity.

Urry, J. (2011) *Climate Change and Society*. Cambridge: Polity.

Uzzell, D. (1989) *Heritage Interpretation* (Vol. 2). London: Belhaven Press.

Van House, N. (2007) 'Flickr and public image-sharing: distant closeness and photo exhibition', *CHI*, April 28–3 May: 2717–22.

Van Maanen, J. (1991) 'The smile factory: work at Disneyland', in P. J. Frost, L. Moore, M. Louis, C. Lundberg and J. Martin (eds), *Reframing Organizational Culture*. London: Sage. pp. 58–76.

Veijola, S. and Jokinen, E. (1994) 'The body in tourism', *Theory, Culture and Society*, 6: 125–51.

Veijola, S. and Valtonen, A. (2007) 'The body in tourism industry', in A. Pritchard, N. Morgan, I. Ateljevic and C. Harris (eds), *Tourism and Gender: Embodiment, Sensuality and Experience*. Wallingford: CAB International. pp. 13–31.

Venturi, R. (1972) *Learning from Las Vegas*. Cambridge, MA: MIT Press.

Verstraete, G. (2010) *Tracking Europe*. Durham, NC: Duke University Press.

Villi, M. (2007) 'Mobile visual communication: photo messages and camera phone photography', *Nordicom Review*, 28: 49–62.

Vulliamy, E. (1988) 'Squalid renaissance', *Guardian*, 16 April.

Waitt, G. and Head, L. (2002) 'Postcards and frontier mythologies: sustaining views of the Kimberley as timeless', *Environment and Planning D: Society and Space*, 20: 319–44.

Walter, J. (1982) 'Social limits to tourism', *Leisure Studies*, l: 295–304.

Walton, J. (1978) *The Blackpool Landlady*. Manchester: Manchester University Press.

Walton, J. (1979) 'Railways and resort development in Victorian England: the case of Silloth', *Northern History*, 15: 191–209.

Walton, J. (1981) 'The demand for working class seaside holidays in Victorian England', *Economic History Review*, 34: 249–65.

Walton, J. (1983) *The English Seaside Resort: A Social History, 1750–1914*. Leicester: Leicester University Press.

Walton, J. (1997) 'Seaside resorts and maritime history', *International Journal of Maritime History*, 9: 125–47.

Walton, J. (2000) *The British Seaside*. Manchester: Manchester University Press.

Walton, J. and Poole, R. (1982) 'The Lancashire wakes in the nineteenth century', in R. Storch (ed.), *Popular Culture and Customs in the Nineteenth Century*. London: Croom Helm. pp. 100–24.

Walvin, J. (1978) *Beside the Seaside*. London: Allen Lane.

Wang, N. (2000) *Tourism and Modernity*. Oxford: Elsevier.

Ward, M. and Hardy, D. (1986) *Goodnight Campers! The History of the British Holiday Camp*. London: Mansell.

Warhurst, C., Nickson, D., Anne, W. and Cullen, M. A. (2000) 'Aesthetic labour in interactive service work: some case study evidence from the "new" Glasgow', *Service Industries Journal*, 3: 1–18.

Waters, S. (1967) 'Trends in international tourism', *Development Digest*, 5: 57–61.

Wates, N. and Krevitt, C. (1987) *Community Architecture*. Harmondsworth: Penguin.

Wearing, B. and Wearing, S. (1996) 'Refocusing the tourist experience: the "flâneur" and the "choraster"', *Leisure Studies*, 15: 229–43.

Weaver, A. (2005) 'Interactive service work and performative metaphors: the case of the cruise industry', *Tourist Studies*, 5: 5–27.

Wells, L. (2001) 'Introduction', in L. Wells (ed.), *Photography: A Critical Introduction*. London: Routledge. pp. 1–8.

Welsh, E. (1988) 'Are locals selling out for a bowl of gruel?', *Sunday Times*, 11 December.

Welsh, E. (1989) 'Unmasking the special agents', *Sunday Times*, 26 February.

West, B. (2006) 'Consuming national themed environments abroad: Australian working holidaymakers and symbolic national identity in "Aussie" theme pubs', *Tourist Studies*, 6: 139–55.

West, N. (2000) *Kodak and the Lens of Nostalgia*. Charlottesville, VA: University of Virginia Press.

Whitaker, R. (1988) 'Welcome to the Costa del Kebab', *Independent*, 27 February.

White, D. (1987) 'The born-again museum', *New Society*, 1 May: 10–14.

Whittaker, E. (2009) 'Photographing race: the discourse and performance of tourist stenotypes', in M. Robinson and D. Picard (eds), *The Framed World: Tourism, Tourists and Photography*. Aldershot: Ashgate. pp. 117–38.

Whyte, W. F. (1948) *Human Relations in the Restaurant Industry*. New York: McGraw-Hill.

Wickers, D. and Charlton, G. (1988) 'Oh, we do like to be by the seaside', *Sunday Times*, 5 June.

Williams, A. and Shaw, G. (1988) 'Western European tourism in perspective', in A. Williams and G. Shaw (eds), *Tourism and Economic Development*. London: Belhaven Press. pp. 12–38.

Williams, R. (1972) 'Ideas of nature', in J. Benthall (ed.), *Ecology: The Shaping Enquiry*. London: Longman, pp. 146–66.

Williams, R. (1973) *The Country and the City*. London: Paladin.

Williams, S. (1998) *Tourism Geography*. London: Routledge.

Wilson, A. (1988) 'The view from the road: nature tourism in the postwar years', *Borderlines*, 12: 10–14.

Wilson, A. (1992) *Culture of Nature*. Oxford: Blackwell.

Winter, T., Teo, P. and Chang, T. C. (eds) (2009) *Asia on Tour: Exploring the Rise of Asian Tourism*. London: Routledge.

Wittel, A. (2001) 'Towards a network sociality', *Theory, Culture and Society*, 18: 31–50.

Wolff, J. (1985) 'The invisible *flâneuse*: women and the literature of modernity', *Theory, Culture and Society*, 2: 37–48.

Wolff, J. (1993) 'On the road again: metaphors of travel in cultural criticism', *Cultural Studies*, 7: 224–39.

Wong, Jehn-Yih and Wang, Chih-Hung (2009) 'Emotional labor of the tour leaders: an exploratory study', *Tourism Management*, 30: 249–59.

Wood, K. and House, S. (1991) *The Good Tourist*. London: Mandarin.

Wood, M. (1974) 'Nostalgia or never: you can't go home again', *New Society*, 7 November: 343–6.

Wordsworth, W. (1984) *The Illustrated Wordsworth's Guide to the Lakes*. London: Book Club Associates (orig. 1810).

Wouters, C. (1989) 'The sociology of emotions and flight attendants: Hochschild's *Managed Heart*', *Theory, Culture and Society*, 6: 95–124.

Wright, P. (1985) *On Living in an Old Country*. London: Verso.

Xiang, Z. S. and Gretzel, U. (2009) 'Role of social media in online travel information search', *Tourism Management*, 31: 179–88.

Younger, G. (1973) *Tourism: Blessing or Blight?* Harmondsworth: Penguin.

Zukin, S. (1991) *Landscapes of Power*. Berkeley, CA: University of California Press.

Index

Page numbers in *italics* refer to non-textual matter, such as photographs